GENDER JUSTICE

Women's Rights Are Human Rights

By Elizabeth Fisher and Linda Gray MacKay

Unitarian Universalist Service Committee

Gender Justice: Women's Rights Are Human Rights
by Elizabeth Fisher and Linda Gray MacKay

© 1996 Unitarian Universalist Service Committee
All Rights Reserved.
Printed in the United States of America

ISBN 0-9655622-0-4

Gender Justice: Women's Rights Are Human Rights
is published by:

Unitarian Universalist Service Committee
130 Prospect Street
Cambridge, MA 02139-1845
617-868-6600

About the Unitarian Universalist Service Committee

The Unitarian Universalist Service Committee (UUSC) is an independent, nonprofit human rights agency that has confronted political, cultural and economic oppression throughout the world for more than 56 years. The Unitarian Universalist Service Committee is recognized for its innovative and comprehensive approaches to social change.

UUSC advances human rights by combining support for grassroots organizations overseas with education and mobilization of U.S. citizens and Washington, D.C.-based advocacy. As an independent, nonsectarian organization, UUSC builds on the strength of its 20,000 members and supporters worldwide to foster justice in the United States, Central America, the Caribbean, Africa and South Asia.

Overseas, UUSC challenges political repression and promotes women's rights, health and reproductive rights. In the United States, the Service Committee defends children's rights and provides volunteer service opportunities for constituents. While specific programs may change, the guiding principle of the Unitarian Universalist Service Committee remains always to work for justice at home and throughout the world.

Table of Contents

Why Gender Justice: Women's Rights Are Human Rights?

The title *Gender Justice: Women's Rights Are Human Rights* is derived from two sources:

First, point 14 in the Beijing Declaration produced at the Fourth World Conference on Women affirms that "women's rights are human rights."

Second, "A Pledge for Gender Justice" was drafted by a working group of nongovernmental organizations in preparation for the Women's Linkage Caucus at the Preparatory Committee meeting for the United Nations Fourth World Conference on Women, held March 15 - April 5, 1995. It was endorsed by organizations from around the world.

The pledge begins: The Fourth World Conference on Women comes at a time when women's leadership is urgently needed in the face of challenges to our collective survival. Over the past decade, women have demonstrated that gender is central to all contemporary and cross-cutting debates on global issues, such as development, human rights, democracy, population, peace and the environment. They have shown that the empowerment and equal participation of women in decision making are necessary to the advancement of solutions to the world's crises.

> What will be important as we end the forum and the conference at the end of this week, is that it will be NGOs who will hold governments to the commitments that they make. It is important that the final Platform for Action that is adopted be distilled down into words that every woman, no matter where she lives, or how much education she has, can understand. I think we should want every woman, no matter where she is, to believe that there are women all over the world who care about her health, who want her children to be educated, who want her to have the dignity and respect that she deserves to have.
>
> Hillary Rodham Clinton, First Lady of the United States
> Speech to NGO Forum on Women
> September 1995
> Huairou, China

Acknowledgements

Producing a document of this scope is indeed a formidable task. We would like to thank the many individuals who have played a critical role in its development. Rachel Slocum and Laurel Jackson con-

More than 30,000 women and men from around the world came together to set a course for women's rights at the U.N. women's conference, including UUSC President Dorothy Smith Patterson (left, center).

tributed invaluable insight, input and hard work in the final stages of its production, and Heather Robert, Katy Ellison, Maryama Atoine, Eileen Reynolds and Lynne Curran provided important contributions in its earlier stages. Carmen Vázquez contributed enthusiastic help throughout the process. Mary Lania, Shalini Nataraj, Guadelupe Lopez, George Ann Potter, Heather Foote, Denise Moorehead and Theresa Driscoll also played key roles. Pam Sparr graciously provided invaluable feedback and input at various stages of its development.

Carol Burton, Cathy Briggs, Susan Klaseus and Christine Brotman (who also developed the "Gender-Based Violence Quiz") provided important comments and suggestions. Carmelita Logerwell and Vail Weller of the Center for Women and Religion, Graduate Theological Union, generously provided valuable feedback, encouragement and support during the development process and a pre-release presentation of the workshops. Linda Rose contributed important facilitation aids and educational design elements. We are also grateful to the following readers: Doris Duarte, Leith Dunn, Nancy Flowers, Betsy Hartmann, Terri Hawthorne, Jean Hueston, Margi McCue, Reverend Judith Mannheim, Rita Maran, Anne Olson, Reverend Tracey Robinson-Harris, Elizabeth Shippee, Dr. Tamsen Stevenson and Jennifer Yenco. We would also like to extend a special thanks to Rosemary Matson for her encouragement, supply of resources and special support.

We are also grateful for the input and comments provided by the Center for Women's Global Leadership, the Women's Environmental and Development Organization, the Women's Tribune Center and ISIS, organizations that generously granted permission to use some of their beautiful sketches and graphics. Debra Beck of Beck Designs provided the design and layout. Thanks also to the staff of Ten Days for World Development in Toronto for allowing us to reprint excerpts from their fine book, *Doing the Gender Boogie*. We are also grateful to Pat Mora and Beacon Press for allowing us to reprint her powerful poem "Let Us Hold Hands" and to Carolyn McDade and Stuart Stotts for allowing us to reprint their beautiful lyrics and music. We also wish to thank the United Methodist Church's Friendship Press for allowing us to reproduce the video "A Matter of Interest"; Jenny Kilbourne and Margaret Lazarus of Cambridge Documentary Films for allowing us to use a segment from the excellent film "Still Killing Us Softly"; and Gary Rogers, Augusta Productions and Women Make Movies for allowing us to use a segment from their award-winning film "The Vienna Tribunal" in the video produced to accompany *Gender Justice: Women's Rights Are Human Rights*.

We would also like to thank UUSC Executive Director Richard S. Scobie for deciding to undertake this project in the first place and to UUSC Board President Dorothy Smith Patterson for supporting it along the way. Finally, we would like to thank our husbands, families and friends for their patience and support during the challenging stages of this process.

Foreword

Challenging Assumptions

Shortly after the conclusion of the Fourth World Conference on Women held in Beijing, China, in the fall of 1995, I visited the Great Wall. There, I met a young Chinese high school girl. She recognized one of the conference buttons on my hat because she had been given one by some Americans visiting her school. She asked if I had been at the conference. When I answered "yes," she looked at me closely for a moment. "But you are not a woman." "That's true," I answered, "but my organization is committed to women's rights and I was honored to be able to attend." And then she said something that was very telling, and very sad. "Ah, but you were at the top! Right?" "No," I explained, "at this conference women were at the top; I was there mainly to listen and to learn."

UUSC Executive Director Dick Scobie and President of UUSC's Board of Directors Dorothy Smith Patterson at the opening ceremonies of the Fourth World Conference on Women, Beijing.

The assumption that, as a man, I must have been at the top — one that is made daily by men and women in all countries — shows us how far we have to go before women's rights will truly be embraced as human rights. Gender doesn't just have to do with sexuality and reproduction. Gender brings with it multiple layers of socially prescribed expectations, roles, prohibitions and barriers that oppress and limit the hopes and possibilities of women and men everywhere.

Building a More Inclusive World

For the Unitarian Universalist Service Committee, an organization whose mission is to advance justice, the struggle for women's rights is a major priority. Our programs include: 1) direct support to grassroots women's organizations in Asia, Africa and the Americas; 2) advocacy for women's rights in Washington and in the international community; and 3) work with our members and supporters in the United States to help them become more effective advocates for women's rights at the local, state and federal level.

This workshop series, *Gender Justice: Women's Rights Are Human Rights*, has been created to help women and men better understand the impact that gender has on all of our lives, to connect with the international movement for women's rights as it grows in power and diversity, and to take effective action to build a better world; one in which men and women will be at the top together.

Richard S. Scobie
Executive Director
Unitarian Universalist Service Committee

Preface: Beyond Beijing

Advancing Women's Rights

For people unfamiliar with the global women's movement, Beijing is a world class city just like Mexico City, Copenhagen, Nairobi, Cairo and Vienna. But for women around the globe who have been ana-

Young Salvadoran women, like the one to the right, now consider options in addition to motherhood for the future.

lyzing obstacles to the advancement of women worldwide, these cities represent critical international women's conferences organized by the United Nations during the last 20 years. These gatherings produced documents that identified a wide range of problems affecting women, and offered strategies for remedying them.

A document issued by the United States State Department in July 1995, just prior to the United Nations Fourth World Conference on Women held in Beijing, China, in September 1995, states that:

In the United States, women make up too large a percentage of those in poverty and constitute too small a percentage of those in power. These inequities exact an unacceptable cost in human potential and in the well-being of individuals, families and communities. They warrant our attention and action.

Americans have a stake in how women live around the world. Improving the status and lives of girls and women is an important goal in its own right. It is also the key to building a safer, more secure and peaceful world.

Policies that improve the status of women enable communities to alleviate poverty, develop local economies, expand the number of educated and healthy citizens, sustain the environment and strengthen families. Educating girls and women is one of the best development decisions any country can make. Serious problems facing the world will never be solved until women are able to use their full potential on behalf of themselves, their families and their global and local communities.

Providing a Moral Force for Change

At the Beijing conference, delegates from more than 180 countries met to finalize the "Platform for Action," a blueprint for women's advancement around the world. The Platform for Action lists "12 Critical Areas of Concern" that provide normative guidance for governments that bear the primary responsibility for implementing its strategic objectives. Though it is not a binding treaty, this document represents a global consensus on the issues and commits each nation to goals, standards of behavior, and specific legal, regulatory and enforcement actions. It offers corresponding strategic objectives and actions to be taken by governments, the international community, nongovernmental organizations and the private sector for removing existing obstacles. Each section of a U.N. document is generally adopted by consensus among the delegates present. Each nation's delegation receives instructions from its capital on whether to accept, accept with reservations, or reject the entire document.

Since the United Nations conferences do not produce legally binding documents, U.N. documents have only the moral force of consensus among the nations drafting them, and many U.N. conference goals are not achieved because of failure to implement them. To ensure that the Platform for Action achieves its potential, member governments were challenged to pledge specific commitments for implementation. The U.S. Department of State, on behalf of the United States of America, made eight commitments to the Platform for Action, which are outlined in this book. Because the most effective mechanisms for advancing the status of women are women's nongovernmental organizations (NGOs) at the international, national, state and local levels, the State Department, before the Beijing conference, solicited input from U.S. nongovernmental organizations concerning priorities for U.S. commitments.

These NGOs often hold forums at approximately the same time that official U.N. conferences are held. The forum held in Huairou, China, was attended by more than 30,000 women, men and children from around the globe. Like other NGO forums held parallel to major U.N. conferences, this forum consisted of workshops, seminars, exhibits and briefings, and it drew international celebrities and public figures. NGOs financed their own events and participation.

Securing Justice for All People

An estimated 5,000 to 7,000 U.S. citizens made the trip to the NGO forum in China. I was lucky enough to be one of them. As I listened to workshop presenters, engaged in personal conversations with women from around the world, and studied carefully crafted displays, the women's movement for global social change assumed a concrete authenticity for me that I had only imagined prior to taking part in this international experience. I learned firsthand that there are women everywhere who are determined to secure justice for all people. These women know that there is ample proof that as conditions improve for women, the quality of life for everyone rises.

Unitarian Universalist women at a workshop at the NGO forum in Huairou, China.

Many of the women who came to Beijing work in their home countries with nongovernmental organizations. They came anxious to meet other women at the NGO forum and at the official U.N. conference. Since the 1992 Earth Summit in Rio de Janeiro, NGO participants have played an increasingly more visible and effective role at official U.N. conferences as well as at their own forums. As NGOs have attained status as observers, lobbyists, advisers and members of national delegations, their input has proved useful and often essential to U.N. decision making.

Gender Justice: Providing Understanding and Developing Strategies and Plans for Action

Gender Justice is a workshop series produced by the Unitarian Universalist Service Committee (UUSC), an NGO committed to women's empowerment, which has made one of its primary commitments recognition and promotion of the fact that "women's rights are human rights." This slogan grew out of the U.N. World Conference on Human Rights held in Vienna in 1993 (explored in session one of this workshop series), which was an important turning point for the global women's movement.

Providing a method for gaining a basic understanding of issues that are critical for women worldwide today, this workshop series supports efforts by women to:

- reduce violence against women
- control their personal health and reproductive capacities
- achieve economic independence and justice
- achieve equal access to education, mass media and communications
- actively contribute to environmental sustainability
- gain knowledge of their legal rights and ways to exercise them

Developing local actions that can be undertaken by groups of people who come together during these workshops is one of the key components of this series. During the workshops, ways to use the ideas contained in the Platform for Action and to strengthen and expand already existing efforts on behalf of women will be explored at the local, national and international levels.

Welcome to *Gender Justice: Women's Rights Are Human Rights!*

Elizabeth Fisher
June 1996

Introduction

Now Is the Time for Gender Justice

Many of us who were born female rejoice in our destiny while at the same time we categorically reject the "socially accepted" customs, practices and policies that demean, devalue and violate the rights of women and girls. Many of these practices are based on cultural beliefs or customs that suggest that women or girls, by virtue of their gender, should behave or be treated in certain ways. Such conventions are culturally determined. They change over time and vary widely from one country to another. Many women have dared to live lives that have defied gender stereotypes, but by doing so they have often put themselves in line for merciless assaults.

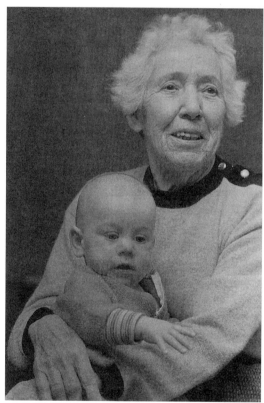

Margaret Saunders, a UUSC volunteer from First Parish Church of Duxbury, Mass. holds an infant at the "Transition to Independent Living" Program of Old Colony YMCA in Plymouth, Mass.

The lives of Madame Marie Curie, George Elliot, Susan B. Anthony, Sojourner Truth, Eleanor Roosevelt, Amelia Earhart, Rigoberta Menchu, Aung San Suu Kyi or Hillary Rodham Clinton, to name just a few, provide ample evidence of the virulence of such attacks. Yet, such retribution has never been able to overcome the desire for gender justice and equality of opportunity that stirs within the heart of most women.

I believe that this desire for justice and equality is usually one that extends beyond a concern for women's rights, to a commitment to the struggle for the rights of all people, especially those who are most vulnerable. I suggest that this commitment stems, in part, from each woman's personal experience of oppression and injustice.

Progress for Women, Progress for All

According to Christina Hoff Sommers, the author of *Who Stole Feminism?*, at one time or another every woman has the "click experience," a moment when a light goes off and a girl or a woman has her first "blazing realization" that women have been cheated and silenced. Although this experience often results in feelings of anger, outrage or even depression, it can often lead to a deep commitment to justice. Many women take a personal interest in leveling the scales of justice. It is one reason why you often find a preponderance of women in the ranks of those who work for social justice whether it be the civil rights movement, the environmental justice movement or the peace movement.

Furthermore, many women believe that by forcing changes in oppressive patriarchal structures they will be leading the way to important changes in society. Such changes include a rejection of military solutions to conflicts and support for sustainable development strategies based on efforts to meet human needs, not just short-term corporate gains. Such changes, many women believe, will lead to a more peaceful and just world order that will truly benefit all the world's people, not just the 50 percent of us who happen to be born female. This belief is captured in the phrase that appears on a U.N. poster: "Progress for women is progress for all."

Today we live in a period of transition, comparable to the period that followed the Industrial Revolution. It presents us with enormous challenges and extraordinary opportunities brought about by several factors: unprecedented technological advances, economic globalization, corporate downsizing, government restructuring and an emergence of conservative political and religious ideologies. In this period of upheaval it is critical that women's voices be heard at the table. Fortunately, today's women are ready, willing and able to take on this leadership role.

A Unique Opportunity

Our experience in the global struggle for women's rights has prepared us well for this opportunity. This reality was clearly demonstrated at the Fourth World Conference on Women in August 1995 when more than 30,000 women from all corners of the globe gathered in China for this conference and the NGO forum, which paralleled it. The Unitarian Universalist Service Committee sent its Board President Dorothy Smith Patterson, Executive Director Dick Scobie and Washington office Staff Director Heather Foote. UUSC also subsidized the participation of several of its project partners who represented women's organizations in Haiti, Eritrea and India. Some UUSC partners from Central America also attended. They provided the important perspective of women from the South[1] to these deliberations.

This unprecedented gathering, the largest U.N. conference ever held, was a spectacular illustration of the power of the international women's movement. Doctor Krishna Ahooja-Patel, president of the Women's World Summit Foundation in Geneva, Switzerland,

---

1 The term South, or global South, refers to the poor nations of the world; the term global North refers to the wealthy industrialized countries. These terms are merely descriptive, as the split between rich and poor nations and people does not fall along strict geographic lines.

described the incredible growth in this movement in just two decades:

> Looking at the history of the past 20 years — this being the Fourth World Conference on Women — and having been to all other conferences, I am completely amazed and fascinated how within two decades this women's revolution has spread to all corners of the world. The international women's movement has helped unleash what we must consider one of the most important social movements of this century...If we start from the Mexico Conference in 1975, in the government delegations there were few women. Those who were there were the wives of the political representatives who held political power. But the women who came to Beijing, as a part of more than 170 delegations, were women leaders in their own rights. I do not know of any other area where such fundamental change has taken place in 20 short years; we have actually forged a whole cadre of women leaders in just 20 years.[2]

Dick Scobie of UUSC echoed this sentiment and suggested that it is this movement that will lead the struggle for human rights in the next century:

> I believe that at different moments in history the leadership of the broader movement for human rights passes from one group to another. The issues have sometimes been defined primarily in terms of race, at other times in terms of class. At this moment they are being defined in terms of gender. I believe that the international women's movement is currently the vanguard of the human rights movement and I am proud to be part of an organization that is engaged in this struggle.

Fulfilling the Promise of Beijing

It is this conviction that prompted the Unitarian Universalist Service Committee to launch a major initiative to engage the women and men of this country in efforts to fulfill the promises and commitments made at Beijing. UUSC is a membership organization, rooted in and inspired by liberal religious principles, that has worked to advance human rights in the United States and abroad for more than five decades. UUSC has supported locally-based groups in Asia, Africa, Latin America and the Caribbean that have addressed issues of women's empowerment, education, health and family planning since the 1960s. UUSC's approach, which stresses individual human rights, has always emphasized the importance of providing women with knowledge and services to empower them to make informed

---

2 "Women Are Changing the World - A 20 Year Record," Women's International Network News, Winter 1996, Vol. 22, No. 1.

choices about their lives. From early on in its history, UUSC recognized that these choices are not made in a vacuum, but in a broader context that includes women's roles and participation in the economic, social and political life of their communities.

Tibetan women demonstrate at the NGO forum.

We hope that this workshop series will be a useful tool for providing participants with a taste of what went on at Beijing and an understanding of the agenda for action that was articulated there. We also hope that those who use it will be moved to take steps to join in the struggle for gender justice and human rights for all the world's people.

The theme of the NGO forum was: "Look at the World Through Women's Eyes." Its purpose was to provide an opportunity for sharing experiences, ideas and concerns and lobbying official government delegates to support particular language in the Platform for Action. The platform contains a global plan for women's empowerment, which was negotiated over a two-year period involving both preparatory conferences and regional meetings in several countries.

The document that finally emerged from this process is a consensus document adopted by more than 180 countries, which contains some major breakthroughs, including the reaffirmation and extension of previous commitments to promote and protect women's human rights negotiated at recent U.N. conferences in Vienna, Cairo and Copenhagen. These human rights include the right to be free from violence; the right to sexual and reproductive health — free from discrimination or coercion; access to information about sexual and reproductive health; equal rights to inheritance; and the obligation of governments to pursue and punish rape and sexual violence in situations of armed conflict as war crimes. It is a major achievement, though it has been criticized by some because it does not effectively deal with many of the concerns expressed by the world's women concerning poverty, especially those related to the globalization of the economy, economic restructuring and structural adjustment.[3] These oversights clearly point to the need for action to change these policies that have led to major cutbacks in education, health care and government subsidies for the poor in both the North and the South. These cutbacks have been felt most directly by poor women and their families.

A Valuable Tool in Advancing the Rights of Women

Despite these shortcomings, the platform is an important tool for promoting the advancement of women. It represents the culmination of many years of work by dedicated women from every corner of the globe who make up the international women's movement — women who have fought for food, shelter, comprehensive health care, schools, rape crisis centers, shelters for battered women, abortion rights, legal services, affirmative action, equal pay for equal work, educational and training opportunities, day care, credit, land, family planning services, access to political power and influence in their societies and an end to violence against women, forced marriages, sexual slavery, sexual harassment and environmental degradation.

The women who gathered at Beijing also called for changes in the ways that governments allocate their resources. They want cutbacks in military expenditures that continue to take the lion's share of the discretionary budget in this country and in many other nations. In addition, they are concerned about the role of multinational corporations that often ignore environmental and labor laws and whose activities have adversely impacted women's lives.

In the pages that follow, you will find a description of many of the problems that women face on a daily basis. You will also find profiles of several programs and organizations that have been formed by women to deal with their problems. We hope that these examples will provide you with some idea of the energy, strength and wisdom that the international women's movement represents.

The Spirit of Beijing

I would also like to share with you an excerpt from a talk by Barbara Zeckhauser, a Unitarian Universalist woman from New Hampshire, one of more than 50 who participated in the NGO forum. I hope it

---

3 Structural adjustment refers to the changes in government policies and practices which typically lead to cutbacks in government services, increases in unemployment, privatization of government industries or services and export-led development. Many of these changes have been forced on the governments of the South by the World Bank and International Monetary Fund to free up funds to pay back interest on old loans made by previous governments. In Northern countries, similar government austerity measures have been enacted to deal with budget deficits resulting from high military budgets and tax cuts that have benefited corporations or those in high-income brackets. Many of these changes impact most acutely on the lives of poor women and their families.

will give you an idea of the spirit and flavor of who went to Beijing and what went on there.

> From Korea they came: old women, in their 70s and 80s to speak about being forced to serve as "comfort women" for Japanese soldiers during World War II.
>
> From India they came: with stories of girls sold as brides at nine, condemned to be uneducated slaves for the rest of their lives, and about women killed by their husbands so they could marry again for larger dowries.
>
> Women came from Bosnia, Serbia and Croatia to keep communications open, sharing stories about the horrors of war. Women from the former Russian republics did the same. Besides sharing their pain, women came to share solutions to the problems they face.
>
> They shared ideas about how to cook with the sun, how to save trees. They taught each other successful pregnancy prevention methods and about sterile birthing practices.
>
> Women from Palestine and Israel learned mediation skills in a workshop led by the Queen of Belgium. Women from the Scandinavian countries came to tell about the work they're doing to work toward balanced gender representation in their parliaments. They held strategy sessions for women who want to run for office.
>
> Women learned about monitoring the media for the coverage of issues that are important to them. They also strategized about how to get the media to frame the issues and debates of our time from a woman's perspective.
>
> Women came to demonstrate: Cambodians protesting land mines, Poles wanting access to abortion, South Sea Islanders opposing atomic testing, Filipinos demanding protection for migrant workers, women protesting all kinds of violence.
>
> There were workshops about the all too common practice of selling young girls to be used as sexual slaves for tourists and businessmen in the Far East and about the fact that thousands of poor young women from countries like the Philippines are promised jobs that trap them into this most cruel kind of slavery.
>
> The theme of the conference was: "Look at the World Through Women's Eyes." See this practice through a frightened young women's eyes, and you'll understand why it's so important for those of us who went to China to tell these stories to some of you who didn't, and why it's so important for all of us to work together to put into practice the Platform for Action adopted there.

We hope that these materials and the videos that supplement them will provide you with an opportunity to look at the world through women's eyes, to look at gender issues and how they impact all of our lives, and to learn more about the international women's movement and the many important steps that women have taken along the road to Beijing. We also hope that after completing the series, participants will join together to begin to act on the steps envisioned in the platform so that we can begin to grapple with what we as individuals or as members of a group can do to end gender bias and reorient our national and international priorities to create a world based on equality, development and peace for all the world's people.

We also hope that after participating in the workshop series you will join UUSC's International Human Rights Network: Focus on Women. By doing so you can keep connected to the ongoing struggle for women's rights around the globe.

The world's women have placed an impressive agenda before us. They need allies to help put it into practice. Come, let us walk with them. *Together we will transform the world!*

Linda Gray MacKay
June 1996

Facilitator's Guide

How to Facilitate These Workshops

The word "facilitator" comes from the Latin root meaning "one who makes things easy." A good facilitator ensures that the group achieves its aims and encourages active participation from everyone. This series consists of six two- or three-hour workshops designed to provide participants with an overview of complex social issues and to help them gain an appreciation of how these issues are interconnected. Developing local actions, strengthening and expanding already existing efforts on behalf of women's rights, furthering personal education on key issues and deepening individual commitment to global social welfare are all potential benefits of this workshop series.

The material in this series may elicit strong emotions from some members of the group. Session one contains a section entitled "Feelings and Action" that suggests ways to help group members deal with their emotional reactions.

Here are a few key questions and answers that will make the job easier.

What about co-facilitators?

It is usually easier to facilitate and plan a workshop if two people work together. While one leads an exercise, the other can keep an eye on group dynamics, provide logistical support and so on.

What is the ideal size for a group?

This will vary depending on the nature of the participants. Often 12 to 20 individuals assure sufficient attendance at each session (everyone cannot always come each time), while also allowing for good group participation.

How important is it to prepare for the sessions?

Facilitating is an adventure. Surprises usually occur during any facilitation experience. When a facilitator is prepared, she/he is better able to react appropriately and manage successfully most unanticipated occurrences. Being familiar with the flow of the activities and the time allotted to each one is key to making the experience a successful one.

How should the facilitator prepare for the workshop sessions?

- Review all materials before each session, including the resource and reference materials that follow the workshop text, to become fully comfortable with the process and the content of the particular session.

- Write lists on flip charts. Instructions on what to write is under "Preparation" on the first page of each session. Preparing these pages in advance of the session will not only help to make the class run more smoothly, it will also increase the facilitator's familiarity with the workshop material prior to the session.

- Review background material to be able to elaborate on flip chart points. Participants should be encouraged to read this material as well.

- Check out the physical surroundings: the arrangement and comfort of chairs, ability to hear, temperature of the room and so on. Arrange chairs in a circle if possible.

- Have the necessary video equipment available. Check out the tape before the session to prepare the group for its contents. The videos are available from UUSC for rental ($10) or purchase ($20). One videotape per group is recommended.

- Supply refreshments for the first session. Invite the participants to share this responsibility in the following weeks. During the first session, send around a sign-up sheet asking for volunteers to supply drinks or snacks for the succeeding sessions.

- Arrive early to make sure everything is in order and to welcome participants.

Why are centering exercises included in the series?

The decision to participate in a workshop series on women's rights is one that involves a level of commitment that can be enhanced by activities that allow time for reflection and personal sharing. Accordingly, each session begins and ends with a time to center the group's thoughts and envision a brighter future. The vision statement developed at the NGO forum in China, poems, and personal sharing exercises are used for this purpose. In addition, in the resource section there are several songs that can be used to end the sessions if desired. See the final resource section for information on the *Sister Carry On* audiotape that is available to those who would like to hear some of the songs sung before introducing them to the group.

What if the group would like to schedule longer sessions?

The directions allow for two- or three-hour sessions.

What are some important points to remember about using flip charts?

- Keep an ongoing flip chart page posted to list topics that members of the group might want to pursue following the workshop series.

- In later sessions, attach lists from previous brainstorming sessions to the walls. Encourage participants, before or after the sessions, to add ideas or resources to any of the lists. All the lists will be used in the last session when the group develops an action plan.

- Write only the bold-face words, not the entire sentence, on flip charts.

- When reviewing the flip chart pages verbally during the sessions, share the entire explanation contained in the text, not just the shortened phrase.

What are the rules for brainstorming?

- No criticism, evaluation, judgment, or defense of ideas during the brainstorming session.
- No limit on "wild" ideas, no matter how outrageous or impractical they may seem. Express every idea.
- Quantity is better than quality.
- "Piggybacking" — building on ideas — is encouraged.[1]

What are ways to aid participants' retention?

Each session contains a page for participants to write down what they wish to remember or investigate after the session is over. A short journal writing period (two to five minutes) is suggested just before the "Closing Circle" to allow time for reflection during the session, while ideas are still fresh. Participants might also be encouraged to keep a longer journal.

Why are learning styles important?

Learning styles of adults vary considerably. The attention span of the average adult for any given form of educational presentation is about 15 to 20 minutes. This is why changing the form of the experience frequently improves retention and motivation. Some individuals learn from information, others by empathizing with another's situation. Participatory activities help most adults retain information and empathize, thus being one of the more effective teaching styles. This is why this program suggests involving participants in a variety of ways.

What is the best way to keep the group moving through the activities?

Each activity is allotted a specific amount of time. These times may seem insufficient. However, because this series is designed to give participants a sense of the interconnection among the Critical Areas Of Concern that form the basis of the Platform for Action, the structure of the workshops provides the opportunity to touch on multiple subjects rather than dwell on any one topic for a long period of time.

Before and during the workshop series, remind participants that the purpose of this experience is to gain an overview of the many aspects of the global situation for women, not to pursue in depth any one area of concern.

Modify the prescribed format of these workshops if the group needs fewer activities and more time. Preselect the most appropriate activities for the group. Facilitators are more effective if they are comfortable with the format. Altering the format requires re-crafting the entire session to ensure sufficient time for the opening and closing.

---

1 Pfeiffer, J. William (ed.) *Theories and Models in Applied Behavioral Science*, Vol.3.

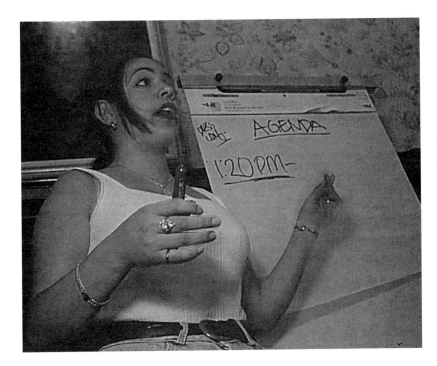

Sonia Ramirez from Oakland, Calif., leads a UUSC-sponsored workshop on conflict resolution.

Is it important to start and end at the agreed upon time?

In order to make the best use of the time available, it is important to start at the time agreed upon even if everyone is not there. If latecomers continue to be a concern, invite the group to discuss it, or perhaps renegotiate the starting time. Ending on time is also important. Be sure that there is closure time for the group, and always allow time for brainstorming about action. This will require setting a time, approximately 20 minutes before the end of the workshop, to stop all activities and begin brainstorming for action (five minutes), journal writing (two minutes) and forming the "Closing Circle" (five minutes).

What about a break?

A 10-minute break has been included in the overall timing of each session. This is an important feature and should be maintained if possible. It is also important to resume as close to the end of 10 minutes as possible. This usually leaves the group refreshed but not distracted.

How does a facilitator keep the group on track?

- Ask for a volunteer to keep track of the time allotted for the workshop segments.
- If a discussion is not going anywhere, the facilitator should ask questions to give the discussion direction.

- The facilitator should manage the discussion rather than getting emotionally involved. For example, she/he could say: "I'm not clear what you mean when you say..."
- If the group is spending a long time on a small point, the facilitator should note it on the flip chart as something that could be pursued later, but move on to the next step in the process.
- The facilitator should not take sides.

How does a facilitator encourage participation?

- Create a sense of fun, especially at the beginning of an exercise.
- Draw on people's experiences.
- Create an atmosphere of collective inquiry.
- Give feedback in a way that is clear and specific.
- Make everyone feel valued.
- Ensure that every person has a chance to give her/his viewpoint.

UUSC volunteers at a skills training program for teenage mothers held in Plymouth, Massachusetts.

How do you deal with conflict?

There will often be differences of opinion and conflict when people exchange their thoughts and feelings honestly. Facilitators should encourage participants to explain their points of view and give others the opportunity to do the same. Recognize that conflict is happening and bring it out into the open by saying something like: "We seem to have a difference of opinion on this issue." Decide if this is something that should be dealt with in the group or later, possibly with a mediator from the group.

Some ways of dealing with conflict in a group are:

- Ensure that conflict never becomes a personalized attack. People can say: "I am not clear about what you mean," rather than: "You're not making sense." Move the discussion away from personalities to the actual problem at hand.
- Rephrase the comments made into general questions for the group.
- If two/three people are involved in the exchange, ask the rest of the group to comment on the exchange: "What do others think/feel about this?"
- Restate the issue, clarifying it and giving a breathing space: "Are you saying...?"

- Sometimes simple misunderstandings of each other's position is at the base of the argument. Ask each of the parties involved in the conflict to summarize the other's point of view. For example, ask those who are in conflict:

  "How do you understand what Sue said?"

  "Sue, is that what you said?"

- If the conflict persists, ask the rest of the group if they want to pursue the question further or if they would like to move on.

How do you deal with painful feelings that are brought out?

If an exercise or discussion brings out painful personal experiences (for example an abusive situation), it is important to allow the person space to feel what they are feeling. Remind the person to focus on her breathing as this will calm and center her. Keep the name of a counselor available should participants need to talk to a professional.

Are special instructions for the facilitator included in the text?

Yes. The facilitator should read aloud or paraphrase the various parts of the text as follows:

Activity Title: Read aloud.

Objective: States the aim of the activity and the amount of time required to complete it. Read aloud.

Process: This word indicates the beginning of the directions that guide the facilitator through the steps of the activity.

Facilitator's Note: These notes contain instructions on how to proceed in order to help the activity run smoothly.

 The flip chart icon indicates the information that the facilitator needs to write on a flip chart prior to the session. Other uses of flip charts are mentioned in *Facilitator's Note*.

Indented Paragraphs: These indicate material that the facilitator should read or paraphrase aloud. These paragraphs are typically preceded by words such as: "Explain, Discuss or Share." Key words appear in boldface type to make it easier for the facilitator to glance at the sentences and emphasize the most essential information.

Information Contained in Boxes: The facilitator reads or paraphrases this information.

Quotes: Quotes that are contained in shaded boxes and set off from the rest of the text do not need to be read aloud, unless indicated in directions.

Volunteer Readers: Sections for volunteers to read are marked "Reader 1," etc., and appear in a different typeface. The facilitator should invite members of the group to be readers for particular sessions before the session begins.

Assignments for Next Week: Review assignments with the group at the end of each session. In the case of sessions two, three and six, specific readings are given. It is highly recommended that all participants complete these assignments in advance of the next session. The facilitator will ask for volunteer presenters to share the highlights of the readings assigned for sessions two and three.

Background and Resource Material: This is essential reading for the facilitator. Encourage all participants to read this information as well before each session.

EXAMPLE OF USE OF FACILITATOR INDICATORS

The Global Women's Movement
(15 minutes)

Objective

To become acquainted with the nature and importance of the Platform for Action that was adopted at the U.N. Fourth World Conference on Women and its place in the historical development of women's movements around the globe.

Process

1. Share the information below:

    The efforts of women at all levels of society to improve their lives and to form alliances with women from other countries has been called the "Global Women's Movement." This movement is based on belief in the equal rights of women and men, a concept enshrined in the U.N. Charter, the Universal Declaration of Human Rights and the Convention on the Elimination of All Forms of Discrimination Against Women (CEDAW). The women's movement has also been strengthened by several major United Nations conferences, four of which focused on women. Read aloud or paraphrase.

Facilitator's Note: Write the following on a flip chart in advance. Review "The Road to Beijing: A U.N. Chronology" (page 40) in advance so that you can mention a few facts as you point to the dates and events on the chart. Prepare a flip chart with the following information in advance.

The Road to Beijing

1945	U.N. CHARTER
1948	Universal Declaration of Human Rights
1975	MEXICO CITY - First World Conference on Women
1979	Convention on the Elimination of All Forms of Discrimination Against Women (CEDAW)
1980	COPENHAGEN - Second World Conference on Women
1985	NAIROBI - Third World Conference on Women
1992	RIO - U.N. Conference on Environment & Development
1993	VIENNA - World Conference on Human Rights
1994	CAIRO - International Conference on Population and Development
1995	COPENHAGEN - World Summit for Social Development
1995	BEIJING - Fourth World Conference on Women

Workshop Activities

This guide contains guidelines for six workshops filled with hands-on activities. While each session contains unique elements, they are generally built around these key segments:

Opening Circle — To begin each workshop, participants have an opportunity to share something personal that relates to the focus of the workshop.

Exploration of a Central Issue(s) — Each workshop focuses on a topic or topics that are supported by one or more of the 12 Critical Areas of Concern contained in the Platform for Action produced at the Fourth World Conference on Women, such as: violence, education, or economic equity. This segment of each workshop gives participants an opportunity to explore these central topics.

Role Play (Sessions two and five) — In order to develop a deeper appreciation for situations affecting women around the world, members of the group, during these two sessions, will portray positions held by a range of individuals who represent different perspectives and various regions of the world.

Video Segments — The Unitarian Universalist Service Committee has developed a 40-minute video that includes four segments from longer videos that are relevant to the discussions that will take place during sessions one, three and four. Using them during these sessions will greatly enhance the learning experience of the workshop participants. The videos are available from UUSC for a seven-week rental ($10) or for purchase ($20). For more information contact UUSC at (617) 868-6600.

Brainstorming for Action — During each workshop, aspects of the Platform for Action pertaining to the concerns of the workshop will be reviewed and a brief period will also be included to list possible activities relating to the focus of the workshop. Action ideas the group brainstorms will be listed at this time so they can be utilized during the final session when the group develops its plan of action, which will include concrete activities the group commits to undertake. In addition, community contacts participants already have or know about that relate to the focus of the session will be recorded.

Successful Strategies for Action — Each session also contains a description of a successful action that has been taken relating to the Critical Areas of Concern of the Platform for Action focused on during the session to provide ideas for action that might be adaptable.

Closing Circle — This final segment gives participants a chance to be together for a few moments of meditation, reflection and inspiration before ending each workshop.

Gender, Human Rights and Global Organizing

Critical areas of the platform covered in this session:

Human Rights of Women (Section IV. I)

Violence Against Women (Section IV. D)

Women and Armed Conflict (Section IV. E)

Two-Hour Workshop

Activities	Minutes
Opening Circle	15
Orientation to the Series	10
Feelings and Action	3
Central Issue: Gender Typing	25
The Global Women's Movement	10
Break	10
Central Issue: Women's Rights Are Human Rights (includes 10-minute video)	30
Platform for Action Positions	5
Brainstorming for Action	5
Journal Writing	3
Assignments for Next Week	2
Closing Circle	2
Total Time:	**120**

Materials

One *Gender Justice* guide for each person

Objects, such as textiles, used by women around the world

Pictures or statues of women from a variety of cultures

A candle and matches

Two flip charts

Masking tape

Video

Preparation

Write on separate flip chart pages the words that appear in the following sections of text:

Goals for gender justice chart (page 6)

Definition of sex and gender (page 8)

Gender typing of girls and boys (page 10)

Blank page to list typical girl/boy adjectives

The road to Beijing (page 12)

Questions relating to "women's rights are human rights" (page 16)

Set up centerpiece

Check VCR and tape

Ask for four volunteers to read parts of the closing poem

Three-Hour Workshop

Activities	Minutes
Opening Circle	15
Orientation to the Series	10
Feelings and Action	3
Central Issue: Gender Typing	35
Global Women's Movement	10
Central Issue: Women's Rights Are Human Rights (includes 10 minute video)	30
Break	10
Mind Map: Violence Against Women*	45
Platform for Action Positions	5
Brainstorming for Action	10
Journal Writing*	3-5
Closing Circle	2
Total Time:	**180**

Materials

One *Gender Justice* guide for each person

Objects, such as textiles, used by women around the world

Pictures or statues of women from a variety of cultures

A candle and matches

Two flip charts

Masking tape

Video

Preparation

Write on separate flip chart pages the words that appear in the following sections of text:

   Goals for gender justice chart (page 6)

   Definition of sex and gender (page 8)

   Gender typing of girls and boys (page 10)

   Blank page to list typical girl/boy adjectives

   The Road to Beijing (page 12)

   Questions relating to "women's rights are human rights" (page 16)

   Causes of violence against women (page 29)

Set up centerpiece

Check VCR and tape

Ask for four volunteers to read parts of the closing poem

*exercises and/or time added

Opening Circle

(15 minutes)

Objective

To focus the group and allow for a brief period of personal sharing.

Process

Facilitator's Note: This will be the first time participants meet in this setting. If possible, place chairs in a circle. At the center of the circle put objects or pictures relating to women from around the world as well as a candle to be lit when the session begins. Use the centerpiece for each session.

1. Welcome participants and then explain:

    > This opening circle is a time for us to introduce ourselves and **share briefly what has brought us** to this workshop series. This might include any international or local experiences you have had that have prompted your interest in women's human rights and concern about conditions important to women globally.

2. Make it clear that men are welcome to be members of the group and that one of the premises of this program is that everyone will benefit from gender equity and equality for women.

3. Share the following quote that highlights this point of view:

    > "Empowering women around the world is **not just a women's issue.** It is important for both men and women. **Progress for women is progress for everyone.** We must respond to this vision: the future of our children depends on it."[1]

4. Provide a model to the group by being the first to share. Keeping in mind the size of the group, be sure to keep your sharing brief to assure that this segment can be completed in the allotted 15 minutes.

5. Make a circle, light the candle and read together, "Look at the World Through Women's Eyes," which appears in the box on the following page. Share the reasons why you have decided to facilitate this workshop series. Invite the person next to you to share why she or he is attending the workshops.

---

1 Baroness Chalker, Britain's Minister for Overseas Development; Address to the Fourth World Conference on Women, September 1995.

Look at the World Through Women's Eyes
Theme of the NGO Forum on Women held in China, September 1995

Visualize a world where all conflicts — domestic violence, gun fights on the streets and civil wars — are solved through negotiation. When women and families feel safe in their homes, on the street and in their communities.

Visualize a society where clean water, food and housing are priorities for each citizen in every village, town and city. Where women can get credit and access to other resources they need to be fully economically productive.

Visualize nations where girls are educated and valued as much as boys, and all people are free to develop their full potential. Where men, too, are responsible for their fertility and sexuality, and family planning is transformed into comprehensive reproductive health care. Where women's knowledge and experience are integrated into every day decisions And legislation is passed through parliaments with a critical mass of women representatives.

Visualize the globe where the massive amounts of money spent on guns and weapons is used instead to end poverty, preserve health and well-being and create sustainable human development.

This is the kind of world women organizing for the NGO Forum on Women in Beijing want to build.

Look at the world through women's eyes.

Orientation to Series
(10 minutes)

Objective
To clarify the approach and goals of the *Gender Justice* workshop series.

Process
1. Once the personal sharing is completed, ask the group to think about their expectations for the workshop series and write these on the flip chart.

Facilitator's Note: When jotting down ideas or statements on the flip chart, remember to simplify, recording key words or simple phrases that accurately reflect the comment. Have the person who originated the idea correct the wording if it is not accurate.

2. After everyone has had a chance to speak, display the following list of goals for this workshop series (write these on a flip chart before beginning). Compare the participants' workshop expectations to

these goals, pointing out where the workshop series is designed to meet the goals expressed, and where participants' expectations might go beyond what can be accomplished in this program.

Workshop Series Goals

To discover the holistic approach to the Beijing Platform for Action

To connect with others around women's human rights

To plan for future study, action and support

3. While displaying the above goals on the flip chart, paraphrase the following summaries, which provide fuller explanations.

> **Educate ourselves** about the movement to promote the concept that women's rights are human rights.

> **Explore** the most important issues affecting women today and how they interconnect.

> **Build relationships** with others who are working on local, regional, national or international plans of action.

> **Develop practical ways** to support one another in our individual and collective work by cooperating with one another in alliances and coalitions for greater effectiveness.

4. Discuss the following:

> Psychologists have long noted that individuals exhibit **varied learning styles**. Learning may occur through presentations, participation in simulated real life situations, discussions, watching videos, reading and so on. Most people learn best from a mixture of these. For this reason, the workshop series contains a variety of **educational experiences** so that we can maximize what we learn.

> While we may want to stay with a topic longer than is scheduled, we will often need to **move on** before we have completely exhausted a topic.

> Part of what we will do is keep track of those **areas to which we might want to return** as part of our continuing study and action on these issues that could extend beyond the six workshops.

Facilitator's Note: Remember to keep a flip chart where you list topics that some members of the group might want to pursue after the workshop series is complete.

5. Explain the structure and process of the program:

    The **structure** of this program consists of six two- or three-hour workshops that include a variety of participatory activities such as:

    - Discussion, role play, story telling, personal sharing, and video viewing

    The **process** used is designed to bring a group together for exploration and study of issues that are key to women's empowerment in order to lead to planning, actions and ongoing advocacy by:

    - **Identifying** and exploring **central issues**

    - **Considering strategies** and actions included in the Platform for Action

    - **Brainstorming about possible actions** on the international, national, state and local levels

    - **Compiling information about** participants' **local contacts** and current venues of involvement

    - Designing a **plan for action** to which group participants will commit

Feelings and Action
(3 minutes)

Objective
To acknowledge the emotional power the material in these workshops contain and to suggest methods for dealing with personal reactions.

Process
Facilitator's Note: The material that will be covered may elicit strong feelings that need to be acknowledged. One way to handle these emotions is to keep a journal noting issues and feelings. There will be a journal page at the end of each session to jot down feelings, reactions or ideas.

1. Discuss the following:

    As we study the varied injustices that women are subjected to around the globe, it can be difficult to deal with our **reactions.** We may feel frightened, angry, victimized or overwhelmed. **Writing in the journal** can help people deal with these strong feelings. **Taking action** to remedy problems can transform those feelings into **self-esteem.**

2. Pass out the books and briefly review with the group the structure of

this book, which includes in sequence: workshop activities and background and resource material grouped by session.

3. Make participants aware of the page entitled, "What's in the Workshop?" on page xxix for those who want a more detailed orientation to the activities included in each workshop. If you feel the entire group needs this orientation, review the various elements together.

The transition from elementary to middle school may be the most damaging period of a girl's young life.

Myra and David Sadker, *Failing at Fairness*

Exploration of a Central Issue: Gender Typing
(25 minutes)

Objective
To explore the realities and effects of gender typing.

Process

1. Explain:

    The way we see ourselves and others is often influenced by our attitudes toward **sexual differences**. To explore this aspect of our identity, think about how you would **differentiate** between the words **"sex" and "gender"** and jot down your definition of each on the journal page for this session in your book.

Facilitator's Note: Allow about one minute for participants to develop their own definitions of sex and gender and have pencils or pens available.

2. Ask one or two participants to share their descriptions. Later compare them with these definitions that you have written on the flip chart:

Facilitator's Note: Prepare a flip chart in advance with the following definitions of sex and gender. Add any additional ideas offered by the group.

Definition of Sex and Gender

Sex is an analytical category that distinguishes males from females exclusively by their biological or reproductive characteristics.

Gender is a cultural construct that refers to the different roles, responsibilities and activities that societies or cultures prescribe for females and males.

3. Explain the difference between sex and gender:

    Biological differences are universal and unchangeable except through the most modern methods of medical science. **Gender differences**, on the other hand, **vary by culture and over time**. Typically they include attitudes toward the division of labor and distribution of resources, which are based on culturally determined perceptions of differences in men's and women's natures and capabilities. **Gender biases** are often so **deeply embedded psychologically** that they are sometimes thought to be biologically[2] not socially determined.

It is the division of labor dictated by gender-based stereotyping that has led to the fact that **"women's work" is frequently undervalued** or taken for granted in most societies. Furthermore, such work is **rarely "counted"** in the way that other productive activities are when they are included in a nation's gross national product.

In addition, even when women have jobs outside the home they are still held responsible for most **child rearing and housekeeping tasks.** Also, because women are usually held responsible for tasks for which they are either not paid, or underpaid, they are often **economically dependent.**

These realities have made women **vulnerable to discrimination, exploitation, and abuse,** factors that form the basis of the so called **gender gap** that is apparent in most societies. This gap is manifested in women's unequal access to resources and political and economic power. The following chart[3] illustrates the impact of gender bias on women's lives around the globe.

THE GENDER GAP: WOMEN'S SHARE OF...

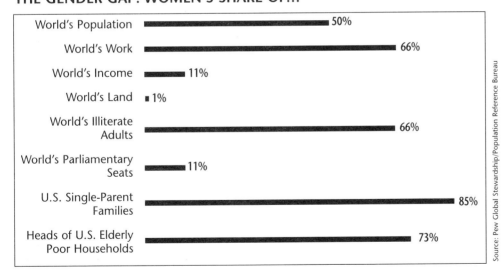

World's Population	50%
World's Work	66%
World's Income	11%
World's Land	1%
World's Illiterate Adults	66%
World's Parliamentary Seats	11%
U.S. Single-Parent Families	85%
Heads of U.S. Elderly Poor Households	73%

Source: Pew Global Stewardship/Population Reference Bureau

2 During the negotiations of the Platform for Action, debates over whether to substitute the word sex for the word gender took place. Some representatives argued that the use of the word gender was inappropriate because it does not acknowledge biologically determined behavior or responsibilities, which, they maintain, exist. The issue was resolved during negotiations prior to the Beijing conference and the word gender was retained.
3 "A Matter of Simple Justice: Women's Rights Are Human Rights," Center for Policy Alternatives, 1996. Reprinted with permission.

4. Ask participants to think about the differences between girls' and boys' experiences during the most impressionable years of their lives.

The Delhi community health workers hold up panels on which they've written statements on a range of women's rights issues — from gender discrimination to the dangers of Norplant. Women raise awareness by singing these statements in their communities.

5. Ask them to suggest ways that boys and girls are socialized. The categories below may be helpful, but see if the group can come up with them before uncovering them on the flip chart.

Gender Typing of Boys and Girls

ways they are **dressed**

kinds of **toys** they are given

types of **tasks** they are expected to perform at **home**

ways they are expected to **interact** with others

ways they are expected to handle **conflict**

role models they are given

types of **subjects** they are expected to do well in **at school**

ways they are encouraged to get **recognition** from peers and parents

kinds of **careers** they are encouraged to choose

ways their sex is **portrayed in the media** or school texts

6. Ask participants to briefly brainstorm adjectives to describe "typical" boys or "typical" girls, allowing about two minutes for each brainstorm. On the flip chart write **Girls** on one side and **Boys** on the other, with a line down the middle.

7. Another aspect of gender stereotyping is **prejudice against homosexuals.**[4] Homosexuals are often subjected to harassment and discrimination based on their sexual orientation.[5] For more information on how these issues were raised at the Fourth World Conference on Women see page 58 in the background and resource section.

The Global Women's Movement

(10 minutes)

Objective

To become acquainted with the Platform for Action that was adopted at the U.N. Fourth World Conference on Women and its place in the historical development of women's movements around the globe.

Process

1. Share the information below:

> The efforts of women at all levels of society to improve their lives and to form alliances with women from other countries has been called the **"Global Women's Movement."** This movement is based on a belief in the **equal rights of women and men,** a concept enshrined in the U.N. Charter, the Universal Declaration of Human Rights and in the Convention on the Elimination of All Forms of Discrimination Against Women (CEDAW).[6] The women's movement has also been strengthened by several major United Nations Conferences, four of which focused on women.

Facilitator's Note: Write the following on a flip chart in advance. Review "The Road to Beijing: A U.N. Chronology" on page 40 in advance so that you can mention a few facts as you point to the dates and events on the chart.

Have you noticed how at puberty the Amazon-like energy we are born with fades and we turn into doubt-filled creatures with clipped wings? The female condition...Isabel, it's like having rocks tied to your ankles so you can't fly.

Isabel Allende, *Paula*

4 The Unitarian Universalist Association was one of the first religious groups to support the rights of homosexual and bisexual persons. For more information about resources available to counteract homophobia in your congregation or community contact the Unitarian Universalist Association's Office of Lesbian and Gay Concerns at UUA, 25 Beacon Street, Boston, MA 02108, (617) 742-2100 x465.
5 Sexual orientation is the "deep seated or predispositional direction of one's sexual response toward partners of the same sex (homosexuals- lesbians and gays), other sex (heterosexuals), or both sexes (bisexuals)," from *Beyond Pink and Blue*, Tracey Robinson-Harris and Ritch Savin-Williams, Unitarian Universalist Association, Boston, MA, 1994.
6 A convention is a legally binding treaty or agreement among nations that have agreed to it. The CEDAW convention was passed by the United Nations in 1979 and has been adopted by more than 150 nations. The United States is the only major industrialized nation that has not ratified it. Though it has been signed by President Clinton, it must be ratified by the U.S. Senate in order to become law.

The Road to Beijing

1945   U.N. CHARTER

1948   Universal Declaration of Human Rights

1975   MEXICO CITY - First World Conference on Women

1979   Convention on the Elimination of All Forms of Discrimination Against Women (CEDAW)

1980   COPENHAGEN - Second World Conference on Women

1985   NAIROBI - Third World Conference on Women

1992   RIO - U.N. Conference on Environment & Development

1993   VIENNA - World Conference on Human Rights

1994   CAIRO - International Conference on Population and Development

1995   COPENHAGEN - World Summit for Social Development

1995   BEIJING - Fourth World Conference on Women

2. Continue discussing the following:

The role of the U.N. has been to provide a forum for **dialogue,** which has helped to produce hope, vision and new solutions to difficult problems. The **agreements** produced at U.N. conferences are adopted by consensus and represent agreed-upon **international standards.** These are used in many countries **to confront government officials** and **demand redress** of situations that do not conform to these standards.

The **First United Nations Conference on Women** was held in **Mexico City** in **1975.** In addition to the three other international women's conferences held, several world conferences on topics such as environment, human rights, population and social development all contributed to the articulation of internationally agreed upon positions on issues relating to women. The Beijing Conference produced the Platform for Action, which is central to this workshop series.

At the **Fourth World Conference on Women,** held in Beijing, China, the world had an opportunity to **review and appraise the advancement of women** since the U.N. held its Third Conference on Women (Nairobi, 1985).

The official U.N. conference included 4,000 delegates from 189 countries who adopted a **Platform for Action** that integrated **12 Critical Areas of Concern** into a vision that supports the concept that "women's rights are human rights."

Parallel to this conference the **Nongovernmental Organization Forum on Women** was held, which was attended by more than 30,000 representatives of nongovernmental organizations as well as individuals from around the globe. It took place in Huairou, a suburb of Beijing. The NGO forum consisted of a wide range of activities including: plenary sessions, workshops, art displays, dance presentations and demonstrations that explored concerns central to women. It was a **major networking event** for women from around the globe.

Those assembled for these events concluded that in the 20 years between the U.N. International Year of Women (1975) and the Fourth World Conference on Women in China (1995), **the situation of women worldwide has deteriorated significantly.** They also identified 12 Critical Areas of Concern developed through a review of progress since the Nairobi Conference (1985). These concerns are areas of particular urgency that stand out as **priorities for action.** Paragraph 45 of the section "Critical Areas of Concern" calls for action and resources on the strategic objectives relating to these critical areas of concern, which are interrelated, interdependent and of high priority. Paragraph 46 of the Platform for Action states:

"To this end, governments, the international community and civil society, including nongovernmental organizations and the private sector, are called upon to take strategic action in the following areas of concern."

These 12 Critical Areas of Concern will form the **basis of our explorations** during this workshop series.

3. Read the description of each of the 12 Critical Areas of Concern and invite group members to alternately read the facts associated with them.

Like the Universal Declaration of Human Rights, the Beijing agreement will be a tool for education and mobilization on women's rights for the coming decade.

Dick Scobie, executive director, Unitarian Universalist Service Committee

As stated in the platform, the 12 Critical Areas of Concern are:

1. The persistent and increasing burden of poverty of women

    More than 1 billion people in the world today, the great majority of whom are women (about 70 percent), live in poverty.

2. Inequalities, inadequacies and unequal access to **education and training**

    Since the mid 1980s, educational and social services available to women have decreased.

3. Inequalities, inadequacies and unequal **access to health care** and related services

    Each year approximately 500,000 women die from complications related to pregnancy and childbirth.

4. **Violence** against Women

    In the U.S., domestic violence is the leading cause of injury to adult women.

5. The effects of armed and other kinds of **conflict** on women, including those living under foreign occupation

    More people (mostly women and children) have died in wars each year of the 1990s than any year since 1945; women and their dependents constitute 75 percent of the world's 23 million refugees.

6. **Inequality in economic structures and policies,** in all forms of productive activities and in access to resources

    Including unpaid work done in the home, women perform more than two-thirds of the world's work, yet receive less that one-tenth of its income.

7. Inequalities between men and women in **power and decision-making** at all levels

    Only 10 percent of parliamentary seats and 6 percent of cabinet positions are occupied by women today. Political representation of women has decreased in most countries in the last decade.

8. **Insufficient mechanisms** at all levels **to promote** the advancement of women

Women still constitute less than one-seventh of top administrators and managers in developing countries. Women put in
longer work hours than men in almost all countries that have
been surveyed, but most of their work remains unpaid,
unrecognized and unvalued in national income accounts.

9. Lack of respect for, and inadequate promotion and pro-
    tection of the **human rights of women**

    The rise in religious fundamentalism and its backlash against
    women has caused a decrease in women's rights and free-
    doms in many countries.

*A Unitarian Universalist,
Dr. Catherine Briggs
speaks out at the
NGO forum.*

10. **Stereotyping** of women and **inequality in women's access
     to,** and participation in all communication systems, espe-
     cially in the **media**

     Male prime time television characters outnumber females
     three-to-one. Front-page female references dropped from an
     average of 25 percent in 1994 to 19 percent in 1995.

11. Gender inequalities in the management of natural
     resources and in the safeguarding of the **environment**

     As consumers and producers, caretakers of families and educa-
     tors, women play an important role in promoting sustainable
     development, yet remain largely absent from decision-making
     and their experience and skills are often overlooked.

12. **Persistent discrimination against** and violation of the
     rights of the girl-child

     65 percent of illiterate adults are women.[7]

7 Adapted from the Minnesota International Network for News and Action for Women,
1995.

Break
(10 minutes)

Exploration of a Central Issue: Women's Rights Are Human Rights
(30 minutes, including a 10 minute video clip)

Objective
To become aware of the importance of including women's rights as an integral component of fundamental human rights.

Process

1. Ask the group to consider the following questions on human rights:

Facilitator's Note: Prepare a flip chart in advance with the following questions.

Women's Rights Are Human Rights

What is a human right?

Do rights apply to what takes place in private spaces such as homes?

Is a right something every person is entitled to?

2. Break the larger group into subgroups of three. After about 10 minutes of small group discussion, bring all participants together. Ask each group to share a few reactions to each question. Record them on the flip chart.

3. Share the following perspectives on human rights:

    The **Universal Declaration of Human Rights**, adopted by the United Nations General Assembly in 1948, asserts that every human being has the right to **life, liberty** and **security of person**, **equal pay for equal work**, **a standard of living adequate for health** and **well-being**, **education**, **freedom from slavery** and **equal protection of the law.**

    Human rights have been defined as:

    - An international **ethical vision of principles** to live by

    - A **value system** that promotes the dignity and worth of all human beings

    - The universal **rights of all** regardless of class, sex or ethnic background by virtue of one's humanity[8]

8 Adapted from *Our Human Rights: A Manual for Women's Human Rights*, a publication of the Organizing Committee for the People's Decade for Human Rights (see bibliography for ordering information).

4. Ask why is it so important to have women's rights viewed as human rights.

5. Ask the group to briefly consider and discuss the following realities and problems that the human rights community is now addressing by pointing out that women's rights are human rights.

> Human rights reality: Women as much as men are entitled to full protection of their rights.
>
> Problem: Women often do not receive the same protection as men.

> Human rights reality: The advancement of women depends on their rights being recognized and protected.
>
> Problem: The unequal status of women results in gender discrimination.

> Human rights reality: Describing an incident as a human rights violation, not just as an unfair practice, gives it greater significance.
>
> Problem: Human rights for women are not guaranteed, but must be articulated and recognized.

6. Explain the following:

> Until recently, human rights groups did not focus on violations of women's human rights because what happens to women was considered to take place largely in the private sector and therefore considered to be outside of human rights considerations. **Violations against women's human rights were also often justified in the name of culture or religion.** Thus, when human rights were considered, violations of women's rights were historically invisible. Rights for women were not included in the mainstream human rights movement until the 1990s.
>
> During the last five years, women and men concerned about assuring equality for women have worked diligently to have human rights extended to women. This struggle was advanced by the conclusions reached at the **Vienna World Conference on Human Rights** in 1993, which declared **human rights** to be **universal** and **indivisible**.[9]

The NGO Forum on Women '95 and the Fourth World Conference on Women are... an historic opportunity to present the global community with a vision for the 21st century, one that is human-centered and informed by looking at the world through women's eyes.

From a flyer distributed at the Beijing conference

---

9 This also means that "economic rights do not have priority over political rights nor political rights over economic rights as had been argued by the East and West respectively during the Cold War." Betty Reardon, *Educating for Human Dignity*, University of Pennsylvania Press, Philadelphia, 1995.

The evolution of this movement has produced a growing understanding that women's rights issues must be understood from a **holistic perspective**. The Platform for Action is an important embodiment of the concept that "**women's rights are human rights.**"

Facilitator's Note: Review the chart entitled, "Platform for Action: An Integrated Holistic Vision." This chart shows how the 12 Critical Areas of Concern are all considered parts of the concept captured in the phrase "women's rights are human rights." It also shows the areas that constitute basic human rights as used in the platform. Encourage participants to review the 12 Critical Areas of Concern in the background and resource material on pages 52-53.

PLATFORM FOR ACTION: INTEGRATED HOLISTIC VISION
Fourth World Conference on Women

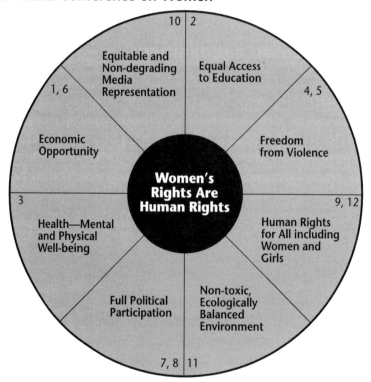

Numbers refer to Critical Areas of Concern

This perspective underlies the Unitarian Universalist Service Committee's approach to women's rights as outlined in the essay, "Reframing the Population Debate," included in the assignments for next week.

7. Explain the following point:

   At the **Vienna** Human Rights Conference, the phrase

"women's rights are human rights" came into use. Violence against women is one of the most prominent human rights abuses women experience. During the Vienna conference, more than a thousand people listened to women testify at the Global Tribunal on Violations of Women's Human Rights.

8. Show the 10-minute video clip of Vienna Tribunal and ask for reactions.

    A video containing this video clip, along with three others suggested for use in later sessions, is available on loan from the UUSC for $10. For more detailed information about this videotape, see page 319 in the resource section. Since there are a limited number of copies available, please contact UUSC as soon as you know you will need it.

A Chinese woman holds up one of the most important messages of the Fourth World Conference on Women in a demonstration organized by UUSC project partner Vimochana at the closing ceremony of the Beijing conference.

9. Discuss these points on violence:

    International and national efforts have been undertaken since 1993 to create **official mechanisms** for dealing with **violence against women.**

    In December **1993,** the **United Nations General Assembly** adopted a landmark resolution on gender violence called, "The Declaration on the Elimination of Violence Against Women." This declaration **defined** for the first time what constitutes an act of **violence against women** and calls on governments and the international community to take specific measures to **prevent such acts.** It defined violence as "any act of gender-based violence that results in, or is likely to result in, **physical, sexual or psychological harm** or suffering to women, including threat of such acts, coercion or arbitrary deprivations of liberty, whether occurring in **public or private life.**"

In **1995**, President Clinton announced the creation of the **Violence Against Women Office at the Justice Department**, following the passage of the 1994 Crime Bill, which included the **Violence Against Women Act**. The goal of this office is to develop a comprehensive national effort to fight domestic violence and other crimes against women.

10. Encourage participants to review the section entitled, "Violence Against Women Act" (page 46) and "National Office" (page 64) in the background and resource section for more details.

> Three-hour session: Add the "Mind Map: Violence Against Women" exercise, page 28. (45 minutes)

It is time for us to say here in Beijing, and for the world to hear, that it is no longer acceptable to discuss women's rights as separate from human rights.

Hillary Rodham Clinton at the Fourth World Conference on Women.

Platform for Action Position on Human Rights, Violence Against Women and Armed Conflicts
(5 minutes)

Objective
To become acquainted with the platform's positions on human rights, violence against women and armed conflicts.

Process
1. Share information on violence against women in conflict situations.

    In addition to concerns for women's rights as human rights as well as freedom from violence, the Platform for Action paid specific attention to the plight of women and children in armed conflict situations. Though women may have no role in the decisions leading to such conflicts and seldom are combatants themselves, they are often responsible for keeping family units intact when social and economic life is disrupted. Often women are also **victims of torture, disappearance, forced prostitution and systematic rape as a weapon of war.**

    "Human Rights of Women," "Violence Against Women," and "Women and Armed Conflict" are three of the 12 Key Areas of Concern in the Platform for Action. The strategic objectives relating to these concerns include:

    - Applying norms and standards to safeguard the full enjoyment of human rights for women

- Eliminating violence against women

- Increasing the participation of women in conflict resolution

- Protecting women in armed and other conflicts

Two of the most **contentious issues** at Beijing platform negotiations that illustrate differing theories of gender and women's human rights involved whether or not to include language explicitly **prohibiting discrimination** on the basis of **sexual orientation** and whether or not to include a footnote in the health section, which qualified governments' commitments to implement that section according to a **nation's religious and cultural values**. These two issues were not resolved until the final hour of negotiations in an informal group by a ruling of the chair on "majority" sentiment — **not to include "sexual orientation" and not to include the footnote in the health section**.[10]

2. Explain:

In Beijing, **the U.S. Government made eight specific commitments to implement the** platform. It is important to hold government agencies accountable for the implementation of their commitments.

Facilitator's Note: For an overview of these commitments, see the box entitled, "Summary of the Eight Major U.S. Commitments to the Platform for Action."

10 The Center for Women's Global Leadership Report of the Women's Human Rights Caucus. See the background and resource section for more detail.

Such violent treatment of women must be seen as a violation of human rights. We must condemn it, we must indict it, we must prosecute it and we must stop it.

Edward Broadbent, president of the International Centre for Human Rights and Democratic Development

Summary of the Eight Major U.S. Commitments to the Platform for Action

1. Establish a White House council on women to plan for the effective implementation within the U.S. of the Platform for Action, which will build on the commitments made at the conference and the work with the NGO community.

2. Launch a six year, $1.6 billion initiative to fight domestic violence and other crimes against women. The Department of Justice will apply funds for specialized police and prosecution units and to train police, prosecutors and judicial personnel.

3. Lead a comprehensive battle through the Department of Health and Human Services on threats to women's health and security — AIDS, smoking and breast cancer.

4. Conduct a grassroots campaign to improve conditions for women in the work place. The Department of Labor will work with employers to develop more equitable pay and promotion policies and to help employees balance the twin responsibilities of family and work.

5. The Treasury Department will take new steps to promote access to financial credit for women, with presidential awards given to outstanding U.S. microenterprise lending organizations.

6. The U.S. Agency for International Development will establish initiatives to increase women's participation in political processes and to promote the enforcement of women's legal rights.

7. Continue to speak out openly and without hesitation on behalf of the human rights of all people.

8. The Department of Education will take action to remove barriers placed upon girls and women of different backgrounds, including persons with disabilities, those of low income, and those from ethnic and racial minorities.

Brainstorming for Action
(5 minutes)

Objective
To collect ideas that can be used to formulate a local plan of action.

Process
Facilitator's Note: Urge participants to look later at the background and resource section that highlights some of the specific recommendations of the platform in these areas.

1. Use two flip charts to begin to formulate a local plan for action.

2. Ask participants to make a **theoretical list** of possible activities they would like to undertake that relate to the topics of this workshop. Encourage them to mention whatever comes to mind, regardless of their ability to perform the action.

3. On the second flip chart, list any **organizations** that participants know about that address these issues.

Facilitator's Note: In subsequent sessions, attach the lists from previous brainstorming sessions to the walls. Encourage participants to add ideas or resources to any of the lists as the series progresses. All the lists will be used in the last session when the group develops an action plan.

4. Read aloud the information in the following box entitled, "Successful Strategies for Action." Remind participants that additional information about these programs, which could be helpful for local action planning, is included in the background and resource section.

Successful Strategies For Action

Violence against women is being addressed by organizations worldwide. The Clothesline Project, a hands-on personal empowerment project as well as an effective media device, is being used across the United States to heighten awareness about this issue. The Asian Women's Human Rights Council (AWHRC) organized a women's rights Tribunal and a Women in Black demonstration at the Fourth World Conference on Women. These campaigns can be used as models to raise consciousness about women's rights issues at the local or state level.

Join UUSC'S International Human Rights Network: Focus on Women

Building on the momentum of the U.N. conferences at Cairo and Beijing, the Unitarian Universalist Service Committee has launched an effort to establish a network of women and men who are willing to join in UUSC's efforts to work for justice, equality and human rights for women around the world. This network will provide action alerts, access to additional educational materials and connections with women's rights activists.

Sign-up sheets for this network will be collected during the last workshop session.

For more information, contact UUSC at (617) 868-6600.

Journal Writing
(3-5 minutes)

Objective

To give participants an opportunity to record issues that touched them in a particular way or about which they wish to write.

Process

1. Ask participants to take a few minutes to write on the journal page for this session any reactions, questions, action ideas or possible contacts they wish to pursue. If time is short, encourage them to write these down between sessions. When appropriate, invite them to add them to the flip chart pages that will be posted during each session.

Assignments for Next Week
(2 minutes)

Process

1. Encourage participants to review the information in the background and resource section including, "U.S. Commitments to the Platform for Action" for details.

2. Point out the box entitled, "Successful Strategies for Action" (page 23) and remind participants that additional information about these projects and organizations, which could be helpful for local action planning, is included in the background and resource section.

3. Refer participants to the section on sexual orientation and lesbian rights on page 58.

4. Urge participants to take the "Gender-Based Violence Quiz" on page 31 before the next session.

5. Urge all participants to read "Reframing the Population Debate" on page 66. Ask for a volunteer presenter to read and summarize this material in five minutes during the next session.

6. Encourage participants to review the background and resource material that follows Session Two in advance of next week's workshop. It will help prepare them for their role play exercise experience.

Closing Circle
(2 minutes)

Objective

To provide an opportunity to connect symbolically with others before separating.

Process

1. Encourage participants to gather in a circle around the centerpiece, holding hands. Ask someone to share their experience of the session. Invite participants to bring items to future sessions that remind them of women's lives or that honor women.

2. To close, ask for volunteers to read the poem, "Let Us Hold Hands" from the book *Agua Santa: Holy Water* by Pat Mora.

Facilitator's Note: Since the poem is long, it can be read by three readers with the group joining in for the last verse. If time is short, the group could read it together beginning with the third reader's part and continuing until the end.

Women's power will develop and one day — not very long from now — all these atrocities and injustices will be stripped away.

Justice A.N. Bhagwati, Vienna Tribunal Judge

Let Us Hold Hands
by Pat Mora[11]

First reader:

Let us now hold hands
with the Iroquois woman who slipped berries into children's lips
while her sisters planted stars with a wooden hoe,

with the woman who rubbed warm oil into her neighbor's feet-
when Plymouth's winter prowled and howled outside their doors,

with the woman who sewed faith into each stitch, cloth
comforters
pieced to the rhythm of español for babies born al silencio
del desierto,

Second reader:

with the woman who seasoned soups with pepper and hope
as her days took her further from sighs of trees she loved,

with the woman who parted her parched lips and sang
for her mother when they staggered onto these shores in chains,

with the woman who trained her stubborn tongue to wrap
around that spiny language, English, to place her child in school.

Let us now hold hands with the woman
who croons to the newborn left amid orange rinds and newspaper,
who teaches grandmothers to link letters into a word, a word,
who whispers to the woman dying with one breast,
who holds a wife whose face is more broken than any bone,
who bathes the woman found sleeping in black snow.

Third reader:

Let us hold hands
with the woman who holds her sister in Bosnia, Detroit, Somalia,
Jacksonville, Guatemala, Burma, Juarez and Cincinnati,
with the woman who confronts the glare of eyes and gunbarrels,
yet rises to protest in Yoruba, English, Polish, Spanish, Chinese,
Urdu.

continued on next page

11 From *Agua Santa: Holy Water*, 1995 by Pat Mora, reprinted by permission of Beacon Press, Boston. Pat Mora, a native of El Paso, Texas, speaks about multicultural literature, creative writing and leadership at conferences, schools and universities. Her work is included in anthologies, journals, textbooks and reading series. For more information, contact her at 3423 Oakview Place, Cinncinnati, OH 45209, (513) 533-0811.

Let Us Hold Hands *(continued)*

Third reader (continued):

Let us hold hands
with the woman who cooks, with the woman who builds,
with the woman who cries, with the woman who laughs,
with the woman who heals, with the woman who prays,
with the woman who plants, with the woman who harvests,
with the woman who sings, with the woman whose spirits rise.

All together

In this time that fears faith, let us hold hands.
In this time that fears the unwashed, let us hold hands.
In this time that fears age, let us hold hands.
In this time that fears touch, let us hold hands,
brown hands, trembling hands, callused hands, frail
hands, white hands, tired hands, angry hands, new
hands, cold hands, black hands, bold hands.

In towns and cities and villages, mano a mano, hand in hand,
in mountains and valleys and plains, a ring of women circling
the world, the ring strong in our joining,
around our petaled home, this earth, let us join hands.

*Human rights
are not worthy
of the name if they
exclude the female
half of humanity.
The struggle for
women's equality is
part of the struggle
for a better world for
all human beings,
and all societies.*

Boutros Boutros-Ghali,
secretary general
of the United Nations

ADDITIONAL ACTIVITIES FOR THREE HOUR SESSIONS

Mind Map: Violence Against Women
(45 minutes)

Objective

To explore feelings about violence against women.

Process

1. Do a word association to the key phrase "violence against women." Write this key phrase in the middle of a piece of paper with a circle drawn around it. Jot down other words and phrases you associate with this central phrase in other circles on the page and connect them to lines drawn to the central circle containing the key phrase. (This exercise is an effective way to facilitate the focusing of diverse emotions.) See mind map directions below.

2. After everyone has had time to make several associations, ask them to write one sentence representing their matrix.

3. Invite participants to gather in groups of four and share their sentences.

4. Ask each group to come up with a combined statement that includes their individual understandings.

5. Depending on the size of the group, use about 10 minutes at the end of this segment to allow each group to share its statement with everyone.

6. Review flip chart list.

SIMPLE MIND MAP

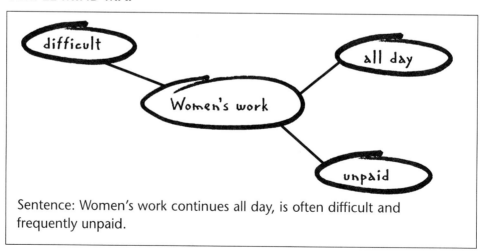

Sentence: Women's work continues all day, is often difficult and frequently unpaid.

Facilitator's Note: Prepare a flip chart in advance with the following information.

Causes of Violence Against Women:

Lower status accorded to women in the family and in society

Ignorance

Lack of laws to prohibit violence

Inadequate enforcement of existing laws

Absence of education that addresses its causes

Toleration and promotion of violence in society

Dehumanization and objectification of women

Facilitator's Note: Refer participants to the box entitled "Gender-Based Violence" in the background and resource section.

While the public hearings listen to the voices of the victims/survivors, they also listen to the voice of women who resist, who rebel, who dare to dream differently. They also attempt to challenge the dominant human rights discourse which is based on the legitimated discrimination of women.[12]

Asian Women's Human Rights Council

12 An Asian Women's Human Rights Council publication excerpt.

Journal Page

Gender-Based Violence Quiz

Directions: Make your best guesses. Then check the answer sheet for details and data sources.

1. In the U.S. and almost every country in the world, the leading cause for severe injury among women is _____.

2. More than _____ women are "missing" worldwide, based on what would be expected from the standard male-female ratio. This is due to: selective abortion of female fetuses, female infanticide, and selective withholdings of food and medical care from girls and women.

3. The number of dowry deaths ("bride-burnings") in India in 1993 was officially ___; however, the burnings are notoriously under-counted because they are typically reported as _____.

4. In the U.S. a woman is raped every ____ minutes. The rate of rape in the U.S. is ____ times higher than Germany's, ____ times higher than Britain's, and ____ times higher than Japan's.

5. In the U.S., one out ____ of girls will be sexually abused by the age of 18.

6. The _____ of women is used as a tactical weapon of war, to terrorize, to get revenge, to degrade populations, to force ethnic groups to flee, in every modern conflict on the planet.

7. International trade in child prostitution is growing because clients believe older prostitutes are more likely to be infected by _____. The average age of girls from Nepal who are forced into prostitution in India has dropped from _____ to _____. (1994 statistics)

8. Every year _____ young girls are subjected to female genital mutilation (part or total removal of the clitoris, vulva or labia).

9. The majority of people killed in wars today are: ____ (a) soldiers or (b) women and children.

10. Women and children make up _____ percent of the world's 49 million refugees fleeing conflict situations.

Answers to the Gender-Based Violence Quiz

1. In the U.S. and almost every country in the world, the leading cause for severe injury among women is **domestic violence**.[13] Domestic violence in the U.S. causes three times more injuries to women than auto accidents.[14]

2. More than **100 million** women are "missing" worldwide, some 49 million in China alone.[15] Every year, according to UNICEF, more than a million infant girls die because they are born female. These deaths are largely due to female infanticide or the withholding of food or medical care from girl babies.[16]

3. The number of dowry deaths ("bride-burnings") in India in 1993 was officially **5,000**; however, the burnings are notoriously under-counted because they are typically reported as **kitchen accidents**.[17] These women are most often killed after being doused with kerosene and being burned alive (for bringing an inadequate dowry to the husband's family). Data from two Indian cities shows that 19 percent of all deaths of women aged 15-44 are due to "accidental burnings." This contrasts with less than 1 percent in other developing countries such as Ecuador, Guatemala and Chile.[18]

4. In the U.S. a woman is raped every six minutes. The rate of rape in the U.S. is four times higher than the rate in Germany, and is **13** times higher than Britain's and **20** times higher than Japan's.[19]

5. In the U.S., one out three girls will be sexually abused by age 18.[20]

6. The **rape** of women is deployed as a tactical weapon of war — to terrorize, to get revenge, to degrade populations, to force ethnic groups to flee — in every modern conflict on this planet.[21] Rape remains the least condemned war crime, according to U.N. Special Rapporteur on Violence Against Women.[22]

7. International trade in child prostitution is growing because clients believe older prostitutes are more likely to be infected by **AIDS**. The average age of girls from Nepal who are forced into prostitution in India has dropped from **14** to **10** years. Female trafficking victims in India are subjected to virtual slavery and are an estimated 20,000 to

13 Amnesty International, 1995, and Human Rights Watch, 1995.
14 The U.S. Surgeon General.
15 U.S. Dept. of State, Bureau of Public Affairs: "Focus on Fourth World Conference on Women," 1995, U.N. Development Program Survey, 1995.
16 Human Rights Watch, 1995.
17 Amnesty International, 1995.
18 World Watch, "The Global War Against Women," 1989.
19 Newsweek, July 16, 1990.
20 Russell, Diana. "The Incidence and Prevalence of Intrafamilial and Extrafamilial Sexual Abuse of Female Children," *Child Abuse and Neglect: The International Journal*, October 1982.
21 Amnesty International, 1995.
22 Human Rights Watch, 1995.

50,000 in Bombay alone. These girls are abducted, lured or sold by their families into forced prostitution.[23]

8. Every year **2 million** young girls are subjected to female genital mutilation (FGM) which is part or total removal of the clitoris, vulva or labia. The purpose this procedure is to eliminate sexual pleasure which is thought to "save" women from infidelity. The mutilations occur in Africa, parts of the Middle East and Asia, as well as other countries where there are immigrants who practice FGM. FGM can cause serious, even life-threatening, injuries throughout women's lives.[24]

9. The majority of people killed in wars today are **(b) women and children**. During World War I, 80 percent of causalities were civilians, most of them women and children.[25]

10. Women and children make up **80 percent** of the world's 49 million refugees fleeing conflicts. In 1995, 23 million refugees fled their countries (up from eight million in 1981), and 26 million were internally displaced in their own country — for a total of 49 million. Refugee women are particularly vulnerable to sexual assaults during their stay in refugee camps.[26]

23 Ibid.
24 World Bank.
25 Amnesty International, 1995, quoting UNICEF, "State of the World's Children 1992."
26 Human Rights Watch, 1995.

Journal Page

Background and Resources
on Women's Human Rights

Discrimination Against Women

- In 1993 only six countries had women as heads of government, while the average proportion of women in the world's parliaments had dropped to 10 percent — from 12 percent in 1989.

- Three-fourths of women over age 25 in much of Africa and Asia are illiterate (a much higher rate than for men) as a result of ongoing discrimination. Women account for two-thirds of the world's illiterate population.

- On the average, women receive between 30 to 40 percent less pay than men for the same work. At the same time, much of women's daily work is unremunerated and the value of all household labor goes unrecorded.

- More than half a million women, nearly all of them in the South,[27] die each year from pregnancy-related causes. Thirty percent of them are teenagers.

- One-fourth of all families worldwide are headed by women.

- In many parts of Asia and the Pacific, inferior health care and nutrition for girl children, coupled with maternal mortality and discrimination against girl babies (even in the womb), have caused men to outnumber women by five in every 100. This is in contrast to demographic trends in the rest of the world, where women as a rule outnumber men. (United Nations statistics)

- Despite a two-thirds increase in female literacy during the last two decades, women's participation in the formal employment sector has increased by only three percentage points — from 37 percent in 1970 to 40 percent in 1990.

- In many African countries, women account for more than 60 percent of the agricultural labor force and contribute up to 80 percent of total food production — yet receive less than 10 percent of the credit to small farmers and one percent of total credit to agriculture.

- Women constitute less than one-seventh of top administrators and managers in developing countries.

27 Global South is a term that refers to the world's poor countries. The term North refers to the world's industrialized, wealthy nations. These terms are merely descriptive, as the split between rich and poor nations does not fall along strict geographic lines.

UUSC Partners and Others: Working Against Violence

Images Asia

UUSC is supporting a program called Images Asia, which is a nongovernmental organization dedicated to the human rights of the people of Burma. Images Asia investigates and documents the exploitation and atrocious situations of many Burmese women who have been forced into the sex trade in Thailand. Its activities include an analysis of conditions in Thailand and Burma that have resulted in the egregious exploitation of Burmese women and girls, many of whom were forced to flee their homes because of the brutal military dictatorship that has ruled Burma for 34 years.

The military junta, the State Law and Order Restoration Committee (SLORC), targets minority ethnic communities in ethnic cleansing campaigns and subjects everyone in these communities, including women, children and the elderly, to arbitrary arrests, torture, rape and forced labor. Since the early 1990s, there has been an unprecedented influx of Burmese women to Thailand. In addition to suffering from human rights abuses, these women have also suffered from extreme poverty caused by the deterioration of the Burmese economy under the corrupt military dictatorship's mismanagement. Vulnerable Burmese women are frequently targeted by pimps, posing as representatives of employment agencies in Thailand. When these women reach Thailand, hoping to find jobs, they are locked up and forced into prostitution. In many cases, they are kept as virtual slaves, forced to take up to 20 customers a day. Often they must pay bribes from the paltry sums they are allowed to keep to corrupt Thai officials who threaten them with arrest. According to a Human Rights Watch report on Burmese women in the flesh trade, women and girls suffer a wide range of abuses, including debt bondage, illegal confinement, forced labor, rape, physical abuse, exposure to HIV/AIDS and, in some cases, murder.

UUSC seeks support for advocacy efforts in the U.S. to focus attention on human rights in Burma, especially the rights of Burmese women who are suffering from this outrageous form of abuse. For more information on the struggle for democracy and human rights in Burma, read the excerpts from the keynote speech delivered on videotape at the NGO forum in Beijing by Aung San Suu Kyi, the leader of the pro-democracy movement in Burma and recipient of a Nobel Peace Prize in 1991.[28]

---

28 Contact UUSC's International Programs department for information on how you can support this struggle as well as additional efforts to stop the trafficking of women in South East Asia now at (617) 868-6600.

The Clothesline Project

This project was created to bring the truth about violence against women out into the open. The Clothesline Project commemorates both victims and survivors of violence. Each shirt bears witness to the experience of one individual and is decorated with her name and a date. The shirts are painted by a friend or a loved one, sometimes even by the women herself. The colors of most of the shirts are symbolic as follows:

- White for women who have died as a result of violence
- Yellow or beige for women who have been battered or assaulted
- Red, pink or orange for women who were raped or sexually assaulted
- Blue or green for survivors of incest or child sexual abuse
- Purple or lavender for women who have been attacked because of being lesbian

More than 125 clotheslines have already been hung in the U.S. and in places as distant as Vienna and Tanzania. Unitarian Universalists Acting to Stop Violence Against Women supports this project and can provide more information about how to become involved. This organization was created after the Violence Against Women Resolution passed at the 1993 Unitarian Universalist Association's General Assembly.[29]

The Asian Women's Human Rights Council

A UUSC partner group, the Asian Women's Human Rights Council (AWHRC) speaks out on human rights abuses against women through public hearings, tribunals, workshops in Asia and at NGO forums and world conferences. This group attended the NGO forum at the Fourth World Conference on Women in Huairou, China, to hold the "Court of Women: A World Public Hearing on Crimes Against Women." The AWHRC has these specific program goals:

- Developing and promoting a critical and feminist perspective on human rights in order to focus attention on the gender dimension in the dominant human rights discourse
- Providing an analysis of the roots of violence against women in order to create possibilities for dialogue with women, human rights groups and other social movements
- Fostering solidarity and concrete action among women's groups, leaders, and advocates in the region in order to promote women's human rights as integral to the struggle for universal human rights
- Working to change the existing socioeconomic, political and patriarchal systems that continue to result in severe forms of exploitation, inequality and violence against women

29 Contact Jody Shipley and Marilyn Gentile, Co-Chairs, 3221 Snyder Ave., Modesto, CA 95356, (209) 545-1837 for more details.

- Promoting conversations across cultures based on the knowledge and wisdom of women, in order to enter into a dialogue of transformation the challenges that dominant world view

- Developing new visions of a just and peaceful world for women and men

The Road to Beijing: A U.N. Chronology

1945 The United Nations charter affirms "faith in fundamental human rights, in the dignity and worth of the human person, and in equal rights of men and women."

1947 The United Nations Commission on the Status of Women is established.

1954 General Assembly urges governments to eliminate laws and customs specific to women that violate the Universal Declaration of Human Rights.

1974 Bucharest: First U.N. World Conference on Population. The West, led by the U.S., advocates strict population control policies. U.S. links economic assistance to development of family planning programs.

1975 Mexico City: First World Conference on Women, International Women's Year. Equality, development and peace are the principle themes. Mexico City led to the declaration by the U.N. General Assembly of the United Nations Decade for Women 1975-1985.

1979 General Assembly adopts the Convention on the Elimination of All Forms of Discrimination Against Women (CEDAW or the Women's Treaty). It includes commitments to equal political, economic, social, cultural and civil rights. As of May 1996, 151 nations have ratified the CEDAW Treaty. The U.S. is the only major industrialized nation that has not.

1980 Copenhagen: Second World Conference on Women. 1,326 official delegates from 145 countries attend; 8,000 people participate in the NGO forum's parallel conference. Review progress of U.N. Decade for Women (1975-1985) and adopt a Program of Action for the second half of the Decade for Women.

1984 Mexico City: Second World Conference on Population. Significant number of countries identify growing population as a key restraint to national development and call for more family planning programs. The Reagan Administration's Mexico City Policy signals cutbacks in U.S. support for family planning programs.

1985 Nairobi: Third World Conference on Women. 1,400 delegates from 157 nations adopt the "Forward-Looking Strategies for the Advancement of Women to the Year 2000," which provides a framework for action at the national, regional and international levels to promote greater equality and opportunity for women based on the three objectives of the U.N. Decade for Women: Equality, Development and Peace. (These also served as the objectives of the Fourth World Conference on Women held in Beijing, China, in September 1995.)

The goals of the strategies include: equal rights for women, the abolition of slavery and prostitution, establishment of a legal minimum age for marriage and punishment for female infanticide. At the social policy level, the strategies call for access by all women to maternity leave, maternal health care, family planning, nutrition and education, as well as increased national health budgets; shared parenting responsibilities, recognition of women's unpaid work, wage equity, participation of women in society beyond the domestic sphere, and an end to the abuse of women and children.

1990 A mid-decade evaluation of the Forward-Looking Strategies by the Commission on the Status of Women reveals that the world community had become more conscious and sensitive to issues affecting women, however, there seems to be a loss of momentum in implementation.

1992 Rio de Janeiro: United Nations Conference on Environment and Development (UNCED), known as the "Earth Summit," recognizes the essential role of women in environmental management and sustainable development.

1993 Vienna: World Conference on Human Rights. The Global Tribunal on Violations of Women's Rights and the Vienna Declaration condemn all forms of violence against women and affirms that "the human rights of women and of the girl-child are an inalienable part of universal human rights."

1994 Cairo: International Conference on Population and Development (ICPD) recognizes women's health and rights as the cornerstones of effective population and development policies. Acknowledges linkages between population, environment, development and economics. Program of Action calls for education, empowerment, comprehensive health and reproductive health programs for women and girls, and efforts to eradicate poverty and share family responsibilities.

1995 Copenhagen: World Summit for Social Development. Agenda reflects full range of women's issues. Declaration confirms commitments to assuring equality, and determines that women's political and economic empowerment is essential to combat poverty and social disintegration.

1995 Beijing: Fourth World Conference on Women. More than 4,000 delegates from 189 countries attend conference, and 30,000 participate at the NGO forum. The official Platform for Action addresses 12 Critical Areas of Concern including violence and discrimination against women and girls, reproductive and sexual rights, economic empowerment (including access to credit and inheritance rights), equal access to education and the need for family supports.

UUSC offered a series of workshops at the Cairo conference which stressed the importance of women's rights to population and development policy decisions.

World Conference on Human Rights
Vienna, Austria, June 1993

The historic presence of women as a well-organized constituency at the U.N. World Conference on Human Rights (WCHR) was emphasized often in the media coverage of the conference as well as by delegates to the conference. In addition to those women working for more inclusive treatment of female human rights violations within the human rights community, thousands of women from diverse organizations — often seen as outside of the human rights community — came to Vienna to demand women's human rights. This included women from organizations addressing battery, rape, reproductive rights, and female sexual slavery, as well as those striving for women's economic empowerment, lesbian rights and the rights of indigenous women.

The effective global collaboration of women over the two-year period preceding the conference was evident in both NGO events and the government conference. The Global Tribunal on Women's Human Rights was a pivotal event that drew more than a thousand people to a jammed auditorium where 33 women from 25 countries testified to abuses they had suffered or witnessed. News media worldwide took notice. The tribunal provided a forum for women to protest the failure of existing human rights laws and mechanisms to protect and promote women's human rights. This event concluded a worldwide petition drive calling upon the U.N. to comprehensively address violations of women's human rights at the Conference. The petition, initiated in November 1991 by the International Women's Tribune Centre and the Center of Women's Global Leadership, had more than 900 sponsoring organizations internationally. Women gathered close to half a million signatures in 124 countries and translated the petition into 23 languages.

The tribunal featured sessions in the following theme areas: human rights abuses in the family, war crimes against women in conflict situations, violations of women's bodily integrity, socioeconomic violations of women's human rights and political persecution and discrimination. Women argued that religion, tradition, and culture are used constantly to justify the subordination of women and to rob them of human rights protections. They argued that the right not to be raped, tortured, mutilated, sexually coerced, or killed cannot be dependent upon culture or religion and must be made universal.

Most importantly, violence against women in both public and private settings was recognized explicitly as an abuse of human rights. The conference urged the United Nations General Assembly to name a special rapporteur on violence against women, to strengthen the Women's Convention on the Elimination of All Forms of Discrimination Against Women (CEDAW), and to integrate women's concerns into every area of U.N. operations. In March 1994, the Commission on Human Rights appointed Radhika Coomaraswamy, a Sri Lankan lawyer and activist, to a three-year term. Her mandate is to be carried out "within the framework of the Universal Declaration of Human Rights and all international human rights instruments" including the women's treaty.[30]

Excerpt from Section One of the Vienna Declaration and Program of Action
Adopted at the World Conference on Human Rights June 25, 1993

The human rights of women and of the girl-child are an inalienable, integral and indivisible part of universal human rights. The full and equal participation of women in political, civic, economic, social and cultural life at national, regional and international levels, and the eradication of all forms of sexual discrimination are priority objectives of the international community.

Gender-based violence and all forms of sexual harassment and exploitation, including those resulting from cultural prejudice and international trafficking are incompatible with the dignity and worth of human beings and must be eliminated. This can be achieved through legal measures as well as through national action and international cooperation in areas such as economic and social development, education, safe maternity and health care, as well as social security provisions.

Women's human rights should form an integral part of the United Nations human rights activities, including the promotion of all human rights instruments relating to women. The World Conference on Human Rights urges governments, institutions, intergovernmental and nongovernmental organizations to intensify their efforts to protect and promote the human rights of women and the girl-child.

30 This report on women's organizing at the U.N. World Conference on Human Rights (Vienna, 1993) was excerpted from The Center for Women's Global Leadership, Rutgers University.

Gender-Based Violence[31]

- Until 1989, the United States did not report violence against women and gender discrimination in its annual Country Reports on Human Rights Practices — studies used to help determine eligibility for foreign aid.

- In Pakistan, reports show that a woman is burned alive by her husband at least once a day, and that there are many more cases that go unreported.

- A recent study indicates that based on expected sex ratios, the world population is short by about 60 million women, apparently because of the selective abortion of female fetuses, female infanticide, the withholding of medical care and food from girls and women, and from beatings and wife murder.

- Amnesty International has documented sexual violence by soldiers (in war and peace) in 90 countries since 1992. Many women abused in wars are from the most marginalized and vulnerable sectors of society, such as indigenous, refugee or displaced women.

- Women and children make up the majority of the world's 49 million international and internal refugees.

- A U.N. report states that 200,000 women die every year from unsafe abortions where safe, sanitary procedures are illegal. These procedures are the leading cause of death for Latin American women aged 15-39. In Cochabamba, Bolivia, 79 percent of child prostitutes questioned said they had run away from violent homes where male relatives had beaten and raped them.

- At a police station in Sao Paulo, Brazil, 70 percent of all reported cases of violence against women took place in the home. In Santiago, Chile, three fourths of all assault injuries to women were caused by family members.

- Contrary to popular belief, the majority of people killed in wars are not soldiers. More women and children than soldiers have died in every war since World War I.

continued on next page

31 These facts and statistics were drawn from material compiled by: the National Association of Social Workers, The Global Campaign for Women's Human Rights (Rutgers University), and the Minnesota International Network for News and Action for Women.

Gender-Based Violence *(continued)*

- Domestic violence rates are twice as high in U.S. military families than in civilian families.

- In the U.S., domestic violence is the leading cause of injury to adult women, according to a 1989 report by then U.S. Surgeon General C. Everett Koop. Nine of 10 female homicides are committed by men, half of them by the woman's partner. A rape is committed every six minutes. In Massachusetts, a husband or partner murders a woman every 22 days.[32] One woman is physically abused every eight seconds, and one is raped every six minutes.

Declaration on the Elimination of Violence Against Women

Adopted by the United Nations, November 1993. The United States is automatically in agreement with this declaration by virtue of U.N. membership.

In December 1993, as a consequence of the World Conference on Human Rights in Vienna in June 1993, the United Nations General Assembly adopted a landmark resolution on gender violence called the Declaration on the Elimination of Violence Against Women. This declaration defines for the first time what constitutes an act of violence against women and calls on governments and the international community to take specific measures to prevent such acts. It defined violence as, "any act of gender-based violence that results in, or is likely to result in, physical, sexual or psychological harm or suffering to women, including the threat of such acts, coercion or arbitrary deprivations of liberty, whether occurring in public or private life." Violence against women is one of the social mechanisms by which women are forced into subordinate positions to men.

The declaration lists abuses that fall into the category of violence against women:

1. Physical, sexual and psychological violence occurring in the family and in the community, including battering, sexual abuse of female children, dowry-related violence, marital rape, female genital mutilation and other traditional practices harmful to women

2. Non-spousal violence

3. Violence related to exploitation

4. Sexual harassment and intimidation at work, in educational institutions and elsewhere

5. Trafficking in women

32 *The Boston Globe.*

6. Forced prostitution

7. Violence perpetrated or condoned by the state.

The Violence Against Women Act

The Violence Against Women Act, passed in 1994, resulted in the creation of the Violence Against Women Office at the U.S. Department of Justice dedicated to fighting domestic violence and other crimes against women. The act provides for $1.6 billion in federal resources to be expended over the next six years on this effort.

In 1995-96, the office devoted about $200 million to the effort, concentrating on helping U.S. jurisdictions across the country establish specialized police and prosecution units for sexual and domestic violence and enhancing the training of police, prosecutors, judges and court personnel. The effort will combine new federal laws with assistance to states and localities to make real progress in law enforcement, victim assistance, prosecutions and crime prevention.

Through outreach, collaboration and public education initiatives, the office will work to transform public attitudes toward these crimes and dispel the notion that acts of violence against women are private disputes not fit for public scrutiny or legal judgment.

Warning Signs (That Often Precede Violence Against Women)[33]

1. Partner is overly possessive and extremely jealous; may accuse you of flirting, call to check on you often and insists on knowing where you are or where you are going.

2. Partner seems to lack own interests and is overly dependent on relationship.

3. Partner discourages your own outside interests and friendships, and attempts to isolate you from family and friends.

4. Partner is overly critical, finding fault with your dress, talents and conduct.

5. Partner has poor communication skills and refuses to or is unable to settle differences with words.

6. Partner's abuse increases with use of alcohol or drugs.

7. Partner tries to sabotage your work or school efforts, possibly forcing or convincing you to quit against your wishes.

8. Partner tries to control the money and decisions for both of you.[34]

33 Information packet, YWCA, Sonoma, California.
34 Ibid.

Discussions on Violence Against Women at Beijing[35]

Vimochana, a Unitarian Universalist Service Committee overseas partner and a member of the Asian Women's Human Rights Council (AWHRC), organized a powerful, all day tribunal at the Beijing conference. The morning session was devoted to women who have experienced war, fundamentalist or ethnic violence and the globalization of the economy. The afternoon was devoted to presentations from women on how they have resisted these forces. The tribunal concluded with a call to create a new matrix for a more caring, compassionate and just society for all.[36]

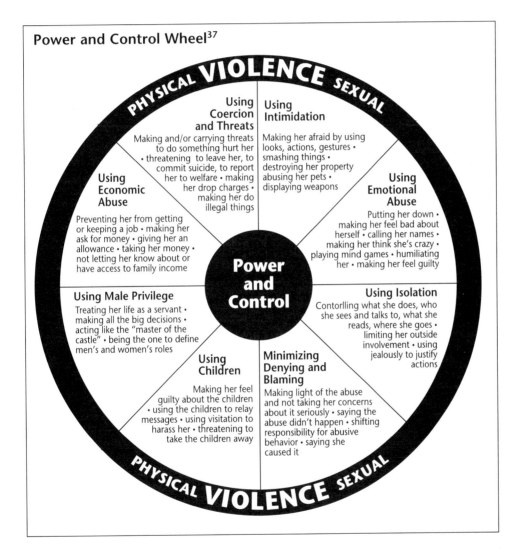

Power and Control Wheel[37]

PHYSICAL VIOLENCE SEXUAL

Power and Control

Using Coercion and Threats
Making and/or carrying threats to do something hurt her • threatening to leave her, to commit suicide, to report her to welfare • making her drop charges • making her do illegal things

Using Intimidation
Making her afraid by using looks, actions, gestures • smashing things • destroying her property abusing her pets • displaying weapons

Using Economic Abuse
Preventing her from getting or keeping a job • making her ask for money • giving her an allowance • taking her money • not letting her know about or have access to family income

Using Emotional Abuse
Putting her down • making her feel bad about herself • calling her names • making her think she's crazy • playing mind games • humiliating her • making her feel guilty

Using Male Privilege
Treating her life as a servant • making all the big decisions • acting like the "master of the castle" • being the one to define men's and women's roles

Using Isolation
Contorlling what she does, who she sees and talks to, what she reads, where she goes • limiting her outside involvement • using jealously to justify actions

Using Children
Making her feel guilty about the children • using the children to relay messages • using visitation to harass her • threatening to take the children away

Minimizing Denying and Blaming
Making light of the abuse and not taking her concerns about it seriously • saying the abuse didn't happen • shifting responsibility for abusive behavior • saying she caused it

PHYSICAL VIOLENCE SEXUAL

35 Smith Patterson, Dorothy, president of the UUSC Board of Directors, in a conference retreat from Oct. 1995.
36 Ibid.
37 "Power and Control Wheel." From a YWCA information packet, Sonoma, Calif.

Fourth World Conference on Women
Goals of the Conference

- To adopt a Platform for Action, concentrating on key issues — the "Critical Areas of Concern" — identified as obstacles to the advancement of women.

- To review and appraise the advancement of women since 1985 in terms of the objectives of the "Nairobi Forward-Looking Strategies for the Advancement of Women to the Year 2000." The document proposes and suggests corresponding strategic objectives and actions to be taken by governments, the international community, nongovernmental organizations, the private sector and individuals to remove obstacles to women's full and equal participation in development in all spheres of life.

- To determine priority actions to be taken between 1996 and 2001 for the advancement of women by the international community, including the United Nations system.

- To mobilize women and men at both the policy-making and grass-roots levels to achieve these objectives.

Regional Priorities

In preparation for the Fourth World Conference on Women, the 70-member committee divided the world into five regions, which held a series of regional ministerial meetings and NGO regional forums. Member governments prepared reports on the status of women in their countries and recorded their progress toward enacting provisions of the Third World Conference on Women, held in Nairobi in 1985. These documents informed regional forums that were held in 1994 and early 1995 in:

> Mar del Plata, Argentina (Latin America and the Caribbean)
>
> Dakar, Senegal (Africa)
>
> Amman, Jordan (Western Asia)
>
> Vienna, Austria (Europe and North America)
>
> Jakarta, Indonesia (Asia and Pacific)

These forums developed recommendations for provisions of the Platform for Action and contributed them to the official preparatory committee meetings. They also made plans for further actions and participation in Beijing. Although there was much agreement among the regions concerning key areas of concern, each region determined its own. In summary, they were:

Asia and the Pacific

- Increased feminization of poverty
- Unequal access to economic activities
- Lack of recognition for women's issues in the environment
- Unequal access to decision-making
- Violation of women's human rights
- Inequities, lack of access to health care
- Negative portrayal of women in the media
- Inequities, lack of access to education and literacy
- Inadequate mechanisms for promoting the advancement of women
- Lack of recognition for women's role in peace building

Latin America and the Caribbean

- Gender equity
- Economic and social development with a gender perspective: women's equitable share decision-making, responsibilities and benefits of development
- Elimination of poverty among women
- Women's equitable power in public and private life
- Human rights, peace and violence
- Shared family responsibilities
- Recognition of cultural plurality in the region
- International support and cooperation

North America and Europe

- Insufficient promotion, protection of women's human rights
- Feminization of poverty
- Insufficient awareness of women's contributions to the economy in the context of sustainable development
- Insufficient de facto gender equality in employment and economic opportunity, insufficient policies, and measures to reconcile employment and family responsibilities
- Insufficient participation of women in public life
- Insufficient statistical systems, databases and methodologies to inform policies and legislation
- Insufficient intra- and inter-regional networking and cooperation in the advancement of women

Western Asia

- Safeguard Arab women's rights to participate in power and decision-making structures
- Alleviate poverty
- Ensure equal opportunity for Arab women in education
- Ensure equal access to health services
- Strengthen capabilities of Arab women to enter the labor market and achieve self-reliance
- Overcome the impact of war, occupation and armed conflict on women
- Ensure participation of women in managing the environment
- Eliminate violence against women
- Use communications to change roles in society and achieve equality between the sexes

Africa

- Women's poverty, insufficient food security and lack of economic empowerment
- Inadequate access to education, training, science and technology
- Women's vital role in culture, the family and socialization
- Improvement of women's health and integrated programs
- Women's relationship to the environment
- Involvement of women in the peace process
- Political empowerment of women
- Women's legal and human rights
- Mainstreaming of gender-disaggregated data
- Women, communication, information and arts
- The girl child

Beijing Declaration and the Platform for Action

The Beijing Declaration and the Platform for Action comprise the final document to emerge from the U.N. Fourth World Conference on Women. It began in 1993 as a three-page outline which was to serve as the basis for a policy document of strategic and realistic objectives aimed at accelerating progress on advancing the cause of women to which governments could commit themselves.

Since the beginning of this process, the Platform for Action's text has drawn on information and recommendations in national reports, expert group meeting reports, regional plans of action and the most recent U.N. statistical data. It has been discussed and debated in countless arenas from village meeting halls to U.N. conference rooms including five regional preparatory meetings, numerous expert group meetings, and three full sessions and two intersessional meetings of the Commission on the Status of Women (which serves as the preparatory committee for the Beijing conference). The document has probably been the subject of the most inclusive and participatory process of any of the U.N. global conferences of the 1990s. It was adopted by consensus after round-the-clock negotiations among delegates from 189 participating nations at the Beijing conference.

The document includes two sections: a declaration and a platform. These documents were created as tools to remove obstacles to women's full and equal participation in all spheres of life. The declaration is an inspirational statement that proclaims a commitment to equality and the fair treatment for women and attests to a determination to achieve these goals. The platform is a practical tool designed to support already existing activities as well as suggest new avenues of change. The Platform for Action produced in Beijing is not binding, but it does set a far-reaching standard, which women can take to their respective countries as an agenda for reform. The document includes many specific recommendations for enforcing change and consists of five parts: (I) Mission Statement, (II) Global Framework, (III) Critical Areas of Concern, (IV) Strategic Objectives and Actions (structured around the Critical Areas of Concern), and (V) Institutional Arrangements.

12 Critical Areas of Concern

From the Platform for Action
Fourth World Conference on Women
Beijing, China, 1995

1. Poverty

Create social security systems wherever they do not exist. Develop gender sensitive national and international policies, including those related to structural adjustment. Provide poor women with economic opportunities and equal access to affordable housing, land, natural resources, credit and other services. Devise statistical means to recognize and make visible the work, including unpaid and domestic of women and their contribution to national economics.

2. Education

Close the gender gap in primary and secondary school education by the year 2005. Eradicate illiteracy of women worldwide by the year 2000 or another target date to be agreed at the conference. Improve women's access to and provide funding for vocational training, science and technology. Develop curricula, textbooks and teaching aids free of gender stereotypes.

3. Health

Strengthen and reorient health services in order to reduce maternal mortality by at least 50 percent of the 1990 levels by the year 2000. Strengthen preventive programmes that address threats to women's health. Make efforts to combat HIV/AIDS and other sexually transmitted diseases, and recognize the impact of those diseases on women. Promote research on and increase funding for women's health issues and services.

4. Violence

Take integrated legal and social measures to prevent violence and protect women. Adopt measures to eliminate trafficking in women and eradicate violence against women who are vulnerable, such as those with disabilities and migrant workers. Study the causes of violence against women and effective measures of prevention.

5. Armed Conflicts

Increase and strengthen women's participation in conflict resolution. Promote women's contribution to fostering a culture of peace. Reduce the incidence of human rights abuses in conflicts situations, protect refugee and displaced women and provide assistance to women of the camps.

6. Economic Disparity

Enact laws to guarantee the rights of women and men to equal pay for equal work and adjust work patterns to promote the sharing of family responsibilities. Provide women with equal access to resources, employment markers and trade, as well as to information and technology. Eliminate sexual harassment and other forms of discrimination in the workplace.

7. Power Sharing

Ensure women's full and equal participation in power structures and decision making. Develop education and training to increase women's capacity to participate in decision making and leadership. Aim at gender balance in government bodies and the composition of delegations to the U.N.

8. Institutions

Ensure that responsibility for the advancement of women is invested at the highest level of government. Integrate gender perspectives in all legislation, public policies, programmes and projects. Collect and disseminate statistics showing gender impact of policies and programmes.

9. Human Rights

Encourage ratification of international human rights treaties and promote their implementation. Provide gender sensitive human rights training to public officials. Improve access to legal services and literacy through information campaigns and national training programmes.

10. Mass Media

Take steps to ensure women's access to information and the media on an equal basis. Encourage elimination of gender stereotyping in the media through studies, campaigns and various forms of self-regulation by media organizations.

11. Environment

Involve women in environmental decision making and integrate gender concerns in policies for sustainable development. Assess the impact of development and environmental policies on women.

12. Girl Children

Eliminate all forms of discrimination, as well as negative cultural attitudes and practices, against girls. Ensure that girls develop a positive self-image and have equal access to education and health care. Protect girls from economic exploitation and eliminate violence against them.

Aung San Suu Kyi, Nobel Prize Laureate [38]

Excerpts from the Opening Keynote Address

It is a wonderful but daunting task that has fallen on me to say a few words by way of opening this forum, the greatest concourse of women (joined by a few brave men!) that has ever gathered on our planet. I want to try and voice some of the common hopes which firmly unite us in all our splendid diversity.

But first I would like to explain why I cannot be with you in person today. Last month I was released from almost six years of house arrest. The regaining of my freedom has in turn imposed a duty on me to work for the freedom of other women and men in my country who have suffered far more and who continue to suffer far more than I have. It is this duty which prevents me from joining you today. Even sending this message to you has not been without difficulties.

The opening plenary of this forum will be presenting an overview of the global forces affecting the quality of life of the human community and the challenges they pose for the global community as a whole and for women in particular as we approach the twenty-first century. However, with true womanly understanding the covenant of this forum suggested that among these global forces and challenges, I might wish to concentrate on those matters which occupy all my waking thoughts these days: peace, security, human rights and democracy. I would like to discuss these issues particularly in the context of the participation of women in politics and governance.

For millennia women have dedicated themselves almost exclusively to the task of nurturing, protecting and caring for the young and the old, striving for the conditions of peace that favor life as a whole. To this can be added the fact that, to the best of my knowledge, no war was ever started by women. But it is women and children who have always suffered most in situations of conflict. Now that we are gaining control of the primary historical role imposed on us of sustaining life in the context of the home and family, it is time to apply in the arena of the world the wisdom and experience thus gained in activities of peace over so many thousands or years. The education and empowerment of women throughout the world cannot fail to result in a more caring, tolerant, just and peaceful life for all.

If to these universal benefits of the growing emancipation of women can be added the "peace dividend" for human development offered by the end of the Cold War, spending less on the war toys of grown men and much more on the urgent needs of humanity as a whole, then truly the next millennia will be an age the like to which has never been seen in human his-

---

38 Read on videotape to the NGO Forum on Women, Beijing, August 31, 1995.

tory. But there still remain many obstacles to be overcome before we can achieve this goal. And not least among these obstacles are intolerance and insecurity.

In its Human Development Report for last year, the UNDP noted that human security "is not a concern with weapons — it is a concern with human life and dignity." The struggle for democracy and human rights in Burma is a struggle for life and dignity. It is a struggle that encompasses our political, social and economic aspirations. The people of my country want the two freedoms that spell security: freedom from want and freedom from war. It is want that has driven so many of our young girls across our borders to a life of sexual slavery where they are subject to constant humiliation and ill-treatment. It is fear of persecution for their political beliefs that has made so many of our people feel that even in their own homes they cannot live in dignity and security.

Traditionally, the home is the domain of the woman. But there has never been a guarantee that she can live out her life there safe and unmolested. There are countless women who are subjected to severe cruelty within the heart of the family which should be their haven. And in times of crisis when their menfolk are unable to give them protection, women have to face the harsh challenges of the world outside while continuing to discharge their duties within the home.

Many of my male colleagues who have suffered imprisonment for their part in the democracy movement have spoken of the great debt of gratitude they owe their womenfolk, particularly their wives, who stood by them firmly, tender as mothers nursing their newly born, brave as lionesses defending their young. These magnificent human beings who have done so much to aid their men in the struggle for justice and peace — how much more could they not achieve if given the opportunity to work in their own right for the good of their country and of the world?

In my country at present, women have no participation in the higher levels of government and none whatsoever in the judiciary. Even within the democratic movement only 14 out of the 485 MPs elected in 1990 were women all from my own party, the National League for Democracy. These 14 women represent less than three percent of the total number of successful candidates. They, like their male colleagues, have not been permitted to take office since the outcome of those elections has been totally ignored. Yet the very high performance of women in our educational system and in the management of commercial enterprises proves their enormous potential to contribute to the betterment of society in general. Meanwhile our women have yet to achieve those fundamental rights of free expression, association and security of life denied also to their menfolk.

The last six years afforded me much time and food for thought. I came to the conclusion that the human race is not divided into two opposing camps of good and evil. It is made up of those who are capable of learning and those who are incapable of doing so. Here I am not talking of learning in the narrow sense of acquiring an academic education, but of learning as the process of absorbing those lessons of life that enable us to increase peace and happiness in our world. Women in their roles as mothers have traditionally assumed the responsibility of teaching children values that will guide them throughout their lives. It is time we were given the full opportunity to use our natural teaching skills to contribute towards building a modern world that can withstand the tremendous challenges of the technological revolution which has in turn brought revolutionary changes in social values.

As we strive to teach others we must have the humility to acknowledge that we too still have much to learn. And we must have the flexibility to adapt to the changing needs of the world around us. Women who have been taught that modesty and pliancy are among the prized virtues of our gender are marvelously equipped for the learning process. But they must be given the opportunity to turn these often merely passive virtues into positive assets for the society in which they live.

These, then, are our common hopes that unite us — that as the shackles of prejudice and intolerance fall from our own limbs we can together strive to identify and remove the impediments to human development everywhere. The mechanisms by which this great task is to be achieved provided the proper focus of this great forum. I feel sure that women throughout the world who, like me, cannot be with you join me now in sending you all our prayers and good wishes for a joyful and productive meeting. I thank you.

Human Rights and the Platform for Action[39]

Human rights language permeates both the Beijing Declaration and the Platform for Action. Previous U.N. women's conferences were seen as primarily about women and development or women's rights rather than being about human rights. This expansion of what is generally considered to be "human rights," and its usage to frame a wider set of women's concerns, reflects efforts made over the past several years.

In this sense, Beijing saw the mainstreaming of women's human rights. The entire platform is a document about the human rights of women, including women's right to education, food, health and freedom from violence, as well as the right to exercise citizenship in all its manifestations. Previously, women had to make the case that their concerns are a legitimate part of the international human rights agenda. In Beijing, this legitimacy was assumed.

39 Bunch, Charlotte, Malika Dutt and Susana Fried. "Beijing '95: A Global Referendum on the Human Rights of Women." Center for Women's Global Leadership, Rutgers University, 1995.

The incorporation of human rights language into their work by governments and women's organizations from all regions indicates more than a rhetorical gesture. It signals a shift in analysis that moves beyond single-issue politics and identity-based organizing, and enhances our capacity to build global alliances based on collective political goals and a common agenda. Moreover, since human rights has legitimacy among many governments, the appeal to human rights agreements and international norms can fortify women's organizing.[40]

Hillary Rodham Clinton on Women's Rights Are Human Rights

These abuses have continued because, for too long, the history of women has been a history of silence. Even today, there are those who are trying to silence our words. The voices of this conference and of the women at Huairou must be heard loud and clear.

It is a violation of HUMAN rights when babies are denied food, or drowned or suffocated, or their spines broken, simply because they are born girls.

It is a violation of HUMAN rights when women and girls are sold into the slavery of prostitution.

It is a violation of HUMAN rights when women are doused with gasoline, set on fire and burned to death because their marriage dowries are deemed too small.

It is a violation of HUMAN rights when individual women are raped in their own communities and when thousands of women are subjected to rape as a tactic or prize of war.

It is a violation of HUMAN rights when a leading cause of death worldwide among women age 14 to 44 is the violence they are subjected to in their own homes.

It is a violation of HUMAN rights when girls are brutalized by the painful and degrading practice of genital mutilation.

It is a violation of HUMAN rights when women are denied the right to plan their own families, and that includes being forced to have an abortion or being sterilized against their will.

It is time for us to say here in Beijing, and the world to hear, that it is no longer acceptable to discuss women's rights as separate from human rights...If there is one message that echoes forth from this conference, let it be that human rights are women's rights and women's rights are human rights once and for all.[41]

40 Ibid.
41 Clinton, Hillary Rodham. Remarks at the U.N. Fourth World Conference on Women, Beijing China.

Sexual Orientation and Lesbian Rights at the Fourth World Conference on Women[42]

On September 9, 1995, 25 women stood up during a plenary session of the Fourth World Conference on Women, unfurled a banner that proclaimed "lesbian rights are human rights!" and remained standing in silent protest until United Nations security guards removed them from the room. Government delegates from 189 U.N. member states, along with several official observers (including the Vatican), looked on with varying degrees of interest and astonishment.

Four days later, in the same room, South African lesbian activist Palesa Beverley Ditsie addressed the assembled delegates — but this time from the podium, as the designated representative of several lesbian groups and scores of other supportive organizations that had signed on in support. Ditsie's speech, like all official agenda items, was translated by U.N. interpreters into the official languages of the conference and distributed on paper to every government delegation. It was one of only a few dozen speaking opportunities granted to the thousands of nongovernmental organizations present at the conference.

Never before had government delegates at a U.N. women's conference encountered such a strong presence of gay activists. For the first time, lesbian and gay groups (11 in all, from Mexico, the Philippines, Australia, Canada, the U.S., and several European countries) were accredited to participate as nongovernmental organizations. Every day, the members of the Lesbian Caucus — for the most part grassroots activists with little prior experience in the U.N. — met to educate each other on the esoteric and tedious process by which government delegates were drafting the conference's Platform for Action. Throughout the conference, members of the caucus carefully followed the daily progress of the working groups, cornering delegates in hallways, cafeterias, and hotel lobbies to persuade them of the importance of recognizing lesbian concerns in the Platform for Action, a document which will (in theory) guide national and international action on women's issues for years to come.

The version of the platform being debated in Beijing was the product of several regional and global preparatory meetings. As it stood at the beginning of the conference, the draft document included the term "sexual orientation" in four different paragraphs dealing with discrimination. However, as was the case with 40 percent of the text, the term was "in brackets," meaning that it had been proposed during a preparatory meeting but had not yet met with final approval.

42 Rosenbloom, Rachel. "Beijing and Beyond:International Lesbian Organizing and the World Conference on Women," *Gay Community News*, Boston, Mass., June 1996.

During the conference, as delegates resolved one controversial issue after another, the obstinate brackets around "sexual orientation" came to symbolize just how far outside the U.N. system sexual minorities remain (to the point that the Lesbian Caucus considered plastering the building with stickers reading "A [lesbian] was here"). So controversial was the term that the working groups repeatedly skipped over the four paragraphs in which it appeared and put off discussing them until literally the final hour of the conference: approximately 4 p.m. on September 14.

When the issue finally reached the floor, citizens from a number of countries spoke out against any recognition of this "tiny" and "immoral" minority, with the delegate from Benin going so far as to say, "We do not want this conference to go down as the conference on sexual revolution!" Significantly, however, citizens from countries, including South Africa, Jamaica, Barbados, Canada, the United States, Cuba, Bolivia, Chile, Brazil, Colombia, the Cook Islands, Switzerland, Norway, Slovenia, Latvia, Australia, New Zealand, Israel and the countries of the European Union, spoke out in favor of the language. Although the chair, noting that there was no consensus on the issue, ultimately struck the words from the document, several governments entered formal statements declaring that they interpreted the platform to prohibit discrimination based on sexual orientation whether or not the term itself appeared in the text. It would, of course, have been a tremendous victory if the conference had reached consensus. Yet the debate was in fact important for the opposition because it demonstrated the support of many governmental and non-governmental delegates who had previously been neutral or nominally supportive of these issues.[43]

43 For more information, contact the Unitarian Universalist Association's Office of Lesbian, Bisexual and Gay Concerns, 25 Beacon Street, Boston, MA 02108, Tel: (617) 742-2100, x470, Fax (617) 523-4123, E-mail: olbgc@uua.org. Resources Available on lesbian and gay issues. The Unitarian Universalist Association Office of Lesbian, Bisexual and Gay Concerns has a number of videos, articles and resources including "The Welcoming Congregation," a manual for congregations interested in affirming gay, lesbian and bisexual persons.

Palesa Beverley Ditsie on Lesbian Rights

International Gay and Lesbian Human Rights Commission, United Nations Fourth World Conference on Women, Beijing, China, September 13, 1995

It is a great honor to have the opportunity to address this distinguished body on behalf of the International Gay and Lesbian Human Rights Commission, the International Lesbian Information Service, the International Lesbian and Gay Association, and over 50 other organizations. My name is Palesa Beverley Ditsie and I am from Soweto, South Africa, where I have lived all my life and experienced both tremendous joy and pain within my community. I come from a country that has recently had an opportunity to start afresh, an opportunity to strive for a true democracy where the people govern and where emphasis is placed on the human rights of all people. The Constitution of South Africa prohibits discrimination on the basis of race, gender, ethnic or social origin, color, sexual orientation, age, disability, religion, conscience, belief, culture or language. In his opening parliamentary speech in Cape Town on the 9th of April 1994, His Excellency Nelson Rolihlahla Mandela, State President of South Africa, received resounding applause when he declared that never again would anyone be discriminated against on the basis of sexual orientation.

The Universal Declaration of Human Rights recognizes the "inherent dignity and the equal and inalienable rights of all members of the human family," and guarantees the protection of the fundamental rights and freedoms of all people "without distinction of any kind, such as race, color, sex, language... or other status" (art. 2). Yet every day, in countries around the world, lesbians suffer violence, harassment and discrimination because of their sexual orientation. Their basic human rights — such as the right to life, to bodily integrity, to freedom of association and expression — are violated.

Women who love women are fired from their jobs; forced into marriages; beaten and murdered in their homes and on the streets; and have their children taken away by hostile courts. Some commit suicide due to the isolation and stigma that they experience within their families, religious institutions and their broader community. These and other abuses are documented in a recently released report by the International Gay and Lesbian Human Rights Commission on Sexual Orientation and Women's Human Rights, as well as in reports by Amnesty International. Yet the majority of these abuses have been difficult to document because although lesbians exist everywhere in the world (including Africa), we have been marginalized and silenced and remain invisible in most of the world.

In 1994, the United Nations Human Rights Committee declared that discrimination based on sexual orientation violates the right to nondiscrimination and the right to privacy guaranteed in the International Covenant of Civil and Political Rights. Several countries have passed legislation prohibiting discrimination based on sexual orientation. If the World Conference on Women is to address the concerns of all women, it must similarly recognize that discrimination based on sexual orientation is a violation of basic human rights. Paragraphs 48 and 226 of the Platform for Action recognize that women face particular barriers in their lives because of many factors, including sexual orientation. However, the term "sexual orientation" is currently in brackets. If these words are omitted from the relevant paragraphs, the Platform for Action will stand as one more symbol of the discrimination that lesbians face, and of the lack of recognition of our very existence.

No woman can determine the direction of her own life without the ability to determine her sexuality. Sexuality is an integral, deeply ingrained part of every human being's life and should not be subject to debate or coercion. Anyone who is truly committed to women's human rights must recognize that every woman has the right to determine her sexuality free of discrimination and oppression.

I urge you to make this a conference for all women, regardless of their sexual orientation, and to recognize in the Platform for Action that lesbian rights are women's rights and that women's rights are universal, inalienable and indivisible human rights. I urge you to remove the brackets from sexual orientation. Thank you.

The Platform for Action

Human Rights
(Section I of Chapter IV — Strategic Objectives and Actions)

Strategic Objective

Apply and enforce norms and standards to safeguard the full enjoyment of human rights by women.

Actions by governments:

- Ratify or accede to international human rights treaties, including the Convention on the Elimination of All Forms of Discrimination Against Women (CEDAW)
- Publicize information on existing mechanisms for redressing human rights violations
- Create or strengthen national institutions for protecting women's human rights
- Ratify, accede to and implement the Convention on the Rights of the Girl-Child
- Review national laws and revoke those that discriminate against women
- Provide gender-sensitive human rights education and training to public officials
- Ensure equal rights for women to serve in the courts as police/prison officers

Violence Against Women
(Section D of Chapter IV — Strategic Objectives and Actions)

Strategic Objective

To eliminate violence against women.

Actions by governments:

- Condemn violence against women and not use the excuse of any custom, tradition or religious consideration to avoid their obligation to eliminate it
- Adopt measures to modify the social and cultural patterns of men and women
- Provide well-funded shelters and relief support for victims of violence
- Assist female victims of violence due to prostitution and trafficking; consider ratification and enforcement of international treaties on trafficking and slavery

Actions by governments, employers, NGOs and others:

- Develop programs and procedures to eliminate sexual harassment and other forms of violence in all educational institutions, the work place and elsewhere

- Promote research on violence against women, encourage the media to examine gender stereotypes and take measures to eliminate them

Armed and Other Conflicts
(Section E of Chapter IV — Strategic Objectives and Actions)

Strategic Objectives

To increase the participation of women in conflict resolution, and protect women in armed and other conflicts.

Actions by governments:

- Strengthen the role of women in peace and security activities

- Hasten the conversion of military resources and related industries to development purposes

- Undertake new ways of generating financial resources, through reduction of military expenditure, to provide more funds for social and economic development

- Consider ratifying international treaties on protection of women and children in armed conflicts

Actions by governments, international organizations and NGOs:

- Promote peaceful conflict resolution through education and training

- Encourage peace research involving women

- Take steps to involve women in planning assistance to refugees

- Take steps to ensure the safety and physical integrity of refugee women

- Condemn the systematic practice of rape and other degrading treatment as a deliberate instrument of war and ethnic cleansing

U.S. Commitments to the Platform for Action

President's Interagency Council on Women

The President established an interagency council chaired by Secretary of Health and Human Services Donna Shalala. This intragovernmental body is charged with coordinating the federal implementation of the Platform for Action adopted at Beijing, including the U.S. commitments announced at the conference. The goal of the council is to develop initiatives to further women's progress and engage in outreach and public education to support the successful implementation of the conference agreements.[44]

Violence Against Women Office

Through the Violence Against Women Office at the Department of Justice, the Clinton Administration has taken steps to heighten awareness about the problem of violence against women, including domestic violence and sexual assault. The administration declared October "National Domestic Violence Awareness Month." President Clinton has signed an executive memorandum directing all federal agencies to educate their employees about violence against women.[45]

44 Contact President's Interagency Council on Women, (202) 456-7350 for more information.
45 Contact the Violence Against Women Office at the Department of Justice, (202) 616-8894 for more information.

Assignments for Session Two

Reframing the Population Debate

Poverty, population and the environment are linked, but the relationship is complex. Is population growth the cause of poverty, or is poverty the cause of population growth? Are people hungry because there isn't enough to eat, or is hunger the result of inadequate access for many who are poor to the resources to produce or purchase food? Our answers to these questions determine the solutions that we seek.

Reframing the Debate with a Human Rights Focus

Working on these issues in partnership with community groups and women's organizations for nearly 60 years, the Unitarian Universalist Service Committee is convinced that protecting our environment and improving the quality of life for all people requires a commitment to social justice and human rights. Our partners have challenged us to help reframe the population debate in terms of human rights, and especially women's rights.

Experience has shown that reductions in population growth are more likely to occur in countries that enhance economic and social opportunities and security for their people than in countries with coercive population control programs. Lower birth rates predictably follow improvements in the standard of living, including health care and education. Women gain greater control over their bodies when these improvements occur. These realities underlie UUSC's focus on women's rights and its efforts to combat political repression.

In Africa, Asia, Latin America and the Caribbean, UUSC has supported programs that help to foster the political and social climate necessary for economic development, ones that promote reproductive health rights, safe births and the well-being of the family. These programs have contributed to reducing poverty and improving women's lives where coercive population policies have failed.

Women's Rights Advocacy at Home and Abroad

In addition to our work with overseas partners, UUSC works to shape the U.S. agenda for human rights and sustainable development at home and abroad.

Vienna 1993: The recognition of women's rights by the international community has advanced significantly in recent years. At the 1993 United Nations Conference on Human Rights in Vienna, UUSC's views on development and human rights were strongly affirmed. A consensus emerged that women hold the key to many human rights and development challenges and that women's rights are indeed human rights. UUSC partners from Asia and Africa helped promote this viewpoint in Vienna.

Cairo 1994: The U.N. International Conference on Population and Development (ICPD) and NGO forum held in 1994 in Cairo represented another advance for women's rights. Delegates affirmed that population growth will only be brought under control when women are empowered in their societies. Vice President Al Gore, speaking for the United States delegation to the conference, stated that problems attributed to population growth are not problems of numbers. In fact, calls to end poverty and support women's rights dominated the agenda of the conference.

The Unitarian Universalist Service Committee played an active role in promoting this priority at the ICPD. UUSC sponsorship allowed more than 10 overseas partners to participate in the forum. Many of these women gave testimony to the horrors they, their sisters, daughters and mothers endured at the hands of enforced population control policies and as experimental subjects for invasive contraceptive technologies. They testified about the successes of programs which strengthen the role of women in society and increase their capacity to make informed choices.

The Program of Action adopted at Cairo recognized the connection between population, equal rights, the environment and development. It was significantly different from previous international statements on population in its broader, more comprehensive, more woman-friendly approach. Governments around the world pledged new support to alleviate poverty and empower women. In particular, the conference Program of Action focused attention on the critical need for access to comprehensive health care and education for women and girls at all phases of life.

Beijing 1995: This consensus was echoed at the Fourth World Conference on Women held in Beijing in September 1995. Attended by more than 30,000 women and men, it was the largest U.N. conference ever held. The conference's Platform for Action was a reaffirmation and extension of commitments made at Vienna and Cairo to promote and protect women's human rights, including the right to be free from violence, the right to sexual and reproductive health free from discrimination or coercion, and access to information about sexual and reproductive health care. Although a major achievement for the world's women, the platform does sidestep many economic and environmental issues. Those issues include globalization, economic restructuring and structural adjustment.

Hillary Rodham Clinton addressed the conference and underscored the women's human rights theme: "If there's one message that echoes forth from this conference, let it be that human rights are women's rights and women's rights are human rights, once and for all." It is this focus that underlies the Beijing platform. U.S. Ambassador to the United Nations Madeleine K. Albright has written

> The concept of the human rights of women is so integrated into the platform that it provides the foundation and framework for the broad public policy agenda that the document sets out. For all the painstaking and numerous details, the principles behind them can be simply stated:

- Violence against women in all its forms must be stopped.
- Girls must be protected and valued equally with boys in their families and by societies.
- Women must have access to education and health care of a high quality, and to the levers of economic and political power.
- Family responsibilities must be shared.
- The rights of women to control their own fertility and equality in sexual relations are fundamental to women's empowerment.
- Freedom of expression is a prerequisite to human rights, which are women's rights.

Speaking Out for Justice

UUSC Executive Director Richard S. Scobie, UUSC Board President Dorothy Smith Patterson and Heather Foote, director of UUSC's Washington Office, participated in the Beijing women's conference. More than a dozen representatives of UUSC partner organizations and more than 40 Unitarian Universalist women and men from the United States attended as well. UUSC sponsored two gatherings where project partners and UU women had an opportunity to exchange impressions and talk of follow-up activities.

UUSC overseas partners who journeyed to the conference from India, Eritrea, Nicaragua and Haiti lobbied their own countries' delegations to ensure that the concerns of the women of their countries were clearly represented. UUSC's Patterson, Scobie and Foote also had the opportunity to meet with members of the U.S. delegation to urge their support for the human rights and reproductive health segments of the conference platform.

Beyond Beijing: Advocacy in the United States

UUSC is involved in several national and international efforts that are building on the momentum for progress of women's issues that emerged from the women's conference. These include efforts to develop support for U.S. Senate ratification of the U.N. Convention on the Elimination of All Forms of Discrimination Against Women (CEDAW), a convention signed by President Clinton but not yet ratified by the Senate. One hundred forty-nine nations have now ratified CEDAW, and the United States is the only major industrialized nation that has not. Another UUSC post-Beijing goal is to support moves to ensure that the U.S. government pays its arrears in U.N. dues. The dues can be used to support U.N. programs to follow-up on the priorities established at the ICPD and women's conference.

UUSC also participates in the activities of the President's Interagency Council on Women, which was established following the conference in Beijing. NGOs viewed the establishment of the council and the U.S. commitments made at Beijing as a "down payment" on the development of a national plan that each country will develop to put the platform into practice.

Building Coalitions

UUSC works in coalition with several organizations which focus on international women's rights issues, including the International Women's Tribune Center, the Women's Environmental and Development Organization (WEDO), and InterAction, a coalition of more than 150 development and humanitarian assistance organizations. UUSC is also a sponsor of the "Women's Eyes on the Bank" campaign, which was established at the women's conference to link people from rich and poor nations in efforts to focus attention on the impact of World Bank programs on women in the South, or developing countries. In many cases, loans from the World Bank dwarf the declining bilateral foreign assistance grants from countries like the United States.

The Road Ahead

Although the promises of "human rights for women" made at Vienna, Cairo and Beijing point in a very positive direction, the commitment of resources and policy changes to transform these promises into practice have not yet been made. Concerted action by individuals and groups at the grassroots level will be required to foster such commitments at the local, state, national and international levels.

Your Values Are at Stake

The work of UUSC in Washington – and your support and involvement – will be more important than ever in the months and years ahead. Sharp cuts in foreign assistance and dramatic cutbacks in support for international family planning undermine the course of action set out at Cairo and Beijing.

At stake is the United States' reputation as a responsible member of the world community – concerned about human rights and aware that its own security and economic well-being are linked to the well-being of people throughout the world. In particular, we must stand with those who acknowledge the importance of effective development assistance to some of the poorest nations of the world, especially to the nations of Africa, which have faced some of the largest cuts in U.S. bilateral assistance – including aid to strengthen women's roles as decision makers in local and national politics.

Of concern also is funding of U.S. dues to the United Nations, which are hundreds of millions of dollars in arrears. Such funding would make it possible for the United Nations to follow up on the Beijing and Cairo conferences and to carry out critical peacekeeping missions in countries such as Haiti, Guatemala and El Salvador. UUSC has witnessed first-hand the effectiveness of peacekeepers in those countries, especially in the areas of human rights protection and conflict resolution.

UUSC seeks your help in the challenging times ahead, when we must convince our elected leaders that development aid which supports family planning, health care, education and women's empowerment is sorely needed if we are to create a world that can nurture and sustain future generations.

Health, Sexuality and Reproductive Rights

Critical areas of the platform covered in this session:

Women and Health (Section IV. C)

Two-Hour Workshop

Activities	Minutes
Opening Circle	15
Exploration of a Central Issue: What is Women's Health?	20
Population Role Play	30
Break	10
Discussion of Role Play and UUSC Position Paper	20
Platform for Action Position	5
Brainstorming for Action	10
Journal Writing	5
Assignments for Next Week	3
Closing Circle	2
Total Time:	**120**

Materials

Centerpiece: Pictures and colorful multicultural objects

Two flip charts

Preparation

Write on flip chart pages:

Population growth (page 84)

Needed to guarantee health care and choice (page 85)

This little Haitian girl will have health options her mother and even older sisters lacked as a girl thanks to UUSC partners.

Three-Hour Workshop

Activities	Minutes
Opening Circle	15
Exploration of a Central Issue: What is Women's Health?*	30
Population Role Play *	45
Break	10
Discussion of Role Play * and UUSC Position	35
Platform for Action Positions*	20
Brainstorming for Action *	15
Journal Writing	5
Assignments for Next Week	3
Closing Circle	2
Total Time:	180

Materials

Centerpiece: Pictures and colorful multicultural objects

Two flip charts

Preparation

Write on flip chart pages:

Population growth (page 84)

Needed to guarantee health care and choice (page 85)

*exercises and/or time added

Opening Circle

(15 minutes)

Objective

To focus the group and allow for personal sharing.

Process

Facilitator's Note: Participants will gather around a centerpiece that includes items used in the first session. Encourage them to place any additional items they have brought to share.

1. Light the candle and read this excerpt from the NGO vision statement:

    > Visualize nations where men, too, are responsible for their fertility and sexuality, and family planning is transformed into comprehensive reproductive health care.

2. Explain the focus:

    > With a nudge from women themselves, many societies are getting better at listening to women and looking at the world through women's eyes, to paraphrase the theme of the 1995 NGO Forum on Women. This is a healthy addition to the long-prevailing predominantly male viewpoint, which has often been accepted as applying to all. To look at the world through the eyes of women is to bring hidden issues into the open. It suggests different priorities and alternative solutions.

    > The focus of this workshop is women's health, sexuality and reproductive rights. Let's all take a moment to briefly share what health issues we have observed that are uniquely related to being female. These can be ones that we have directly experienced or ones that have affected a woman whom we know.

Facilitator's Note: Provide a model for the group by sharing something from your own experiences that relates to this topic, such as lack of reproductive choice or inadequate medical research relating to women's health issues.

Exploration of a Central Issue: What Is Women's Health?

(20 minutes)

Objective

To explore the different meanings and associations brought to mind when considering women's health

Three-hour session: Add 10 minutes to this discussion for a total of 30 minutes.

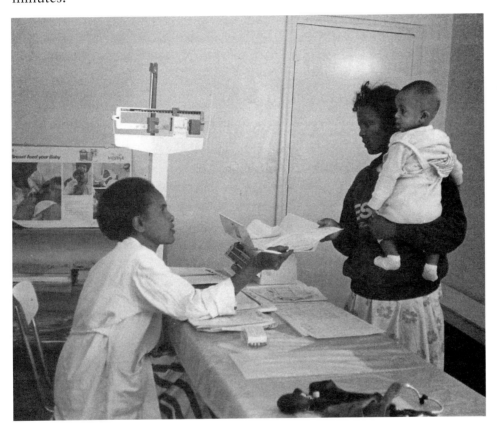

A nurse working with UUSC project partner, the Planned Parenthood Association of Eritrea, consults with a client.

Process

Facilitator's Note: Ask participants to turn to the journal page for this session.

1. Demonstrate the following activity by writing the word "women's work" in a circle in the middle of a flip chart page. Write several words you associate with women's work in circles around the central circle and connect all the circles with lines. (See example of a mind map on page 28 in session one.) After demonstrating this technique, invite participants to write the words "women's health" in the middle of a piece of blank paper and complete the exercise as demonstrated.

2. Ask participants to write a sentence representing their diagram.

3. Invite volunteers to read their sentences aloud.

4. Conduct a brief discussion, inviting participants to share their reactions to the exercise.

5. Read the following definition of health offered by the World Health Organization (WHO).

> Health is a state of complete physical, mental, and social well-being and not just the absence of disease or infirmity.

6. Share the following positions of WHO, which are among those that appeared in a World Health Organization Position Paper distributed at the Fourth World Conference on Women in Beijing.

> The World Health Organization advocates:
>
> - More consideration of **all the factors** that affect women's health, not only biological factors, but social and economic status, cultural, environmental, familial, occupational and political factors
> - **Listening** to what women have to say about health and what they would like to know about it, rather than simply transferring information to women
> - Greater recognition and support of women as **active participants** in the development of health care for themselves, their families and communities
> - More **attention** to the entire **duration** of a women's life, from birth to death — health for everyone is a cumulative matter
> - More **attention** to the **roles and responsibilities** of **men**, and the inequalities between men and women, with an examination of men's roles, perspectives and beliefs in relation to women's health concerns

Population Role Play
(30 minutes)

Objective

To explore a variety of positions about worldwide population issues.

Three-hour session: Add 15 minutes to this discussion for a total of 45 minutes.

Process

1. Explain the exercise:

> To provide you with an idea of what it is like to have been a participant at the nongovernmental forum (held in connection

with the official government conference, just outside of Beijing in Huairou) each of you will be asked to play the role of a person who attended the conference. The role play touches on women's health, reproductive rights and population growth and possible action on these issues.

Role plays help participants to:

- Experience what others might feel in a particular situation
- Understand a concept or problem
- Have fun
- Take part in an active learning experience
- Retain more information than they would if they were just told about an issue

Facilitator's Note: While the groups are engaged in the role play, circulate among the groups and act as a resource on the intention of the exercise.

2. To prepare for the role play:

    - If the group is large enough, break it into several groups of seven and ask the group to count off from one to seven.
    - Tell participants to take five minutes to read one of the role play descriptions.
    - Encourage participants to prepare to speak from their "character's" point of view.

Facilitator's Note: If groups are smaller than seven, select the roles that you find the most provocative and assign them.

3. Introduce the role play by telling the group:

    Several people attending the Fourth World Conference on Women get caught in a torrential rainstorm. They seek shelter in a tea shop and while they wait for the rain to stop, they strike up a discussion about women's health and how it relates to issues of population stabilization, economics and reproductive rights.

    Role 1: You are a woman from Eritrea, Africa. You can speak from your experience about attempts to control population in your country. You are concerned about women's welfare but also aware of cultural attitudes that will take time to change. You want to share your ideas with others you meet at the conference so that those concerned about the welfare of women globally can understand what it will take to improve women's situations.

- At home, girls are traditionally forced to get married, and when they leave school to get married, they cannot return.

- If a girl doesn't get married, people will talk and they will sometimes say that she will end up a prostitute.

- The only thing I hate about marriage is women's oppression within it. In the 70s, I remember that my teenage cousin was forced to marry a much older man because her father had collected a bride price. The man kept beating her and my cousin became ill. She was never allowed to go back to school and now she has to look after four children. She is not allowed to make decisions or say anything to contradict her husband. Most poor women in her village feel they cannot use contraception even if they have 10 babies.

- Knowing these realities, I feel strongly that women-to-women programs at the community level are the only things that can lead to the empowerment of women. These should include: education, health and economic measures. Society will then be able to overcome:
  - The cycles and difficulties of poverty
  - The preference for large families
  - The need for many children to help sustain the household
  - Son preference
  - Lack of education for women and girls
  - The related problems affecting poor communities around the world.

Role 2: You are a staff member from the United States Agency for International Development (U.S. AID), the largest supporter of family planning programs in the world. You are deeply concerned about the trends in the current political climate in the U.S. that will affect your agency. You have learned that Congress is planning to force a drastic cut back in the aid programs your agency administers, which are the mainstay of family planning programs around the world. You feel you need to let others know what is going on. Here are some important facts you want to make others aware of.

- The U.S. actually funds about 45 percent of all family planning programs in the world. If cuts go through, 35 percent will be cut from the population and family planning budget of U.S. AID. (This actually happened in February 1996 though it was partially restored.)

- You and other experts from your agency and from many

of the private organizations who depend on these funds say the cuts will be crippling, not only to birth control programs but also to related activities like maternal health care and AIDS prevention.

- The supporters of the cuts in Congress stated that it is impossible for either side in this debate to prove how many unwanted pregnancies will or will not occur at a given level of funding for population control programs. But you and other family planning advocates say that regardless of arguments about global population and resources, efforts are needed to give more women choice in contraception for reasons of health and personal freedom.

- While the U.S. remains the largest bilateral donor to international family planning programs ($577 million in FY95), on a per capita basis the level of U.S. aid ranks behind Norway, Finland, Sweden, Denmark and the Netherlands.

- Partly because of the U.S. retreat from leadership in population funding in the 1980s, donor funding for population assistance has fallen at least 60 percent below the level of requests for assistance from developing countries.[1]

Role 3: You are an African American woman who is the director of a resource center for women of color in the United States. You have strong feelings about how population control impacts poor women and women of color. Because poor women of color have often been blamed for giving birth to too many children, tensions between women of color and others have developed around the issues of population. Here are some of your opinions that you want to get across.

- Women of color share a common agenda with others who are worried about overpopulation. We agree that the earth cannot sustain an unlimited number of people any more than a woman's body can bear an unlimited number of pregnancies.

- Any population policy that is not based on social justice will not have the support of women of color. Unless those who want to affect population growth link up with those who have access to and the confidence of women at the grassroots, no progress will be achieved. Dialogue is important. The environment, human rights and world

1 Camp, Sharon L. "The Politics of U.S. Population Assistance," in *Beyond the Numbers: A Reader on Population, Consumption and the Environment*, Laurie Ann Mazur, ed., Washington, DC, Island Press, 1994, and personal communication with Population Action International, July 13, 1995.

hunger are all critical issues. How we solve these problems will depend on whether grassroots women are participants in, or objects of, the discussion.

- Population control and sustainable development means working on collateral issues such as homelessness, land rights, AIDS, education, racism, sexism, homophobia, jobs and health care.

- Population means asking why we have a multibillion-dollar crime bill and more jail spaces than college spaces for our children. It means asking why life expectancy for people of color is getting shorter. The future we envision for our children must include living longer and living better, not just surviving.

- Our trust will be based on the expectation that cooperation, not co-optation, is the goal. Our trust will be based on common sense — why coerce a woman into having fewer children when, if she is given an education and a job and ensured that her children will live, she'll make that decision on her own?[2]

Role 4: You are a woman with five children from Bangladesh who is concerned about poverty in your country. You believe that too many children are being born, however, you are well aware of the cultural beliefs of your people about family and women. You are also aware of abuses that have taken place when population control was the only goal. You want others to know what women face in your country and what happened when population control was the only goal. Here are some personal thoughts and experiences you have had that you have decided to share.

- I have experienced how hard it is to overcome many of the realities of male dominance in our society. Often it is considered a matter of shame if a woman cannot have more children, particularly male children. This is especially true because some of our children could die. Actually, many often do.

- It is critical in my country to have a male heir to carry on the family's name. Also I know that if my husband dies, and I cannot bear another child, no one will want to marry me. Without a husband, I cannot survive.

- I know that many women in my country want to regulate the number of children they have, but in my country, family

2 Based on testimony by Loretta Ross of the Center for Democratic Renewal reported in From Information to Education, Panos Institute, 1994.

planning has usually meant sterilization. Many women are fearful of choosing sterilization because their husbands or their husband's families oppose it. I am also afraid that women in my country might be forced to submit to government regulated sterilization campaigns whether they like it or not and whether they understand what is happening to them or not.

- When women and men were offered cash for being sterilized, health workers also received a fee for each client they recruited for sterilization and doctors were paid by the case, encouraging them to rush through operations. Women were the main targets of these campaigns, even though sterilization is far less risky for men.

- I have heard of other ways to prevent pregnancy but I know of women who have suffered severe side effects from long-term contraceptives such as Norplant or from improperly implanted intrauterine devices (IUDs). Follow-up to such procedures are rarely available.

- A comprehensive primary health care system with voluntary family planning would meet Bangladesh's needs far better than top-down population control programs.

Role 5: You are a man from Uganda, Africa. You have come to the conference because you are interested in the role that men can play in solving some of the world's problems. You want women to know that some men are concerned about being part of the solution rather than the problem. You have questions, feelings and insights you hope to share with both women and other men attending the conference. Should family planning be more than a women's issue?

- Men generally have less information than women about reproduction and family planning. In many cultures, family planning is considered a women's issue — even by doctors.

- In Uganda, men don't know what goes on when their wives get pregnant. We need to involve men in overall aspects of family health — not just family planning.

- You believe that one of the elements of a successful, comprehensive population growth policy is to involve men. Where men share equally in the joys and burdens of child-rearing and family life, they also take more responsibility for family planning.[3]

3 Bruce, Judith. "Population Policy Must Encompass More Than Family Planning Services," in *Beyond the Numbers: A Reader on Population, Consumption and the Environment.* Laurie Ann Mazur, ed., Washington, DC, Island Press, 1994.

- Vasectomies for men are cheaper and less invasive than tubal ligations for women. You think vasectomies should become an accepted form of birth control.

- You know, for example, that 49 percent of Kenyan husbands do not want more children, but only one percent have had a vasectomy. This points out the importance of attitude changes in the society. Male participation is needed to help lead the way in educating men.[4]

Role 6: You are a population activist from the Netherlands. You feel strongly that the major issue today is overpopulation and you think providing funds for contraceptives and sterilization is the most effective way to deal with this crisis. You are concerned with what you perceive as inadequate support for family planning services around the world. You are well aware of the following facts and figures about the international family planning movement, and are on a personal mission to make others aware of them.

- In the early 1960s, only 18 percent of women in the developing countries used contraception. Today, 58 percent of all couples of childbearing age in the developing world use either modern or traditional methods of birth control. This is because of the increased awareness of the importance of family planning and the availability of birth control.[5]

- There are still stark differences in contraceptive usage among regions. While 52 percent of couples in the industrialized world use modern birth control, the comparable figure for African couples is only 17 percent.[6]

- At least 100 million women, one in six married women in the developing countries outside China, have an unmet need for contraception. Approximately one in four births in the developing world (excluding China) are unwanted, and even more are unplanned.[7]

- Another rough measure of unmet need for contraception is the estimated 50 million abortions that are performed each year, nearly half of which are illegal and unsafe.[8]

4 Family Planning Counseling: the International Experience, AVSC, 1992.
5 Donaldson, Peter and Amy Ong Tsui, "The International Family Planning Movement," *Population Bulletin*, Vol. 45, No. 3, November 1990.
6 Population Reference Bureau, 1995 World Population Data Sheet, Washington, DC: PRB, 1995.
7 "Population Council Researcher Urges Three Policy Options to Reduce Birth Rates in Developing Countries," press release, The Population Council.
8 Jacobson, Jodi L. "Abortion and the Global Crisis in Women's Health," in *Beyond the Numbers: A Reader on Population, Consumption, and the Environment*, Laurie Ann Mazur, ed., Washington, DC, Island Press, 1994, and "How to Slow Population Growth: The New Approach," Pew Global Stewardship Initiative, April 1994.

Role 7: You are a teenager who has been trained as a sex educator by the Unitarian Universalist Service Committee Nicaraguan project partner Si Mujer (pronounced See Muhair), which is a well-known alternative health program. Si Mujer (Yes, Woman) stands for Servicios Integrales para la Mujer (Integrated Services for Women). The essence of Si Mujer's orientation is to provide services by and for women and girls. You have come to the conference representing Si Mujer, and are anxious to share your work with anyone who is interested.

- The vision of your organization includes gynecology, obstetrics, counseling, education and training from a feminist perspective. Si Mujer's Center for Adolescents and Young People, where you trained, is located in a densely populated slum in Managua.

- You were trained with 36 other young people as health promoters in reproductive health and sexuality. After two years of training, you and others in the program who had been involved in street gangs found a new purpose in your lives. Now you and your friends are sex educators. Here are some of the things that you'd like to tell people.

- Sometimes when I talk about contraceptive methods, kids tell me that they don't need them because they aren't sick. Later they learn that precautions prevent them from catching contagious sexual diseases.

- When I go into the street, the kids treat me well, but they are shy and call me aside to ask questions. Sometimes they are disrespectful and shout at me, "Sell me a condom and try it out with me to see if it works!"

- Here at the center they talk to us about things that our parents don't like to talk about. Thanks to the talks we have had, we understand that our bodies and sex are natural, not something bad. I am preparing for the time when I can have a proper relationship. I want to have a secure relationship, not one in which a boyfriend puts pressure on me. According to my teacher at school, it's taboo to speak about the body. I explained to my classmates that the body isn't vulgar, but some of the ideas that people have about it are. Saying this almost cost me a grade on my report card, but it was worth it.

Facilitator's Note: After five minutes, signal the groups to begin the role play. Allow the role play to run for about 20 minutes. If you are running a three-hour session, allow the role play to run for 30 minutes.

4. Bring the small groups back together and share the following facts about worldwide population growth.

Facilitator's Note: Prepare a flip chart in advance with the following information about population growth and review it with the group.

Population Growth
1800 - 1 billion people
1930 - 2 billion people
1960 - 3 billion people
1975 - 4 billion people
1987 - 5 billion people
1997 - 6 billion people

Break
(10 minutes)

Discussion of the Population Role Play and Reframing the Population Debate
(20 minutes)

Objective

To explore issues that arose in the role play and in the UUSC position paper on population and women's rights.

Three-hour session: Add 15 minutes to this discussion for a total of 35 minutes.

Process

1. Ask participants to share some of the issues that arose during their role plays including: how they felt playing their role, how they felt about the positions advanced by the other participants, and what they learned from the experience. (Allow about 5 minutes.)

2. Explain:

    > Success in helping women to have only the number of children that they want depends on many factors, including:

Facilitator's Note: Prepare a flip chart in advance which lists only the bold-faced words below. When reviewing the flip chart, verbally share the entire explanation of the shortened phrase

Needed to Guarantee Health Care and Choice

Adequate **access** to comprehensive health care

Adequate advanced **methods** so a woman can choose what is best for her; contraceptive methods that do not cause significant side effects or health problems for the user

Good quality **counseling, education, and information** services available both in the community and at health clinics

Outreach and communication efforts

Enabling women to use methods of their **choice** in appropriate and knowledgeable ways

Accessible, **respectful** health care services provided by trusted members of the community[9]

3. Ask the person who volunteered to summarize the UUSC position on population issues, as outlined in the essay Reframing the Population Debate, to do so now. Invite members of the group to share their reflections on the article. (10 minutes)

---

9 Jain, A. "Walking the Walk: Reproductive Health and Family Planning Programs," in Reproductive Health Approach to Family Planning Presentations from a panel held at the U.S. AID Cooperating Agencies Meeting, Feb. 1994. Population Council, New York, NY, Dec. 1994.

Platform for Action Position on Health, Sexuality and Reproductive Rights
(5 minutes)

Objective

To explain the Platform for Action position on health, sexuality and reproductive rights.

Three-hour session: Add 15 minutes to this discussion for a total of 20 minutes.

Process

1. Share with the group:

To control their own reproduction... women must be able to achieve social status and dignity, to manage their own health and sexuality, and to exercise their basic rights in society and in partnerships with men.

**Adrienne Germain
and Jane Ordway,
International Women's
Health Coalition**

The **World Health Organization** has found that women are the cornerstones of the family and assume responsibility for many of its most vital functions, not only in regard to health and education, but also in terms of food production and income generation. Accordingly, the **health of women** is a prerequisite for the **health of the whole family** and, by extension, of communities and societies.[10]

The U.N. takes the position that family planning services need to be integrated into a wider framework that addresses people's overall reproductive and sexual health needs. Women's ability to improve their **reproductive health** also depends on their **ability to make decisions** in other aspects of their lives, and to **participate fully** in the life of the community. In addition to enhanced health services, improving women's health requires **better living conditions** and stronger roles in decision-making at all levels.[11]

The platform states that the right to health is a fundamental human right vital to women's ability to participate in all areas of public and private life. It proposes action to:

- Provide expanded and more accessible comprehensive health care for women

- Strengthen preventive programs that address the main threats to women's health

- Promote research and information dissemination on women's health

---

10 "Health, Population and Development," WHO Position Paper, World Health Organization, Geneva, 1994. Prepared for the International Conference on Population and Development, 1994, Cairo.
11 *Women: Looking Beyond 2000,* United Nations, 1995.

Brainstorming for Action
(10 minutes)

Objective
To collect ideas that can be used to formulate a local plan of action on women's health and reproductive rights issues.

Three-hour session: Add 5 minutes for a total of 15 minutes.

Process
1. Use two flip charts to begin to formulate a local plan for action.

2. Ask participants to make a list of possible activities they would like to undertake that relate to the topics of this workshop. Encourage participants to mention whatever comes to mind, regardless of their ability to perform the action.

3. List any organizations that participants know about that address these issues on the second flip chart.

Facilitator's Note: Attach lists from previous brainstorming sessions to the walls and encourage participants to add ideas or resources to any of the lists. All the lists will be used in the last session when the group develops a viable action plan.

4. Read aloud the boxed information. Remind participants that more information about these programs that could be helpful for local action planning is included in the background and resource section.

> ## Successful Strategies for Action
>
> The Delhi Community Health Workers Program in India and the Women's Secretariat of the Agricultural Workers Union in Nicaragua are two examples of organizations in the South that have reached "ordinary" women and empowered them to act on their own behalf. Women from the North are continually realizing that the organizing being done by women in the South is the source of ideas for many dynamic actions. These activities can often be replicated in the North.

Journal Writing
(5 minutes)

Objective

To give participants an opportunity to record items they wish to remember or process.

Process

1. Ask participants to take a few minutes to write down on the journal page for this session any reactions, additional areas they wish to pursue, questions they want to research or additional action ideas and possible contacts they can think of. If time is short, encourage them to write between sessions and, when appropriate, add items to the flip chart pages posted at each session.

Assignments for Next Week
(3 minutes)

Process

1. Encourage participants to review, between sessions, the background and resource materials, especially the "U.S. Commitments to the Platform for Action." Emphasize that lobbying for the attainment of these commitments is critical.

2. Ask participants to prepare for the next session that covers complex economic issues (including the globalization of the economy, cutbacks in government programs to the poor in the U.S., the global debt problem and the structural adjustment programs of the World Bank and the International Monetary Fund) by reading the background section on economic issues for Session Three that begin on page 157.

3. Ask all participants to read the following:

   - Reading 1 — "Economic Concerns Take a Prominent Place at Beijing," Susal Stebbins, Laurel Parrott, *Minnesota Times*, Vol 17, No. 1, Fall 1995, Minnesota NOW, pages 118-120.

   - Reading 2 — "World Bank and IMF Have Failed, and Poor Pay the Price," by Linda Gray MacKay, *The Boston Globe*, July 14, 1994, pages 121-123. (Read for overall orientation to structural adjustment.)

   - Reading 3 — "Women's Responsibility Increases with Declining Food Production," by Alice Iddi, (native of Ghana), at UUSC Meeting, May 1994, pages 124-125.

- Reading 4 — "Structural Adjustment U.S. Style," Linda Gray MacKay, May 1996, page 125-130.

- Reading 5 — "Dispelling the Welfare Myth," *The Call*, Spring 1995, pages 130-131.

- Reading 6 — "Facts on the U.S. Welfare System, Women and Children   First: A Faith-Based Perspective on Welfare Reform," Summer 1995, pages 132-134.

4. Ask for four volunteers to briefly summarize the highlights of these readings during the next workshop.

    Volunteer Presenter Assignments

    Presenter 1: Describes what the surprise issue was for Susal Stebbins at the Fourth World Conference on Women and what Laurel Parrott thinks should be done about it. (2 minutes) (Reading 1)

    Presenter 2: Describes the impact of structural adjustment programs on a village in Ghana where Alice Iddi grew up. (3 minutes) (Readings 2 and 3)

    Presenter 3: Describes what is meant by "structural adjustment U.S. style," including the origin of our current deficit, what is meant by "corporate welfare" and how the portion of the federal budget that goes toward corporate welfare compares with the portion of the federal budget that goes for welfare to poor families and children (the Aid to Families with Dependent Children Program — AFDC). (4 minutes) (Reading 4)

    Presenter 4: Describes attitudes toward welfare recipients in this country and the inconsistency that a former welfare recipient finds in conservative attitudes towards the task of mothering when it is done by those on welfare as opposed to middle class women who chose to stay home to take care of their children. (2 minutes) (Readings 5 and 6)

Closing Circle
(2 minutes)

Objective

To provide an opportunity to connect symbolically with others before separating.

Process

1. Ask everyone to stand in a circle, acknowledge the work the group has done together and invite people to make a short comment about the experience. Stand, hold hands and read the following section of the poem "Let Us Hold Hands" by Pat Mora. Or sing the song below by Stuart Stotts, "I'm a World Citizen."[12] Substitute the name of your state for Wisconsin in the eleventh line. It is sung to the tune that is similar to the "Wabash Cannon Roll."

> Let us now hold hands with the Iroquois woman who slipped berries into children's lips
> while her sisters planted stars with a wooden hoe,
>
> with the woman who rubbed warm oil into her neighbor's feet
> when Plymouth's winter prowled and howled outside their doors,
>
> Let us hold hands
> with the woman who sewed faith into each stitch, cloth comforters
> pieced to the rhythm of español for babies born al silencio del desierto
>
> Excerpt from the poem *Let Us Hold Hands* by Pat Mora

12 Used with permission.

World Citizen   by Stuart Stotts © 1984

I'm A World Citizen

From Timbuktu to Lima Peru

From Shanghai to Nepal

From the fallen fence between Berlin to the ancient China wall

From Moscow to Jerusalem

From Cairo to Capetown

From Sydney to Seattle

I've got neighbors the whole world round

I'm a world citizen

World citizen

Step up and shake my hand

I'm not just from Wisconsin (substitute your state)

I'm not just American

I'm a world citizen

World citizen

Home the whole year round

You and I can break those borders down

Journal Page

Journal Page

Background and Resources
on Women's Health

Women's Health

- The risk of dying while pregnant or in the process of giving birth is six times higher for a woman in Africa than it is for a woman who lives in the Middle East or in Latin America.

- The death rate of mothers in countries where the least resources are available can be as much as 500 times higher than the lowest rate in affluent countries.[13]

- At least 100 million women — one in six married women in the developing countries outside China — want to use family planning but lack access to contraception. In those countries, approximately one in four births is unwanted and even more are unplanned.[14]

- High levels of maternal mortality and poor maternal health are closely related to the low social and economic status of women.

- One third of all illnesses affecting women of child-bearing age in developing countries is related to pregnancy, childbirth, abortion, HIV and reproductive tract infections.

- Three-fourths of the 500,000 maternal deaths that take place worldwide each year were due to hemorrhage, infection, pregnancy-related hypertension, obstructed labor and the complications from unsafe abortion.

- For every woman who dies in childbirth, as many as 200 or 300 more survive to suffer from chronic illness or physical impairment.

- The major factor in preventing maternal morbidity and mortality is access to appropriate health services, including family planning. Worldwide, some 350 million couples lack access to a full range of modern family planning information and services.

- An estimated 120 million women would practice family planning if an acceptable and affordable modern method were available. Comprehensive reproductive health care can be built on the foundation of family planning programs that already exist in some 155 countries' primary health care systems.[15]

13 "World Military and Social Expenditures," 1989.
14 Population Council, press release, 1994.
15 Cairo: Program of Action International Conference on Population and Development (ICPD), September 1994.

UUSC Project Partners Past and Present: Working for Women's Health

Si Mujer

A UUSC project partner in Nicaragua, Si Mujer (Yes, Woman), is a well known alternative health service. During its first year, 1,600 people attended the workshops, courses and forums developed by the organization. These courses cover sexuality, gender, access to power, AIDS and sexually transmitted disease prevention and cancer prevention. As a non-profit institution, the center is open to all and users pay according to a sliding scale.

In Nicaragua, maternal mortality is a primary concern. Official figures cite 159 maternal deaths per 100,000 live births. In some regions, this number increases to 700, particularly in parts of the Atlantic Coast. Complications from abortion account for 35 to 37 percent of hospital deaths. Si Mujer has tried to confront this problem in various ways, including organizing a controversial public debate on abortion from public health, legal, psychological and feminist points of view.

The Planned Parenthood Association of Eritrea

The Planned Parenthood Association of Eritrea (PPAE), a UUSC partner organization, faces multiple constraints in helping women improve their health and control their bodies. One constraint is that many men resist the concept of family planning because of the traditional status of honor in having large families and the need for a son to pass on the family name. Many families need several children to assist with the many difficult daily chores necessary for survival. Because infant mortality is high, families believe that many children must be born to ensure the survival of even a few. An additional difficulty is that few want to limit births after so many lives were lost during the civil war.

Nationwide, contraceptive use in Eritrea is estimated at 1.5 percent of the population. Only around 5.7 percent of the population have any knowledge of family planning concepts. Generally, public attitudes are favorable towards family planning. No religious, political or other groups have opposed family planning in Eritrea. The major constraints to family planning are the inaccessibility of many rural areas, poor rural health infrastructure, low-levels of awareness of the benefits of family planning, lack of trained family planning service providers, and inadequate funds to carry out this work. Despite these obstacles, the Planned Parenthood Association of Eritrea is taking concrete steps to help Eritrean women improve their reproductive health. These steps include:

- public education campaigns
- family planning services

- psychological counseling services
- training for health care providers in family planning
- research on family planning issues and promoting appropriate public policies
- a health information booklet on breastfeeding, family planning, family life, sanitation, and nutrition has been translated into Tigrinya and circulated to women
- a committee to work on ending harmful traditional practices such as female genital mutilation (90 percent of girls in Eritrea are still genitally mutilated)
- an urban vocational and social education program for young women who have dropped out of school

Gouri Choudhury, founder of Action India and an active participant in the Delhi Community Health Workers at the NGO forum in Huairou.

Delhi Community Health Workers, India

The Delhi Community Health Workers, a project supported by the UUSC, is grounded in a strong commitment to fight women's oppression and protect women's rights in all spheres, particularly in the area of reproductive rights and women's health. It is based on the need for women's access to safe and effective family planning methods.

The Delhi Community Health Workers operate in four slums on the outskirts of New Delhi. The community health workers are "ordinary" women from local communities who have a primary or middle school education. They have emerged as politically conscious and active members of their communities. Through its parent organization, Action India, the DCHW channels insights from poor women to national decision makers on issues like reproductive rights, family planning, economic policies and corruption.

To address the critical need for information and services related to reproductive health, the community health workers have implemented the Fertility Consciousness Program as a safe means of giving a woman control over all aspects of her life, empowered by the knowledge of her own anatomy, biological functions, and the social, cultural and economic structures that are responsible for her subordinate status. This program is complemented by demands from the group for choices in safe and effective family planning methods for poor women.

Gouri Choudhury, a founding member of Action India and an active participant in the DCHW's program stated:

> "Fertility consciousness is not just learning birth control or handing out information on contraceptives. In creating a safe and supportive space, this program gives the women a sense of self-worth and an identity independent of the patriarchal hierarchy."

The program focuses specifically on women in their reproductive years. Its aim is to enable women to know their own bodies and make informed choices regarding reproduction. The Community Health Workers believe that a woman's understanding of her own sexuality empowers her, enabling her to transcend the subordinate role assigned to her by society.

Women's Secretariat of the Agricultural Workers Union (Asociación de Trabajadores del Campo), Nicaragua

The Asociación de Trabajadores del Campo (ATC) is a federation of six rural workers' unions that works to improve the living conditions of rural workers and to promote their participation in Nicaragua's economic, social and political life. Because women make up nearly 40 percent of the ATC's membership, the Women's Secretariat of the ATC was established in 1986. Along with addressing labor concerns of women, the women's secretariat developed a program to overcome traditional taboos in Nicaragua and to promote positive behavior and attitudes toward sexuality. In a culture of machismo, which affects women's attitudes as well as men's, the ATC provides basic sex education and gives men and women opportunities to recognize shared responsibilities regarding sexual activity and its consequences. The Unitarian Universalist Service Committee supported this project for several years.

Two specific programs developed by the women's secretariat in response to reproductive health and empowerment priorities have been in-depth sex education classes and the direct provision of clinical health services.

Leaders of the Agricultural Workers Union of Nicaragua meet with UUSC representative Guadalupe Lopez.

They strongly stress the need for prenatal and postnatal care and family planning. The Women's Secretariat set up a mobile clinic to provide gynecological and obstetric care to women in two northwest municipalities of Nicaragua. The Flor de Sacuanjoche Clinic became the first of five rural clinics that are operated by the ATC, which provide a full range of reproductive and other primary health services to women who do not otherwise have access to such services.

Several indicators point to the reasons behind the success of ATC's sexual education programs, including:

- Women in agricultural settings called for the development of the program themselves.
- The program has created a safe space for reflection and candid discussion of topics not typically examined in the lives of rural women.
- Rural women with little or no prior access to regular health services are now making informed choices about their reproductive health.

Collaboration Across Borders

The Unitarian Universalist Service Committee brought an Indian physician to Nicaragua and a Nicaraguan community health organizer to Eritrea to exchange experiences and ideas. The North-South Institute on Leadership, Development and Sustainability for Grassroots Organizations, sponsored by UUSC in M'Bour, Senegal, in 1991, provided an unprecedented opportunity for representatives of more than two dozen groups from around the world to come together to compare perspectives, experiences and strategies to improve women's lives and health.

Reproductive Rights

Reproductive rights means women's right to decide whether, when and how to have children — regardless of nationality, class, ethnicity, race, age, religion, disability, sexuality or marital status — in the social and economic conditions that make such decisions possible. Reproductive rights means the right and access to:

- Full information about sexuality and reproductive health and health problems, and about the benefits and risks of drugs, devices, medical treatments and interventions, without which informed choice is impossible
- Good quality, comprehensive reproductive health services that meet women's needs and are accessible to all women
- Safe, effective contraception and sterilization
- Safe, legal abortion
- Safe, women-controlled pregnancy and childbirth
- Prevention of and safe, effective treatment for the causes of infertility[16]

Women do not have full reproductive rights anywhere in the world, although the conditions in which women are denied those rights may differ. Reproductive rights depend on achieving basic rights in almost every sphere of life. While reproduction may be an intensely personal experience, it is also a fundamentally social one, at the center of a web of human relations. Reproductive rights are a vital part of struggles for economic, social and gender justice, and cannot be viewed in isolation from them.

Choice/Force: Abortion and Sterilization

Access to Abortion

Often the decision to have an abortion is made by women in desperate situations facing unwanted pregnancies. Deciding to have an abortion is often an emotionally painful decision for a woman. When performed under unsafe conditions, the pain may also become physical and have lasting effects upon the woman's health. The risks associated with the termination of an unwanted pregnancy can be tremendously high for a woman and may include marginalization from society.

Hospitals in developing nations are often filled with women seeking emergency care for complications caused by unsafe abortions performed by unskilled providers in unclean settings. Survivors of unsafe abortions often suffer from debilitating pain, illness and infertility.

- While the U.S. federal government does not permit funding for abortions, it assumes 90 percent of the cost of sterilization operations.[17]

16 "Mission Statement," Women's Global Network for Reproductive Rights, The Netherlands.
17 "Contraception to Control Women," *Third World Resurgence*, No. 2, Nov. 1992.

- Abortion is legally restricted in many countries, leading women to resort to unsafe illegal abortion. An estimated 20 million unsafe abortions take place each year, resulting in up to 100,000 deaths.[18]

- The legal right to choose abortion is under attack in the U.S. Abortion clinics have been targets of escalating violence: three doctors and a clinic escort have been murdered since 1993; of 281 clinics surveyed that year by the Feminist Majority Foundation, 50.2 percent said they had experienced anti-abortion violence, such as death and bomb threats, stalking, arson, invasions and blockades.[19]

- Each year, approximately 50 million women resort to abortion to prevent unwanted births.

- The majority of the world's women, well over 60 percent, are without access to safe, legal abortion.

- Almost 10,000 African women undergo unsafe abortions each day, a procedure that often results in death.

- One in four women live in a country where abortion is banned, or permitted only to save a mother's life.

- About 67,000 women die each year from illegal or unsafe abortions.[20]

Forced Sterilization

A problem that has arisen as a result of overemphasis on population rather than an holistic approach to women's health is forced sterilization. Women were the main targets of a campaign in Bangladesh, which is often cited by population experts as a success story. Bangladesh's fertility rate declined from seven births per woman in 1975 to fewer than five in late 1994 — a considerable achievement in a country that is the world's most densely populated. Yet population agencies fail to acknowledge the human costs of its aggressive family planning policy. In the early 1980s, bodies like the World Bank and the U.S. Agency for International Development called for a drastic reduction in the population growth in Bangladesh. Those calls led to a heavy-handed campaign that emphasized sterilization over temporary birth control methods and all but neglected basic health care. Women and men were offered cash for being sterilized, health workers received a fee for each client they recruited for sterilization and doctors were paid by the case, encouraging them to rush through operations.

Women were the main targets of this campaign, even though sterilization is far less risky for men. A 1983 investigation of government clinics by the World Bank found that doctors operated in appallingly unhygienic conditions and that women sometimes submitted to sterilizations without being

18 Population Action International, "Reproductive Risk: A Worldwide Assessment of Women's Sexual and Maternal Health," 1995.
19 National Clinic Violence Survey, Feminist Majority Foundation, Washington, DC, 1993.
20 *ARAG National Newsletter*, Abortion Rights Action Group, South Africa, October 1994.

told that the operation was permanent. That same year, U.S. Agency for International Development officials complained to the Bangladeshi Government about reports of a coercive campaign by the army to sterilize women who had more than three children in one poor tribal community. A year later, British development workers discovered that officials in flooded areas were withholding emergency food aid from poor women unless they agreed to be sterilized.

The sterilization drive had a devastating impact on the country's fledgling health care efforts. Sterilization fees paid to local health workers, for example, caused them to neglect their other duties. And since the mid-1980s, population control programs have continued to absorb one-third of the country's total health budget. A comprehensive primary health care system with voluntary family planning would meet Bangladesh's needs far better than its present population control program.[21]

Women's Health Risks

HIV-AIDS

Women are very vulnerable to sexually transmitted diseases (STDs). One of the most deadly is Acquired Immune Deficiency Syndrome (AIDS), which is caused by the human immunodeficiency virus (HIV). Heterosexual transmission is the leading cause of AIDS in women. Worldwide, 3,000 women are infected daily with the virus that causes AIDS. This is especially true of the AIDS virus that has hit the people of Sub-Saharan Africa in a tragic way. In some parts of Africa, AIDS is called the "Family Disease" due to a pattern repeated throughout the developing world: men pass HIV on to their wives, who pass it on to their babies. By the year 2000, UNICEF estimates that AIDS will have orphaned 10 million children in Africa alone.

- 15 million people worldwide, including one million children, are infected with HIV. More than half — 8.5 million — live in Sub-Saharan Africa.

- By the year 2000, 40 million people will be infected and 90.7 percent of them will live in developing nations.[22]

- Of the estimated $2 billion spent annually on AIDS prevention, only about 10 percent is spent in the developing world, where 85 percent of infections occur.[23]

---

21 Hartmann, Betsy. "What Success Story?" *The New York Times*, Sept. 29, 1994.
22 "The Gathering Storm: HIV/AIDS in the Developing World," InterAction, *Alliance for a Global Community Newsletter*, Winter; 95/96, v2, n3.
23 "Vital Signs," *The Nation*, September 11, 1995.

Maternal Morbidity and Mortality

In many parts of the developing world, the leading cause of death for women of reproductive age is related to pregnancy and childbirth. Half a million women die each year from pregnancy-related causes, 99 percent of them in developing countries. The majority of these deaths could be prevented if women in developing nations had access to adequate health care. Factors that influence maternal morbidity and mortality include the age at which a woman begins childbearing, the interval between births and the total number of lifetime pregnancies.

Women in Africa have the highest rate in the world of death during childbirth. In various parts of Africa, between 30 to 60 percent of the deaths of women aged 15 to 44 are related to pregnancy or childbirth, compared to two percent in developed countries. Furthermore, the maternal mortality rate for African women may be related to conditions associated with pregnancy such as a woman's living conditions, and/or their physical, social and economic environment.[24]

- Adolescent mothers aged 15 to 19 are twice as likely to die in childbirth as mothers aged 20 to 24.
- Babies born to adolescent mothers are more than twice as likely to die in their first year of life, and that risk is doubled if births are spaced less than two years apart.[25]

Vesico-Vaginal Fistulae (VVF)

A major problem confronting many women in Africa is vesico-vaginal fistulae (VVF), which is an abnormal opening or hole between the urinary bladder and the vagina that results in constant, involuntary leakage of urine through the vagina. Most fistulae are caused by prolonged and difficult childbirth that is unassisted by medical personnel. Estimates show that some 1.5 to 2 million women in Africa are suffering from VVF, with 50,000-100,000 being added to that number each year.

During childbirth, the head of the baby presses hard against the wall of the birth canal for an extended period of time, cutting off the blood supply and killing the tissue. After the birth, the tissue decays leaving a fistula between the vagina and bladder. As urine leaks constantly from the bladder into the vagina, the woman with a fistula is incontinent and smells of urine.

Traditional practice in Africa has been to wait a minimum of three months before repairing the fistula. During this period, the woman waiting for the operation is no longer deemed desirable and in most cases is socially rejected and often divorced by her husband. Women in this state often travel from village to village trying to fend for themselves econom-

---

24 Women's Global Network for Reproductive Rights, Newsletter 49, January-March 1995.
25 "Reproductive and Primary Health: Top Priorities," The Center for Development and Population Activities, July 1995.

ically as their health declines. The wait for the operation may range anywhere from three months to several years. According to surgeon Doctor Kees Waldijl of northern Nigeria, there are many advantages to repairing fistulae at an early stage, which include dramatic improvements in the health and well-being of the women affected with fistulae.[26]

Contraception

Obstacles to Women's Contraceptive Use

The reasons why women do not find a fertility-regulating technology that suits them is not due to the technology itself. More compelling reasons are women's poor health, male control of female sexuality, men's unwillingness to take responsibility for fertility control, poor health infrastructure and a lack of quality of care. What is needed is a search for policies and programs that will remove these constraints.[27]

Offering birth control to women without proper education and follow-up results in medical complications and even death. Programs that try to control women's fertility without attending to their greater health needs do not respect women's rights. No contraception is acceptable without gynecological care.

Another serious problem with family planning programs has been the emphasis on high-technology methods that are extremely effective yet allow women little or no control. These methods require great dependence on family planning services and provide no protection against sexually-transmitted diseases. In the countries of the South, barrier methods such as condoms are used less than in the countries of the North. Priorities in the South are based on reducing population growth and on the belief that women cannot cope with a method that they have to apply themselves, due to lack of education or lack of power in their relationships. In Brazil, as in other countries, the cost of motherhood for women (material and emotional cost, extra work) leads 85 percent of female contraceptive users to opt for pills or surgical sterilization. While these methods might reduce population, they do not protect against HIV infection/AIDS. Even though public opinion surveys show that people believe that HIV infection occurs in at-risk populations, recent worldwide data shows that women represent a considerable proportion of all HIV infected persons.[28]

Even if condoms are available, many women are unable to demand their use. According to Brazilian anthropologist Jane Galvao, "the power women have is to negotiate, plead and beg, while the man has the power to demand, turn down and deny." This puts poor women at increased risk

26 "Surgeons Show Success in Early Fistula Repairs," *Safe Motherhood Newsletter* 14, March-June 1994.
27 World Health Organization.
28 The World Health Organization magazine, special issue for the Beijing conference, September 1995.

of infection or abandonment. A major obstacle for women who wish to protect themselves against HIV infection is the desire for children. Safer sex (non-penetrative or condom-protected) presupposes sex without conception. In many cultures, childless women face stigma; sometimes the penalty is desertion or divorce.[29]

Women are prepared to accept the biological risks of contraception, but often they do so with mixed emotions. Women recognize and appreciate that the increasingly widespread use of modern contraceptives has been beneficial to women's health. The benefits have been won largely through the direct effect of preventing pregnancy and the mortality and illness associated with pregnancy and childbirth. Nonetheless, many women, at one time or another, have had negative experiences using modern contraceptives.

The reasons often have as much to do with the conditions in which contraceptives are made available as with the technology itself. Some of the reasons are dislike of the physical intrusion required for the insertion of some methods, the difficulty of use in the home, costs, inconvenience, dislike of the medicalization of intimate and private acts and of dependence on the provider or partner, mistrust of the longer-term consequences and risks of using a method, and lack of follow-up and concern about side effects on the part of service providers. In short, women take into account a range of concerns, such as safety, privacy, and their ability to control the method, not just the method's effectiveness as a contraceptive. These three factors, the balance of gender power, the ambiguities of women's approach to contraception, and their desire to balance a number of concerns when choosing a method, challenge existing processes of technology development and service provision.[30]

Some women's perspectives on contraceptive technology challenge the belief, deeply embedded in religious and cultural convictions, that men have the right to control women's fertility and sexuality. An age-old fear of unbridled female sexuality not directed toward procreation haunts the debate. The rejection by women of the view that the purpose of their sexuality is to satisfy the sexual needs of men is profoundly threatening to existing patterns of male dominance. Women, however, do not or cannot trust men to take responsibility for protecting them from infection and unwanted pregnancy.[31]

29 "From Information to Education," The Panos Institute, 1994.
30 Jiggins, Janice. *Changing the Boundaries*, Island Press, Washington DC, 1994.
31 Ibid.

Contraceptive Needs

According to the Secretariat of the International Conference on Population and Development held in Cairo, Egypt, in 1994 many countries dramatically expanded the availability of family planning services, accelerating a decline in fertility rates. An estimated 53 percent of couples in developing countries are now using contraception, compared to around 14 percent in 1965-1970. The total fertility rate in developing countries has declined from 6.1 children per women in the 1950s to 3.7 today. Because of markedly different rates of progress among countries and regions, however, there are enormous regional disparities in current contraceptive use levels.

It is estimated that more than 300 million couples do not have consistent and reliable access to safe and effective methods of fertility regulation, or to information on where they are available and how to use them. In many countries, there are cultural, economic and institutional obstacles to correcting this situation, which is often reflected in high abortion rates.

Women trained by the Delhi Community Health Workers use self-help methods for dealing with common ailments and reproductive problems. These women also organize others in their communities to campaign for government action on domestic violence and health care issues.

Family planning contributes to safe motherhood and child survival, but each year more than 500,000 women still die from causes related to pregnancy and childbirth. An estimated 30 percent of pregnancy-related deaths could be averted if all the women who say they want no more children but are not using modern contraception were able to avoid becoming pregnant. Here are some useful facts relating to contraceptive use:

- In the early 1960s, only 18 percent of women in the developing countries used contraception. Today about half of all couples of childbearing age in the developing world use contraception.

- There are stark differences in contraceptive usage among regions. While 71 percent of couples in the industrialized world use birth control, the comparable figure for African couples is only 17 percent.

- Approximately one in four births in the developing world (excluding China) is unwanted, and even more are unplanned. Another rough measure of unmet need for contraception is the estimated 50 million abortions that are performed each year, nearly half of which are illegal and unsafe.

- A recent survey of clinics in Tanzania found that only one quarter of clients were warned about potential contraceptive side effects.

- Partly because of the U.S. retreat from leadership in population, control in the 1980s, donor funding for population assistance has fallen at least 60 percent below the level of requests for assistance from developing countries.[32]

Hormonal Implant Birth Control Methods

Norplant is a hormonal implant that when inserted in a woman's body prevents conception for five years if not removed. While women need access to safe contraceptive technologies, Norplant is not a solution as it is likely to cause imbalance in the menstrual cycle and other side effects. Women's concerns about irregular bleeding while using Norplant contraceptive implants were often dismissed and their requests for removal of the implant were ignored in clinics in the Dominican Republic, Egypt, Indonesia and Thailand.[33]

An attitude expressed about Norplant in the United States reveals how people throughout the world often react to forced use of Norplant. Two days after the U.S. Food and Drug Administration (FDA) approved Norplant, *The Philadelphia Enquirer* ran an editorial suggesting that readers should think about Norplant as a "tool in the fight against black poverty." After protests, an apology was published but the idea behind the editorial was clear. Norplant, in fact, became a tool to inflict punishment on poor mothers. In several states, legislation is being introduced that would make Norplant a part of the sentences women receive when they are convicted.[34]

Anti-Fertility "Vaccines" (Immunological Contraceptives)

According to Judith Richter, who presented her views at a World Health Organization discussion on ethical aspects of research, development and introduction of fertility regulating methods in Geneva in 1994, anti-fertility "vaccines" have an unprecedented high abuse potential. They are relatively long acting (depending on the type, they may last from one year to

---

32 "The Road to Cairo," Pew Global Stewardship Initiative, April 1994.
33 Population Council press release, 1994.
34 "Contraception to Control of Women," *Third World Resurgence*, No. 27, November 1992.

lifelong), they cannot be discontinued by the user herself, they are administered by injection or orally and can be administered far more easily on a mass scale than IUDs, which have to be inserted intravaginally, or Norplant, which requires minor surgery. Researchers claim that the popularity of anti-disease vaccines could facilitate the introduction of anti-fertility "vaccines." But this delivery form harbors the risk of administration without women's knowledge or informed consent.

Moreover, immunological contraceptives present no advantage over existing contraceptives. Because they use the immune system, they are inherently unreliable. Individuals can react completely differently. For example the Indian anti-hCG formula, the most advanced method, did not work for 20 percent of the women, while its effect lasted from six months to more than two years in other women. In addition, stress, malnutrition and disease will cause unpredictable failures of the contraceptive. In women with a predisposition to allergies and autoimmune diseases, the "vaccine" may cause lifelong sterility. There is no outward sign to let women know whether an immunological contraceptive is working for them.

Contraceptive "vaccines" that operate on the immune system are a classic example of the double challenge women face in securing access to safe birth control and health care. The Women's Global Network on Reproductive Rights has launched a campaign against contraceptive vaccine research because it imposes unacceptable health risks and has the potential for widespread abuse in population control programs. At the same time, one of the largest anti-abortion groups, Human Life International, has spread false rumors in Tanzania, Mexico, the Philippines and Nicaragua that WHO-provided tetanus injections are being laced with anti-fertility vaccine. This has had a disastrous effect on public immunization campaigns.

Female Genital Mutilation (FGM)

FGM is the term used to describe procedures that involve partial or total removal of the external female genitalia and/or other injury to the female genital organs for cultural or non-therapeutic reasons. This practice, used in some parts of Africa and Asia, can cause complications in childbirth and increase the risk of reproductive tract infections, including sexually transmitted diseases. It also causes psychological trauma, painful intercourse and menstruation, and lack of sexual pleasure.[35] The health effects of female genital mutilation on girls are numerous and always significant. Death, hemorrhage, anemia, infection, infertility, interrupted schooling, phobia, depression and fear of sex are real and common side effects of FGM.[36]

35 International Women's Health Coalition, "Women's Reality, Women's Power," August 1994.
36 See Research Action and Information Network for the Bodily Integrity of Women (RAINBO), a global action project against female genital mutilation in the women's rights resources section for more information.

Even though there is no reference to FGM in the Koran, more than 50 percent of male respondents to a survey conducted in Sudan in 1983 expressed the belief that female circumcision was a Muslim religious requirement. This mistaken belief is very important to consider when strategies are being devised to abolish the practice.

Dorothy Smith Patterson

Dorothy Smith Patterson, president of UUSC's Board of Directors

President of the Board of Directors of UUSC, on Female Genital Mutilation at the Fourth World Conference on Women

I attended several workshops on female genital mutilation (FGM) which was invisible in the western world when I lived and worked in Nigeria in the 1960s. Many people at that time did not know about the practice. Those who knew had no power or did not want to risk "interfering with local customs," a reason frequently expressed by African Americans.

Being an African American myself, I have a great deal of respect for many aspects of traditional African culture. But having witnessed the damage of this practice, I am personally committed to speaking out against it.

Over the years, I have followed efforts made to eradicate this practice and I am concerned with the slow pace. FGM was opposed by some Christian missionaries as early as the seventeenth century and by colonial governments during the early part of this century. The efforts made then were isolated and scattered, and were met with resistance by local people who saw them as one of many tactics used to destroy indigenous cultures. The practice now occurs in 46 countries.

I was pleased to find a number of workshops at the Fourth World Conference on Women on FGM that focused on the elimination of the practice — some through support of NGO programs to educate families in villages and some through government action to criminalize the practice. One group of presenters encouraged petitions and a letter writing campaign to Egypt's President Mubaruk, whose government recently authorized performance of the procedure in hospitals for health reasons.

The number of NGOs addressing FGM has grown, partly due to the exposure of the subject by a small group of African women, human rights activists and the emergence of the practice in the West.

Cairo: Program of Action

International Conference on Population and Development, September 1994

The International Conference on Population and Development (ICPD) held in Cairo, Egypt, was one of a series of United Nations conferences that will set the world's social development agenda for the 21st century. Its emphasis on reproductive rights and the centrality of women in development was reiterated in the Platform for Action that was produced at the Fourth World Conference on Women in Beijing, China.

Enabling couples and individuals to choose when to have children and freeing women from the health risks associated with reproduction and sexuality are essential to redressing these inequities and fulfilling women's human rights, and make it possible for countries to progress towards sustainable development including the early stabilization of their population size.

This understanding is central to the landmark agreement reached by 185 nations at the International Conference on Population and Development in Cairo in September 1994. The Program of Action adopted by the conference calls for gender equality and equity, for allowing women to have and exercise choices, and for making reproductive health care available throughout the world.

The Program of Action emphasizes human rights and the well-being of individual women and men, and the need to invest in their health and education and in building equity and equality between the sexes.

Population

- World population is now about 5.7 billion. It is increasing at the rate of 88 million per year, and 95 percent of that increase is in the developing world.

- The three chief causes of population growth are: unwanted and unplanned pregnancies where there is unmet demand for contraception and other reproductive health services; a demand for large families where, for example, childhood death rates are high; and population momentum, caused by large numbers of young people entering their childbearing years.[37]

- About a third of the world's people are now under the age of 15. In less-developed nations the figure is higher: 38 percent in Ecuador, for example, compared to 22 percent in the U.S.[38]

- Surveys estimate that voluntary family planning programs could reduce the projected 2100 population by nearly 2 billion simply by helping today's couples avoid unwanted fertility.[39]

37 "The Human Population: A Demographic Profile," Pew Global Stewardship Initiative, April 1994.
38 Population Reference Bureau, World Population Data Sheet, 1995, and United Nations Population Division, personal communication, July 12, 1995.
39 Population Reference Bureau, *A Citizens Guide to the International Conference on Population and Development*, 1993.

Breakthrough on Rights of Women to Control Their Sexuality

The most significant development at the Fourth World Conference on Women may well be the one that received the least comment. Midway through what sometimes seemed like endless round-the-clock negotiations, a working session finally agreed to recognize that the human rights of women include the right to exercise control over their own sexuality — free from coercion, discrimination, and violence. For international diplomats to take on such sensitive subjects — and to assert that full equality for women requires "mutual respect, consent, and shared responsibility for sexual behavior and its consequences" — is a historic breakthrough.

The watershed agreement reached at the International Conference on Population and Development in Cairo in 1994 committed the international community to a wide range of policies and programs addressing the complex relationships between the social status of women and global well-being. For the first time the reproductive and sexual health of women was linked directly to considerations of sustainable population growth and economic development. In Beijing, the equation was extended to explicitly affirm women's rights regarding sexuality. Applying universal human rights standards to women's sexuality also gives women potential legal grounds for refusing unwanted pregnancy and childbearing, along with unwarranted medical interventions or bodily mutilations, such as coercive sterilization or abortions and female genital mutilations.[40]

Call for a Stop to Research on Anti-Fertility Vaccines

More than 350 women's, health action, development and human rights groups from 35 countries have signed a "Call for a Stop to the Research on Anti-Fertility Vaccines." These groups are concerned about the abuse potential of immunological contraceptives.

The "Call for a Stop" states:

Population control ideology should not guide contraceptive development. The aim must be to enable people — particularly women — to exert greater control over fertility without sacrificing their integrity, health, and well being. Contraceptive development must be oriented toward the realities of women's lives. Above all it must consider local health care conditions and the position of women in society.

40 Dunlap, Joan and Ellen Chesler. "Consensus on Woman's Rights Cleared the Skies in China," *The Christian Science Monitor*, Sept. 9, 1995.

Women's health advocates must continually distinguish their critique of population-control-driven contraceptive research from the anti-abortion movement's opposition to virtually all forms of birth control. Demonstrating against hazardous contraceptives, feminists at the NGO forum held up banners proclaiming "Feminists for abortion rights and birth control, not population control" and "We want user-controlled methods of contraception."[41]

Call to Abolish FGM

Women's groups, health professionals, human rights activists and governments are working to stop female genital mutilation. At the international level, the Convention on the Rights of the Child explicitly requires states to take all appropriate measures to abolish traditional practices prejudicial to the health of children. In 1994, the World Health Assembly again called the attention of the world to the detrimental health consequences of FGM, and called for the elimination of FGM. In addition, the World Health Assembly has declared that medicalization of the procedure should not be allowed under any circumstance.[42] At the World Conference in Vienna in 1993 and the International Conference on Population and Development in Cairo in 1994, the international women's movement succeeded in putting women's reproductive health and human rights at the center of the world policy agenda. African women were an integral part of that effort and won a world consensus that FGM and other harmful cultural practices constitute a violation of women's human rights and lead to serious health problems for women and girls. The Cairo Program of Action states that "governments are encouraged to prohibit FGM wherever it exists and to give vigorous support to efforts among nongovernmental and community organizations and religious institutions to eliminate such practices." The Beijing Platform for Action on Female Genital Mutilation states:

- Conditions that force girls into early marriage, pregnancy and childbearing and subject them to harmful practices, such as female genital mutilation, pose grave health risks.

- Prohibit female genital mutilation wherever it exists and give vigorous support to efforts among nongovernmental and community organizations and religious institutions to eliminate such practices. Section 232(h)

41 Hartmann, Betsy. *Reproductive Rights and Wrongs: The Global Politics of Population Control*, South End Press, Boston, 1995. Betsy Hartmann is director of the Population and Development Program at Hampshire College and a founding member of the Committee on Women, Population and the Environment.
42 World Health Organization Position Paper, Fourth World Conference on Women, Beijing, China.

The Platform for Action

Women's Health

(Section C of Chapter IV — Strategic Objectives and Actions)

Strategic Objective

To increase women's full access to appropriate, affordable and quality health care.

Actions to be taken by governments, in collaboration with the U.N. system, the medical community, research institutions, NGOs, media and others:

- Design and implement gender-sensitive health programs.

- Provide affordable primary health care that emphasizes health promotion and disease prevention.

- Give particular attention to the needs of girls.

- Ensure women's involvement in decision making relating to HIV/AIDS and other sexually transmitted diseases, facilitate the development of strategies to protect women from HIV and other sexually transmitted diseases, and ensure the provision of affordable preventive services for sexually transmitted diseases.

- Encourage and support research on prevention, treatment and health care systems related to diseases and conditions that have specific effects on women.

U.S. Commitments to the Platform for Action

Health

The Department of Health and Human Services (DHHS) initiated action on a range of concerns to women throughout the life cycle, recognizing the additional problems faced by women of low income and from ethnic and racial minorities.

Youth and Children: A governing council will develop a comprehensive and coordinated strategy for children and youth that recommends areas for investment of resources, building communications across the government, supporting partnerships with communities and coordinating research and an evaluation agenda.

Disabled Women and Girls: Interagency coordination to integrate health issues affecting disabled girls and women into an overall health agenda.

Older Women: Addressing the health needs of older women through the Women's Health Initiative, the largest clinical research study ever conducted that examines the major causes of death, disability and fragility in postmenopausal women.

Contraceptive Research and Development: Conducting and funding contraceptive research and development, with special emphasis on hormonal implants, immunocontraception and Milepristone (RU-486).

HIV/AIDS: Development of the Women's Interagency HIV Study, a long-term, large-scale study that investigates the impact of HIV infection in U.S. women and a public policy agenda on HIV/AIDS specific to women, adolescents and children.

Clinic Protection: The United States has committed and continues to commit considerable resources to the enforcement by the Department of Justice of the Freedom of Access to Clinic Entrances Act of 1994, including the deployment of three principal investigative agencies. Ongoing task forces directed by the U.S. Attorneys which include federal, state and local law enforcement officials, will continue to develop plans to ensure security for reproductive health clinics.

Additional Programs: Other programs include a comprehensive plan to reduce smoking among children and adolescents by 50 percent; a new initiative to reduce teen pregnancy; the inauguration of the National Women's Health Clearinghouse; and new initiatives on breast and cervical cancer, the impact of poverty-related diseases on women, and the inclusion of women in clinical trials.

Notes

Assignments for
Session Three

Economic Concerns Take a Prominent Place at Beijing

Excerpted from an article by Susal Stebbins, a lobbyist for the Minnesota National Organization of Women, who attended the Fourth World Conference on Women.

The surprise issue of the conference for me, and I think for most U.S. women, was how the globalization of the economy has exacerbated women's struggles everywhere: from girls being sold into prostitution in Southeast Asia, to dowry murders in India, to sterilization abuse in Mexico, to an increase in women's sweatshop labor, and to an increase in poverty for women and children.

The main elements of the globalized economy that became visible at the conference were the increasing power of multinational corporations and the international debt situation.

Technological advances, better communications systems, new trade agreements, tax breaks and other national financial structures that encourage their activity, have allowed multinational corporations to be more plentiful, mobile, spread out and give them more influence on national economies than ever before. Some conference speakers said multinational corporations have usurped the role of governments in setting policies and shaping the lives of citizens. Multinationals are competing on the basis of who can pay the lowest wages to the smallest number of workers, have the cheapest (i.e., poorest) working conditions, the most control over their labor force, and the fewest environmental regulations or responsibilities to the populations. The results have been staggering and consistent worldwide: depression of wages; increases in unemployment and underemployment, increases in sweatshop and child labor; greater exploitation of immigrant, contract and temporary labor; decreases in employer provided benefits, deterioration of working conditions; greater harassment and repression of union organizers and worker's rights advocates; and a growing gap between rich and poor in every nation.

We've seen the impact in Minnesota: a sweatshop discovered in a Minnesota warehouse; Latino immigrants locked in a farmhouse and paid almost nothing for two month's labor; in southwestern Minnesota, a business owner's complaint, echoing hundreds of others, that he can't pay a decent wage because of global competition.

The impact on women has been particularly harsh — not surprising in light of the realities of sexism and the fact that women make up 70 percent of the world's poor. When corporations "downsize," women are the most likely to be laid off.

Then there's the international debt. The World Bank and the International Monetary Fund are owed billions of dollars by industrializing countries. The debts were built up by a combination of military expenditures (weapons purchased mostly from the U.S. and Europe) and development programs designed by U.S. and European advisors. Both expenditures have drained rather than built national economies and moved more wealth outside the countries and into the hands of a few wealthy families within the countries, slowing the timetable for paying back the loans. International monetary institutions place a set of requirements on nations called structural adjustment programs (SAPs) to speed up delinquent loan payments. SAPs require governments to drastically reduce social spending — curtailing vital food, health, education and sanitation programs, and laying off hundreds of thousands of government workers — and to shift local production from products needed in the country to products for export.

The impact is so severe that UNICEF estimates six million children have died each year since 1980 as a direct result of SAPs. Women suffer additional malnutrition and starvation, homelessness, death and disability from disease, die at higher rates from pregnancies that couldn't be prevented due to lack of access to birth control and suffer from higher unemployment. Women must also take over the work abandoned by their governments. When a childcare center or school closes, women care for the children. When a hospital or clinic closes, women nurse the ill. When government food supplements stop, women spend more of their day searching for and preparing food. When a water source becomes polluted or is diverted for industrial use, women walk further each day to carry water for their families. Thus SAPs create a double burden for women.

The U.S. is going through its own form of SAP: the same demands to reduce the debt (built up by military expenditures) are the excuses for drastic cuts in basic services; the same siphoning of wealth into fewer and fewer hands; the same economic hardship for the majority; and the especially harsh effects on women.

As women are hardest hit by the problems, women are also pioneering the solutions. Women are developing standards for multinational corporations' wages, working conditions, environmental impacts, and mechanisms for enforcing those standards, such as a "fair trade" labeling system for all goods. Women are starting to keep track of women's unpaid contributions to the economy: untold hours of housework, cooking, childcare, eldercare, nursing and subsistence farming. Women are creating alternative economic institutions such as the SEWA Bank in India, which started out as a source of micro-loans — under $200 each — for women to set up businesses, and grew to provide its members with childcare, healthcare, life insurance and unemployment benefits.[43]

43 "Women and the Global Economy," Susal Stebbins, *The Minnesota Times*, MN NOW, Vol. 17, No. 1, Fall 1995.

Another Minnesota resident, Laurel Parrott, president of Minnesota NOW who also journeyed to Beijing, sees the global economy as perhaps the primary issue around which women should organize to fulfill the hopes expressed at Beijing:

> Most women in the U.S. plead ignorance on the subject of economics, but we must educate ourselves on it. Money influences every aspect of our daily lives and without money, women are powerless.

> With an obvious recognition that their governments either can't or won't voluntarily act on global economy issues, activists (at the Fourth World Conference on Women) talked about grassroots solutions...getting out the vote, lobbying legislators, pressuring politicians, educational, media, consciousness campaigns, getting progressive women elected...picketing, boycotting... these same strategies must be directed at transnational corporations. Governments can't and shouldn't take the sole blame or responsibility for women's economic plight. We must lobby corporations with the same intensity that we lobby our governments — and with greater intensity than corporations lobby our governments.

> Grassroots efforts and alternative, cooperative economic models are the tools women must use to change the economic crisis and improve women's lives. Our global sisters have called on us to unite, and we must. As long as women do two-thirds of the world's work and receive only five percent of the world's income, the global economy is our issue.

During the 1995 UUSC Haitian Women's Tour, Olga Benoit and Celina Noel described the effects of global economic injustice on women and their families.

BOB DAHM ILLUSTRATION

World Bank and IMF Have Failed, and the Poor Pay the Price

The Boston Globe, July 14, 1994

by Linda Gray MacKay

The World Bank and International Monetary fund were planning to celebrate their 50th anniversary at Bretton Woods, N.H., this month. Now they have called off the celebration, undoubtedly because officials learned it would have been disrupted by protesters against the quiet war that these institutions have been waging against the poor in Africa, Asia and the Americas.

We live in a world that is becoming more and more divided between rich and poor, North and South. Over one-fifth of the world's people, who are in the South, live in abject poverty. Another fifth, who live in the North, consume 80 percent of the world's resources. The World Bank and IMF, funded with our tax dollars, are making the gap even wider.

The Unitarian Universalist Service Committee, Oxfam America and Partners in Health, three locally based human rights and international development organizations, have joined with 35 development, environmental and religious organizations to say "50 Years is Enough." We are part of a national and international campaign calling for a moratorium on funding for the World Bank and the IMF until they become more democratic and accountable and begin to foster sustainable and people-centered development.

The World Bank and IMF were byproducts of the Bretton Woods Conference held a month after D-Day to plan for the postwar economy. These institutions were designed to stabilize world financial markets and provide loans to developing countries to alleviate poverty and stimulate economic growth.

The past 50 years have provided ample evidence that instead of helping Third World nations, these organizations have underwritten projects and imposed policies that have drastically increased global poverty and debt and promoted development that is undemocratic, inequitable and harmful to the environment. In addition, these organizations, which work very closely with each other, function in an atmosphere of secrecy with little opportunity for input by those whose lives their projects and policies affect most directly.

Billions have been spent on poorly conceived projects — dams, roads and power plants — 37 percent of which have been colossal failures, even according to the World Bank's own internal documents. These projects have also severely damaged fragile ecosystems and caused more than 2.5 million people to lose their homes and livelihoods.

In addition, in the aftermath of the international debt crisis of the 1980s, the World Bank and IMF have forced countries to restructure their economies to qualify for additional international loans and grants. These structural adjustment programs were designed to increase foreign investment and promote export-led growth to meet foreign debt payments. These measures have included reductions in import duties and cutbacks in programs for health care, education and agricultural credits for small farmers.

Originally it was anticipated that the structural adjustment programs would be short-term shock treatments that would quickly overcome debt payment shortfalls, but a decade after their initiation, it is clear that they have not yet achieved this goal. This is due to the fact that the adjustment programs were based on the mistaken assumption that the principal cause of the debt problem was excess demand by Third World governments and citizens. This analysis did not factor in external world market influences such as economic recession, plunging export prices and the oil price increases of the '70s, or the inordinate influence of US interest rate increases in the '80s, factors over which the people of the developing nations had no control.

Tragically, even though these harsh programs (cutbacks in health care, education, food subsidies, etc.) failed to solve the debt crisis, the IMF and World Bank continue to require their adoption as preconditions for new loans. These institutions have, in effect, been attempting to balance the world's debt burden on the backs of those who can least afford it.

This crisis prompted former President Julius Nyerere of Tanzania to ask: "Must we starve our children to pay our debts?" A UNICEF document answered that question: "Hundred of thousands of the developing world's children have given their lives to pay their countries' debts, and many millions more are still paying the interest with their malnourished minds and bodies." UNICEF estimates that about 500,000 children die each year from the austerity measures that have been mandated as a result to Third World debt.

Yet it is not facts and figures but the human dimension of these failed policies that have convinced many of the urgent need for taking action on this issue. A development worker from a rural village in Ghana, a country that the World Bank and IMF point to as their success story, offers this observation: "From my experience, things are getting worse for most people. Poverty isn't decreasing, it's increasing and deepening. While more and more cocoa and coffee is being produced in Ghana, the prices have fallen drastically. Now farmers harvest twice as much for the same amount of income. When I was young, about 89 percent of the families in my village had enough food to feed themselves. Today, 99 percent of them, including my own family, don't."

In Nicaragua, an 11 year-old boy is forced to leave school in the fourth grade because his mother couldn't afford the new fees for school materials. Instead, he starts selling gum on the street to help support his family, his father has lost his job and his family doesn't get any more food from his relatives in the country because the government isn't helping small farmers anymore, only large growers who grow crops for export.

In the Philippines a mother discourages her daughter from going on to college so she can go off to work in Japan as an entertainer. The woman's husband has been laid off from his factory job due to trade liberalization policies. The family was hurt further when the cost of rice went up due to cutbacks in government subsidies. The mother then started working in a laundry during the day and selling eggs at night to try to keep the family afloat.

These accounts provide a glimpse of the human suffering and bartered futures exacted daily from the people of the South by the failed polices of the World Bank and International Monetary Fund. They echo tales of family crisis and shattered dreams heard daily in this country as we, too, begin to feel the effects of an increasingly globalized economy that seems to function outside the law.

It is past time to stop funding these organizations and their failed projects and programs. Instead, let us work together to create new institutions that are capable of promoting people-centered development that will respect the right of all the world's families to live in peace with dignity and hope for their children's future.[44]

---

44 Reprinted with permission from *The Boston Globe* and Linda Gray MacKay.

Women's Responsibility Increases with Declining Food Production

by Alice Iddi

It is very difficult to assess the human cost of the shift from subsistence farms to export crop production but observations shared with the Unitarian Universalist Service Committee by Ghanaian women illustrate the impact that such policies had on one rural village. It is important to note that the World Bank and IMF point to Ghana as their structural adjustment success story for Africa.

Alice Iddi, of Oxfam U.K., speaking at UUSC's Advocacy for Africa consultation, May 1994

I am from a small village in Northern Ghana. I am, therefore, intimately aware of what is going on. I can say definitely from my experience that things are getting worse, for the majority of people. While production of export crops has increased tremendously, their prices have fallen drastically, so Ghana now produces twice as much for export but their income has not increased.

My village is a subsistence farming community of about one hundred households. When I was young, about 20 years old, about 99 percent of households had enough food to feed themselves through the year from their own farm produce. There were a handful of families who suffered food shortages during the lean season — three to four months before the new harvest. And everybody knew them. Now, it is the opposite. About 99 percent of households, including my own family, are not able to provide enough food for their families all year round because their time is committed to producing export crops. Those who can afford it have to buy grain for the last four to five months before the harvest. This means reducing food intake during a time when it is needed for energy to prepare and grow the next crop.

Women are particularly hard-hit in this situation of decreasing food production. Traditionally, it's the man's responsibility to provide grain from the farm produce. The woman is responsible for transforming it and preparing it for meals, but when the family granary is empty, and the going gets tough the men often give up and the women are forced to take over, adding to their other responsibilities. It is hard on a man who cannot fulfill his responsibility but it is even harder on the woman because she has to deal with her children crying for food. With the incredible resourcefulness, they manage to get some money together to buy food. In these circumstances, the main concern is to "kill" the nagging hunger and nutritional quality is secondary.

Burning and selling of charcoal and firewood is one of the new income sources for women, and this activity has increased dramatically in my village over the last five years. It causes serious environmental damage, but in their struggle for survival, concern about the environment is a luxury they can't afford.

The primary school in the village has fallen to pieces. Parents now have to pay school fees as well as provide tables and chairs, books and writing materials for their children. Those who manage to finish school can't find jobs so with the prospects so bleak and the struggle for daily survival so intense, I haven't been able to convince my sister to send her children to school. It doesn't hold out much hope for their future.

Structural Adjustment U.S. Style

by Linda Gray MacKay

During the 1980s and 1990s many social program cutbacks took place in the United States that parallel the structural adjustment programs (SAPs) that have been imposed on indebted nations by the World Bank and International Monetary Fund as conditions for receiving new loans.[45] These programs resulted in drastic cutbacks in social safety net programs such as health care, education and food subsidies which have had a devastating impact on poor families. In the United States similar cutbacks were initiated during the Reagan and Bush years which also had a devastating affect on poor families. This was also the time when our own debt crisis began to escalate. Edward Herman has provided an analysis of the origin of this crisis. He points out that it stems, in large part, from both the huge tax cuts which benefited high wage earners and businesses, and the military build up which was financed by high federal borrowing by the U.S. Treasury. He also points out that the current move to cutback on social services and welfare programs championed by the Republican Congress and, to some extent, by the Clinton Administration as well, are being justified by allegations of intergenerational welfare dependence though little attention is being paid to the military budget which was funded above the level requested for fiscal year 1996, at the same time that huge tax breaks are given to corporations. Herman also points out that the health care crisis is responsible for the largest growth in the entitlement[46] budget though neither the Republicans or the so called "New Democrats" seem to want to address this issue. He provides the following analysis to describe the origins of the deficit crisis in the U.S.:

45 Part of the following analysis is adapted from a study entitled, "Reaganomics and Women: Structural Adjustment U.S. Style — 1980-1992: A Case Study of Women and Poverty in the U.S." Alternative Women in Development, Washington DC: Center for Concern, 1992. The study compares the impact of structural adjustment programs in the South to social service and welfare cutbacks in the United States.
46 Discretionary spending is the part of the budget that Congress has the greatest control over. Congress annually decides how to spend approximately $500 billion by cutting, expanding, or maintaining certain programs. Discretionary spending decisions are reviewed in the annual Congressional process of negotiating and debating the federal budget and passing appropriations bills. It includes defense spending, business and agricultural subsidies, grants for students aid, job training and environmental protection.

"Once in office, Reagan produced, by deliberate action, a huge structural deficit via the deep tax cuts of 1981-82. (A structural deficit is one that exists even at high levels of employment because of tax-expenditure policy decisions that result in tax revenues falling short of planned expenditures.) Of course the deficits were rationalized by means of "supply side economics," which forecast a surge of output based on the new work and investment incentives of lower tax rates; but this was nonsense believed in only by a few supply side fanatics.

The national debt tripled during the Reagan years (1981-88), growing from $906 billion to $2.6 trillion.[47]

In 1995-96, the attack on the welfare state could be renewed by selling the deficit as a terrible threat, and by blaming it on social budgets while quietly continuing to reward the same rich constituents who had benefited from the Reagan counter revolution. Now instead of fraudulent supply-side economics and an equally fraudulent huge Soviet military threat justifying large deficits, there are fraudulent claims about intergenerational welfare and an explosion of entitlements that must be brought under control to save our children. In fact the only non-military and non-corporate entitlement threat to the budget lies in the explosion of medical costs, whose solution lies squarely on a reform of the U.S. health care system that the Republicans and New Democrats refuse to make."[48]

When using the term *corporate entitlement*, Herman is referring to the huge benefits that corporations received as a result of the tax benefits to businesses that are currently contained in the U.S. tax code. An excellent new resource called *The Corporate Welfare Guidebook* has been developed by Tax Watch, a coalition of religious organizations, and citizen advocacy groups, including the Unitarian Universalist Service Committee. This group is putting the spotlight on the preferential tax advantages corporations receive through the federal tax code. They point out that although many in Congress are demanding deficit reduction and a balanced budget, most proposals advanced focus on cutting programs that help the poorest Americans while programs that help those in the top tax brackets remain unchanged. This is so even though federal spending on services for the poor represent only a tiny fraction of federal spending. In fact federal spending for welfare, through the Aid to Families with Dependent Children (AFDC) program represents only one percent of the federal discretionary budget. These groups suggest that if the goal is to address the federal deficit, then federal tax benefits to corporations, which outweigh social spending three to one, should be the focus. An excerpt from *The Corporate Welfare Handbook* follows.

47 Max Sawicky, "Roots of the Public Sector Fiscal Crisis," Economic Policy Institute, 1991.
48 Herman, Edward S. "The Balanced Budget Ploy: The Hidden Agenda Behind This Propaganda Campaign," Z Magazine, February 1996.

Corporate Tax Handouts Cost $791; AFDC Costs Only $156 Per Taxpayer

Much of the current budget debate has focused on reducing "welfare" costs to cut the deficit. Total spending on the primary welfare program Aid to Families with Dependent Children (AFDC) has been about $14 billion a year, costing the average taxpayer $156. Adding in costs for food stamps, housing assistance and child nutrition has increased the costs to $415 per taxpayer.

Corporate Tax Breaks Cost More Than Spending on Low-Income Families

In contrast, federal tax benefits for corporations cost almost $70 billion a year, or $791 per taxpayer.

Tax Expenditures Take Many Forms

Tax expenditures include tax deductions, tax exclusion, tax credits, tax loopholes and tax deferrals. Tax deductions allow corporations and individuals to subtract a certain percentage of business expenses from their total taxable income.

WHERE YOUR FEDERAL TAX DOLLARS GO: "WELFARE" VS "CORPORATE WELFARE"

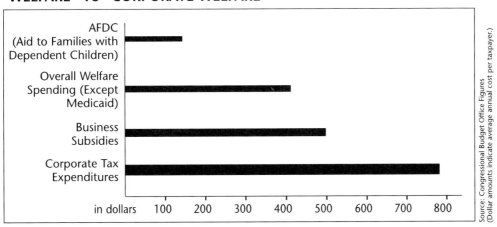

Source: Congressional Budget Office Figures
(Dollar amounts indicate average annual cost per taxpayer.)

Whether cutbacks in programs are motivated by concerns about the deficit, as they are supposed to be in this country, or whether they are motivated by the need to repay government debts under duress from the World Bank and the International Monetary Fund, as they are in the cases of structural adjustment programs in the South, their results have been devastating to the lives of poor women and their families. This is because the premises that underlie both the structural adjustment programs and welfare reform measures have a similar flaw as is pointed out by Shea Cunningham and Betsy Reed in an article entitled "Balancing Budgets on Women's Backs."

Trends in U.S. welfare reform reflect some of the same assumptions underlying Structural Adjustment Programs (SAPs): child-rearing isn't working, and women who do it should also take a paid job...The type of policymaking behind the "Contract with America" and "Structural Adjustment" places debt reduction in front of basic social needs, especially women's needs...

In the United States and abroad, debt relief is nowhere in sight. After years of human sacrifice, the U.S. debt now has a ceiling of $4.9 trillion. The bulk of this accumulated during the Reagan years, under an economic program remarkably similar to that of the Republicans today — fat contracts for military contractors, and tax cuts for big corporate campaign donors and prosperous individuals.

Abroad, the debts of most "structurally adjusted" countries are at least twice as large as they were before the World Bank stepped in with its grand plans for paying them off. And so, to carry their countries further down this fruitless and worn out path, millions of women continue to shoulder the bulk of the burden. Unlike their myopic policies, debt is gender sensitive.[49]

In light of such cutbacks, the safety net for needy citizens in the richest country in the world is now threadbare and problems of the poor in the United States continue to escalate. One out of five children now grows up in poverty and the portion of the homeless population that is made up of women with children has increased from 27 percent to 36 percent.[50]

Today, 39 million U.S. citizens live in poverty, the largest number since 1961. Thirty-eight percent of poor people live in households that are headed by women. This figure has grown from 18 percent in 1960 to 38 percent in 1994, as illustrated in the chart below.

THE FEMINIZATION OF POVERTY
Percent of Poor People Living in Households Headed by Women

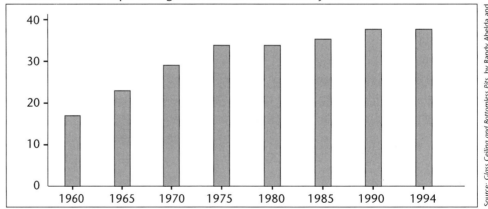

Source: *Glass Ceiling and Bottomless Pits*, by Randy Abelda and Chris Tilley, forthcoming in 1997 from South End Press, Boston, MA.

49 Cunningham, Shea and Betsy Reed. "Balancing Budgets on Women's Backs: The World Bank and the 104th U.S. Congress," Dollars and Sense, 202, Nov/Dec 1995.
50 "Our Responsibility for Children," *The Boston Globe*, March 22, 1996.

In addition, many are plagued by long-term unemployment or underemployment, while others are in jobs that demand long hours and leave little opportunity for recreation or family life.[51] In fact, the amount of leisure time per household has declined 40 percent in the last 20 years. At the same time, quality of life indicators have deteriorated rapidly in the last 20 years.[52]

While those at the bottom of the economic ladder have suffered greatly, those at the top have seen their salaries sore. "The annual salary of the average Fortune 500 CEO is now more than 150 times the annual wages of their company's lowest paid worker." At the same time those in the middle have seen their wages stagnate: "Median family income measured by constant 1993 dollars grew [only] by a total of 0.2 percent between 1973-1993, and it grew by that meager amount only because the proportion of two-income families jumped from 42 percent to 59 percent."[53]

Yet even as more women enter the formal workforce, they continue to shoulder most of the work in the home as well. In addition, at-work women continue to face pervasive economic discrimination as well as racial discrimination in the case of women of color. The deteriorating social conditions in the U.S. are worse for people of color because of the historic legacy of racism. The United States Development Program rates countries by a Human Development Index (HDI) that measures life expectancy, literacy, education, and Gross Domestic Product per capita. In 1993, they found that when the HDI of the U.S. was broken down by race, its ranking changed dramatically: first place for whites, 31st for African Americans (along with Trinidad and Tobago) and 35th for Hispanics (comparable to Estonia).

In addition, real income and wages for women are still usually 25 to 30 percent lower than for men. And though women are working longer hours, their buying power continues to diminish. As women become single heads of household, they end up working harder and longer, leaving little time for themselves or their children.

At the same time the burden that these women must carry has increased significantly, the cumulative impact of cuts in social services has become apparent. (See chart on the next page for changes in selected federal spending programs from 1980 to 1990.)

---

51 Share the Wealth Project, Boston, Massachusetts.
52 Fordham University has developed a composite quality of life index that tracks issues such as child abuse, health insurance coverage, average weekly earnings and the gap between the rich and the poor. The index reached its peak in 1973 at 76.0 points out of 100 and then it began deteriorating. The year Ronald Reagan was elected, the index was at 57 points. By the end of the Reagan/Bush years it was down to 40.6, a fall of 29 percent. The 1994 index warned of the long-term damage to our social fabric because the index has been below 50 since 1996.
53 Farrell, John Aloysius. "Economic Policy Splits Clinton Team," *The Boston Globe*, March 24, 1996.

THE CHANGE IN SELECTED FEDERAL DISCRETIONARY SPENDING PROGRAMS 1980 TO 1990

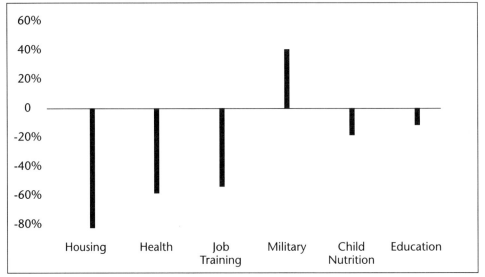

Source: Ways and Means Committee, from Nunez, *Hopes Dreams and Promises*

As the chart above illustrates, the only program area that has increased has been the military budget, while programs for housing, health care, job training, child nutrition and education have experienced significant cuts. Such cuts have directly affected the lives of poor women and their families. These problems are in addition to those that workers are experiencing both in this country and around the world as a result of economic globalization, corporate downsizing and the increasing power of multinational corporations. The power and influence of these corporations have frequently resulted in their receiving special tax treatment by governments, a reality that frequently leads to violations of labor rights and environmental standards both at home and abroad.

Thus, all in all, the situation of poor people, especially women and their children, demands public attention. Hopefully, as women learn more about economic and budget issues, they will demand changes in public policies and programs to reflect the real needs of all citizens including those who are most vulnerable. By doing so they will truly be bringing home the concepts of economic justice for all women and children, which was such an important focus at the Fourth World Conference on Women at Beijing.

Dispelling the Welfare Myth

Motherhood is exalted by the right, but only if practiced according to their formula. (Remain a virgin, go to college, meet Mr. Right, marry, have 2.3 children, work outside the home only after they enter school — and only part-time so you don't interfere with your real job of taking care of the family). The left is still searching for its definitions of motherhood.

We don't want to be misinterpreted as saying that women should stay at home. We talk as though we expect children to raise themselves, or disappear into a daycare factory like little gingerbread people who come out fully formed and perfect every time. We must take care to note the reality of the ideas we support.

This brings us to "work." Women's work in child-rearing, cooking, cleaning, shopping, etc., has always been undervalued. There is no easily attached dollar figure to make domestic work show up in the Gross Domestic Product (GDP) figures. This is not an oversight, it is a deliberate act to keep the value of such work out of the public discourse. Many countries are now calculating this figure and adding it to their GDP reports. Not the U.S., however. We are still not sure that raising children is work. This is evident in the right's rhetoric, now adopted by the mainstream media and centrist politicians, which calls for women on welfare to work. They call it "workfare." They call it the "social contract." Have we grasped how offensive this language is? It completely negates motherhood. This rhetoric says that the work of raising children is of no social value, but don't forget that two paragraphs later these same mothers are blamed for neglecting their children and making them into criminals. I'm confused. Are welfare moms lazy, slothful parasites who refuse to be a productive part of society, or are they neglectful, incompetent parents who don't make the effort to raise their children properly? Clearly the right sees them as both. What do we see?

When you think of the prototypical lazy, neglectful welfare mom, you are programmed to see a woman of color. You tend to see her as helpless, unclean, surrounded by chaos, pregnant for the umpteenth time. You aren't programmed to see me. If you met me in 1977 you would have met the typical American welfare mom: 19 years old, divorced, European American, well-groomed, healthy (maybe a little too thin), mother of a happy, healthy, bright, two-year-old. I held down three different part-time jobs and full-time college classes to make ends meet and to prepare to take care of Heather on my own. But I still needed a welfare check, food stamps, Medicaid, and free childcare from family members to be able to survive. I was atypical only in the fact that I stayed on welfare longer than the average woman does. As a single mom, I needed government assistance at various levels over a period of five years. Seventy percent use assistance for two years or less.

Every one of us who is not currently living in poverty has an obligation to understand the facts, to seek out information, to speak out on behalf of the women, children and men who do know poverty from the inside.[54]

54 An excerpt from *The Call*, a publication of the Unitarian Universalists for a Just Economic Community. "Dispelling the Welfare Myth," *The Call*, Spring 1995.

Facts on the U.S. Welfare System, Women and Children First: A Faith-Based Perspective on Welfare Reform[55]

What is welfare?

More than a dozen programs have constituted the federal welfare package. The nation's primary cash benefits program for poor people has been Aid to Families with Dependent Children (AFDC).

Who has been on welfare?

Fourteen million people have received AFDC annually, including more than nine million children. In 60 percent of these families, the youngest child is under the age of six. Nearly all 4.5 million adults on AFDC have been women.[56]

Have women on AFDC had large families to get more benefits?

Overall, there appears to be no correlation. In the last two decades, as welfare benefits dropped sharply, births to single women have increased steadily. Still, the average welfare family has been slightly smaller than the average non-welfare family, and both groups decreased in size. Nearly three-quarters of all families on welfare have had only one or two children.

The increase in benefits for a child born (on average, $79 per month) has been too small to cover the cost of raising another child.[57]

Why do people go on public assistance?

People who receive assistance are poor and need help. Most poverty occurs because of unemployment, low wages, poor skills and lack of education and training opportunities.[58]

Another cause of poverty is a change in family composition — a child's birth, the death of a spouse, divorce, or becoming a caregiver to an elderly or handicapped relative.

A third factor is poor health and handicapping conditions, which prevent people from working and deplete their resources. Being on assistance has always entitled a family to Medicaid.[59]

55 National Council of Churches, Church Women United, Women's Division, United Methodist Church, Office of Communications, United Church of Christ.
56 U.S. Department of Health and Human Services.
57 U.S. House of Representatives, Ways and Means Committee, Overview of Entitlement Programs.
58 Jencks and Edin. "The Real Welfare Problem," Institute for Research on Poverty, University of Wisconsin, Spring 1990.
59 Bureau of Labor Statistics.

NOTE: AFDC was converted to block grants in legislation that became effective in October 1996.

Why are there so many single-parent families?

Half of all U.S. marriages end in divorce, with a much higher rate in financially stressed families. There was rapid growth in out-of-wedlock births to teenagers in the 70s and 80s. Studies show this was caused by a decline in viable prospects for the future. When young people expect to get education and good jobs, they are more likely to wait until they complete school to marry or have children. If they believe they have no real opportunities, they are more likely to drop out of school, delay marriage and experience out-of-wedlock pregnancies. Despite the increase in youthful childbearing, only 11 percent of all women on some form of public assistance are unmarried teen mothers.[60]

How good have benefits been under AFDC?

The benefits have not been generous. AFDC and food stamp benefits combined have not given a family an income above the federal poverty line in any state. The average AFDC benefit per family in 1993 was $373 per month.[61]

How long do people stay on public assistance?

Nearly 75 percent of all families have left welfare in less than two years. They might have returned briefly in a personal crisis, but they viewed welfare as a helping hand, not a way of life. Only about eight percent have been on AFDC for more than eight years. There is no proof that children who live on AFDC are more likely to be on welfare as adults than anyone else.[62]

Why don't they work?

Nearly half of all mothers on assistance have worked at least part-time. The lack of affordable child care is a problem for all working mothers; but since most AFDC families include a pre-schooler, this has been an especially serious problem for them and has often kept them from working.

Most jobs available to women on assistance have low wages and few or no benefits. Mothers may be reluctant to leave public assistance for a job with no health care coverage when their families can have Medicaid as long as they remain on the aid program.

Working full-time does not assure that a family will escape poverty or the need for support. Women are still victims of wage discrimination, earning $.72 for every dollar earned by men. Seven percent of the active workforce lives in poverty. A minimum wage full-time job leaves a family of three nearly $4,000 below the poverty line.[63]

60 U.S. Census Bureau; Institute for Women's Policy Research.
61 "Statement on Key Welfare Reform Issues: The Empirical Evidence," Center on Hunger, Poverty and Nutrition Policy.
62 House Committee on Ways and Means.
63 Center on Budget and Policy Priorities.

Isn't there a "social safety net" that protects people in hard times?

The "social safety net," created to protect American workers from the harshest effects of recessions, was greatly weakened during the 1970s and '80s and is under attack again. The average monthly AFDC benefit declined by 40 percent from 1970-92. The value of food stamps dropped more than 25 percent. Nutrition programs such as school breakfast and lunch programs have been cut. The number of people getting unemployment insurance reached an all-time low from 1980-90. With all its faults, AFDC has been a crucial transitory safety net for millions of women and children in the last 60 years.[64]

What would help these families rely less on welfare?

In addition to jobs with decent pay, people on welfare need education, job training, placement help and transportation. Like all working parents, they need health care and child care.[65]

Is welfare reform an important factor in reducing the federal deficit?

No. In 1993 the federal share of AFDC cost $17 billion, or less than one percent of the total budget. States spend a similar amount. AFDC and food stamps combined accounted for less than four percent of the federal budget.[66]

How much help do more affluent people get from the government?

Federal subsidies for middle-income and wealthy families total about $140 billion per year, mostly in the form of tax deductions for home mortgages, business expenses and gifts.[67]

64 "Statement on Key Welfare Reform Issues: The Empirical Evidence," Center on Hunger, Poverty and Nutrition Policy.
65 Ellwood, David. Poor Support, Basic Books, 1988.
66 Congressional Budget Office.
67 Congressional Joint Committee on Taxation.

Value of Work and Economic Issues

Critical areas of the platform covered in this session:

Women and Poverty (Section IV. A)

Women and the Economy (Section IV. F)

Two-Hour Workshop

Activities	Minutes
Opening Circle	15
Exploration of a Central Issue: Unwaged Work	20
Exploration of a Central Issue: Global Economics	25
Break	10
Exploration of a Central Issue: The Gap Between Rich and Poor and Structural Adjustment	30
Platform for Action Positions	5
Brainstorming for Action	5
Journal Writing	5
Assignments for Next Week	3
Closing Circle	2
Total Time:	**120**

Materials

Opening circle centerpiece

Two flip charts

Newsprint and markers for small groups' use in global economics section

Preparation

Write on separate flip chart pages:

Typical social roles (page 141)

Blank page: Unwaged work (page 141)

Champagne glass of global economic disparities (page 147)

Results of structural adjustment programs (page 149)

Ask for:

Two volunteers to read in the unwaged work section

Two volunteers to mime in unwaged work section

Four volunteers to read in the global economics section

Two volunteers to read in the structural adjustment section

Three-Hour Workshop

Activities	Minutes
Opening Circle	15
Exploration of a Central Issue: Unwaged Work *	30
Exploration of a Cental Issue: Economic Independence *	20
Exploration of a Central Issue: Global Economics	25
Break	10
Exploration of a Central Issue: The Gap Between Rich and Poor and Structural Adjustment*	60
Platform for Action Positions *	10
Brainstorming for Action	10
Journal Writing	5
Assignments for Next Week	3
Closing Circle	2
Total Time:	180

Materials

Opening circle centerpiece

Two flip charts

Several pieces of newsprint and markers for small groups in global economics section

Preparation

Write on separate flip chart pages:

Typical social roles (page 141)

Blank page: Unwaged work (page 141)

Champagne glass of global economic disparities (page 147)

Results of structural adjustment programs (page 149)

Economic independence for women requires (page 155)

Ask for:

Two volunteers to read in the unwaged work section

Two volunteers to mime in unwaged work section

Four volunteers to read in the global economics section

Two volunteers to read in structural adjustment section

*exercises and/or time added

Opening Circle
(15 minutes)

Objective
To focus the group and allow for brief personal sharing.

Process
1. Light the candle and read this excerpt from the NGO vision statement:

   > Visualize a world where women can get credit and access to other resources they need to be fully economically productive.

2. This workshop focuses on equitable value for work and economic issues. Ask participants to reflect on how the work that women do is valued by those close to them and by society as a whole.

Facilitator's Note: Model this sharing by being the first to speak.

Exploration of a Central Issue: Unwaged Work
(20 minutes)

Objective
To reconsider how work is valued.

Three hour session: Add 10 minutes to this discussion for a total of 30 minutes.

Process
1. Explain:

   > Though women are productive in many ways their work is only considered economically productive when it is done for **monetary compensation**. Valuing and recording unpaid work is an issue of growing concern. We'll now hear about how two women, one from North America and one from Zambia spend their days. Listen to their stories and ask yourself what they have in common.

2. Ask two volunteers to read the stories of Cathy and Selina and two others to mime them.

Cathy's Story

Cathy, a young, middle-class North American housewife, spends her days preparing food, setting the table, serving, dressing, diapering and disciplining her children, taking them to daycare, disposing of garbage, dusting, gathering clothes for washing, doing the laundry, going to the gas station and the supermarket, repairing household items, ironing, making beds, paying bills, caring for pets and plants, putting away toys, books and clothes, sewing, mending or knitting, attending PTA meetings, donating clothes to the Salvation Army, talking with door-to-door salespeople, answering the telephone, vacuuming, sweeping and washing floors, cutting the grass, weeding and shoveling snow, cleaning the bathroom and the kitchen, and putting her children to bed. Cathy has to face the fact that she fills her time in a totally unproductive manner. Economists record her as economically inactive and unoccupied. (Cathy freezes as Selina begins to act out her story.)

The Rural Women's Social Education Center of Madras, India, promotes recognition of women's unpaid work in maintaining the household.

Selina's Story

Selina, a young woman in rural Zambia, wakes up at 5 a.m. After preparing breakfast for her family, she walks 30 minutes to the field with a baby on her back. There, under the hot sun, she spends nine and a half hours ploughing, planting and hoeing to grow food for her family. All the while, she stops to feed and care for her baby. She then spends an hour collecting increasingly scarce firewood and carries it home. For one and a half hours, she pounds and grinds grain or vegetables. It will take 45 minutes to fetch water and an hour to cook the meal for her family. After dishing out food, eating and cleaning up, she will wash her children, herself, the family's clothing and go to bed. Selina is considered unproductive, unoccupied and economically inactive. If she sells any of her crop, her work in the fields may be considered productive. Otherwise, all of the food processing, handicrafts, water carrying, fuel collection and housework she does are not considered to be of economic value.[1]

3. Ask the following questions and discuss briefly:

    Do you think Cathy and Selina work? Why do you think they are considered nonproductive? What effect does their invisibility in their country's economy have on their lives? What effect does it have on national policy?

4. Share the following information on women's work:

    Women's work remains grossly underpaid, unrecognized and undervalued, on the order of $11 trillion a year,[2] the **"invisible" contribution** of women to the global economy.

1 Waring, Marilyn. "If Women Counted: A New Feminist Economics," in *Doing the Gender Boogie*, Ten Days for World Development, Debbie Culbertson, Toronto, Canada, 1995. Reprinted with permission.
2 *Human Development Report*, United Nations Development Program, 1995.

In the jargon of economic statisticians, the yearly output of a country, its Gross National Product (GNP), is measured primarily in terms of the record of the cost of outputs that are sold. As many women researchers have pointed out, these definitions leave out all of the unpaid work that women and many men do. This work is defined as **"non-economic,"** though without it, no economy could function.[3]

5. Discuss the information in the box below. It provides a fuller explanation of the breakdown of social roles by gender in many societies around the globe.

Gender Roles — Women's Triple Role

In most societies, women have a **triple role**: women undertake what economists call **"reproductive, productive and community managing activities,"** while men undertake "productive and community political activities." Women have more work to do than men but less control of the political decisions that determine how resources are allocated and laws are made.

Reproductive Role: Childbearing, childrearing and domestic tasks, done primarily by women.

Productive Role: Work done by both women and men for pay.

Community Managing Role: Activities undertaken, primarily by women, at the community level, as an extension of their reproductive roles to ensure the provision and maintenance of resources such as water, health care and education. This is voluntary unpaid work, undertaken in "free" time.

Community Politics Role: Activities undertaken primarily by men at the at the local, state or national level often within the framework of clubs (Rotary), unions or political organizations.[4]

3 Adapted from Diane Elson "Gender Relations and Economic Issues" in *Women and Economic Policy*, Ed Evers, Oxfam U.K., Focus on Gender Series, 1994.
4 Moser, Caroline O.N. *Gender, Planning and Development: Theory, Practice and Training*, New York: Routledge, 1993.

Facilitator's Note: Prepare a flip chart in advance with the following listing of typical social roles. Add any additional roles that the group suggests.

Typical Social Roles

Roles
Reproductive
Productive
Community managing
Community politics

Women
Reproductive
Productive
Community managing

Men
Productive
Community Politics

6. Ask participants to consider what socially-needed unpaid work they and others they know do, and to share their thoughts about it with one other person (3 minutes).

7. Bring the pairs back together and make a list of the key areas where people feel they have performed unpaid work.

Facilitator's Note: Prepare a blank flip chart page with the heading "Unwaged Work" prior to the session. The examples below may help generate ideas.

Personal/Private/Family: Cooking, nursing the sick, child care, household repairs, shopping, cleaning, financial recordkeeping and planning, elder care, health maintenance for family and continuing education.

Social/Community: Collecting petitions, nonprofit boards, volunteering, Girl Scout leader, Sunday school teacher, car pooling, advocacy, networking and phoning

8. Ask the following questions:

How does the fact that these tasks are unpaid or undervalued relate to the maintenance of family roles and sexual stereotypes?

What are the implications of the fact that these activities are unpaid in terms of self esteem and public policy?

If you are working longer hours for economic reasons, how does this effect your ability or willingness to participate in community maintenance activities?

What changes in business practices and public policies are necessary to lessen women's triple burden?

9. Refer participants to the "Division of Labor in the Developing World" chart in which women's unrecorded workload is illustrated.[5]

DIVISION OF LABOR

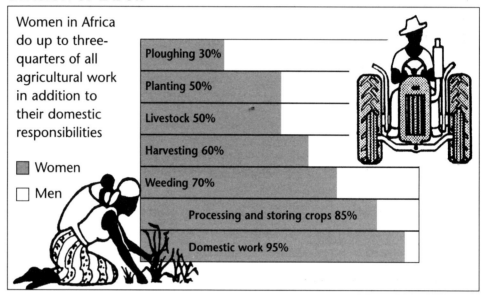

Women in Africa do up to three-quarters of all agricultural work in addition to their domestic responsibilities

☐ Women

☐ Men

Ploughing 30%

Planting 50%

Livestock 50%

Harvesting 60%

Weeding 70%

Processing and storing crops 85%

Domestic work 95%

Three-hour session: Add the "Exploration of a Central Issue: Economic Independence" exercise, page 155 for a total of 20 minutes.

Exploration of a Central Issue: Global Economics
(25 minutes)

Objective

To learn more about the growing influence of government cutbacks, economic globalization and the increasing power and influence of multinational corporations and international financial institutions on women's lives.

Process

1. Discuss these points on the world economy:

Some of the key issues discussed at the Fourth World Conference on Women included government **restructuring,** the **globalization** of the economy, the growing power of **multinational corporations,** and the devastating impact of the **structural adjustment programs** of the **World Bank** and **International Monetary Fund (IMF).**

5 Prepared by the U.N. Economic Commission for Africa.

Participants recognized that it is essential for women to begin to understand these issues so they can exert influence on the political and financial institutions that impact their lives.

Economic conditions today leave many around the globe vulnerable and at risk financially. It is a very different world than it was in the last few months of World War II when representatives of the Allied nations, led by the U.S., held a conference in **Bretton Woods**, New Hampshire to shape a new world economic system. The goal of this conference was to prevent the types of conditions that led to the worldwide economic collapse of the 1930s. This conference led to the **establishment of the World Bank and the International Monetary Fund,** institutions that were designed to stabilize the world economy and provide loans to war torn nations. Later, the mission of the World Bank was expanded to include alleviating poverty and providing loans for poor nations.

The role of these **institutions** and the impact of their programs on the lives of people who live in the poorest regions of the South is a **matter of growing concern.**

The world is increasingly dominated by transnational corporations that are **beyond the reach of national regulation.** At the same time, regional **multinational trading blocs** resulting from the North American Free Trade Agreement and the European Union are growing in strength and almost all barriers to international trade are falling away.

2. Ask the pre-selected volunteers to read the following statements:

Reader 1
Today we are living in a **period of dramatic change**, comparable to the period of the Industrial Revolution, when political, economic and social institutions are changing dramatically. These changes affect everyone's lives differently according to one's race, gender, class and nationality.

Reader 2
Globalization describes the international scope of business operations, information and communications systems, culture, and the media. Globalization is driven by **transnational** corporations' continuous search for bigger markets, lower wages and higher profits, and for technological innovations to reduce costs. The scope and power of these corporations frequently exceed the power of governments that often subsidize these corporations through tax breaks and allow them to bypass labor and environmental laws.

Economic theory pays no attention to the "social reproduction sector" — the unpaid provision of care in the household and the community,... overwhelmingly staffed by women. In the short run, the first response may be for this sector of social reproduction to cushion the impact of public expenditure cutbacks.... The gender division of labor in unpaid "caring" work has proved very resistant to change all around the world, even where men are unemployed and women have new employment opportunities.[6]

Peggy Antrobus

6 Antrobus, Peggy. "Structural Adjustment: Cure or Curse? Implications for Caribbean Development" in *Women and Economic Policy*, Ed Evers, Oxfam U.K., Focus on Gender Series, 1994.

Reader 3

Economic restructuring applies to both companies and nations. One type of business restructuring involves **downsizing** or reducing the number of employees and spinning off production units to areas of the world where labor costs are cheaper in order to decrease costs and increase profits. In addition, many governments are currently restructuring their national economies in several ways:

- Revising their tax codes to benefit businesses and individuals in the top tax brackets

- Deregulating or reducing regulations for businesses

- Reducing the number of government employees

- Selling off public lands or enterprises to the private sector

Reader 4

Government restructuring was officially launched in the 1980s with the election of Margaret Thatcher in England and Ronald Reagan in the United States. Its main goals were to:

- Free businesses from government controls based on the theory that markets work best when they are unregulated

- Stimulate investments which are supposed to trickle down to the rest of the economy

- Reduce government budget deficits (this goal was used to justify huge social spending cuts at the same time that military spending soared)

- Open up trade and financial systems, which resulted in huge increases in profits for transnational corporations

3. Ask the presenters who volunteered at the end of the previous session to share some highlights from the readings assigned for this week.

Presenter 1: Describe what the surprise issue was for Susan Stebbins at the Fourth World Conference on Women and what Laurel Parrott thinks should be done about it. (2 minutes)

Presenter 2: Describe the impact of structural adjustment programs on a village in Ghana where Alice Iddi grew up. (3 minutes)

Presenter 3: Describe what is meant by "Structural Adjustment U.S. Style," including the origin of our current deficit, what is meant by "corporate welfare" and how the amount of money involved in it compares with the portion of the Federal budget that goes to welfare and/or the Aid to Families with Dependent Children (AFDC) Program. (4 minutes)

Presenter 4: Describe attitudes toward welfare recipients in this country and the inconsistency that a former welfare recipient finds in conservative attitudes towards the task of mothering when done by those on welfare as opposed to when it is done by middle class women who choose to stay home to take care of their children. (2 minutes)

4. If the group is larger than 10 people, ask participants to form groups of four to six to discuss the following questions (10 minutes).

    ■ What words come to mind to describe the present political and economic climate and people's response to it? (List words or phrases on flip chart.)

    ■ How secure do you or your friends feel in the present economic and social climate?

    ■ Have these economic realities affected you or anyone you know?

    ■ How do current economic conditions affect attitudes toward welfare recipients, immigrants and affirmative action programs?

As long as women do two-thirds of the world's work and receive only 5 percent of the world's income, the global economy is our issue.

Laurel Parrott, president of Minnesota NOW

Break
(10 minutes)

Exploration of a Central Issue: The Gap Between the Rich and the Poor and Structural Adjustment
(30 minutes – including video segment)

Objective
To become aware of the severe economic disparities in the world today and learn about the destructive economic policies that have been financed by the World Bank and backed by the U.S. government.

Three-hour session: Add 20 minutes to this discussion for a total of 50 minutes.

Process
1. Explain the following and paraphrase the boxed information:

    Clearly the gap between the rich and poor nations is becoming wider, a condition that many believe stems in large measure from the policies that have been implemented by the World Bank and the International Monetary Fund.

Facilitator's Note: Prepare a flip chart in advance showing the champagne glass diagrams or refer participants to the ones in their books that illustrate global and domestic economic disparities. Read the information in the box in preparation for describing the diagrams.

The Champagne Glass of Global Economic Disparities

The UNDP Human Development Report for 1994 uses a champagne glass as a metaphor to depict the extreme economic disparities in the world today. The bowl of the champagne glass represents the abundance enjoyed by the 20 percent of people who live in the world's richest countries, receive 84.7 percent of the world's income, and consume a comparable share of resources. Down at the bottom of the stem we find the poorest 20 percent of the world's people who barely survive on 1.4 percent of the world's total income.

David Korten, author of the provocative new book, *When Corporations Rule the World*, has called this chart the "champagne glass of economic injustice." He believes that it illustrates the success of the Bretton Woods institutions, specifically the World Bank and the International Monetary Fund, in furthering the interests of those with economic power.

The free trade policies advanced by the Bretton Woods institutions give precedence to the interest of money over human and environmental concerns and are thus aligned almost entirely with the narrow interests of the ruling economic elite. It is difficult to conceive of a more powerful proof of this assertion than the rapid growth of the gap between rich and poor. Whether intended or not, the policies so successfully advanced by the Bretton Woods institutions have inexorably strengthened the ability of the wealthy to lay claim to even more of the world's resources at the expense of other people, species, and the viability of the planet's ecosystem.[7]

7 Korten, David. "Sustainability and the Global Economy: Beyond Bretton Woods," October 13, 1994, Bretton Woods, New Hampshire.

GLOBAL ECONOMIC DISPARITIES

Distribution of economic activity, 1991 (percent of word total)

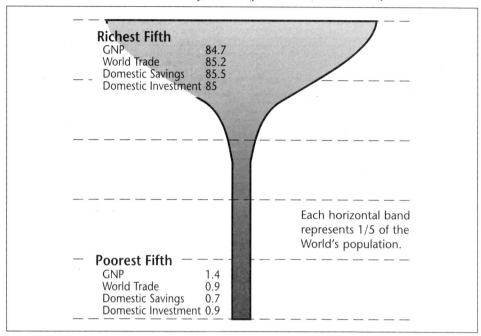

Richest Fifth

GNP	84.7
World Trade	85.2
Domestic Savings	85.5
Domestic Investment	85

Each horizontal band represents 1/5 of the World's population.

Poorest Fifth

GNP	1.4
World Trade	0.9
Domestic Savings	0.7
Domestic Investment	0.9

ECONOMIC DISPARITIES IN THE U.S.

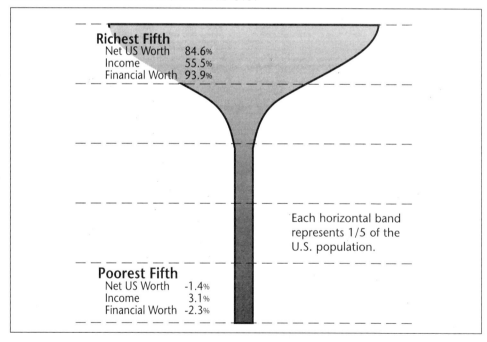

Richest Fifth

Net US Worth	84.6%
Income	55.5%
Financial Worth	93.9%

Each horizontal band represents 1/5 of the U.S. population.

Poorest Fifth

Net US Worth	-1.4%
Income	3.1%
Financial Worth	-2.3%

In the eighties, we can clearly see that the structural adjustment policies have benefited the rich. Forty-six percent of our population in India is below the poverty line. What is happening is the privatization of profit, and the nationalization of losses.

Kavaljit Singh, coordinator of the Public Interest Research Group, India.

SOURCE: *Top heavy: A Study of the Increasing Inequility of Wealth in America*, Edward N. Wolff, Twentieth Centruy Fund Press, 1995. All stats: 1989

2. Briefly comment on the champagne glass diagram that depicts "Economic Disparities in the U.S." and its similarity with the worldwide graphic.

3. Explain the following points:

Women in Mindoro Province, the Philippines, have organized their own federation to defend the rights of rural women to own land and earn equal wages.

One of the most critical economic realities of today's world is the staggering international debt burden that is now being carried by the countries of the South. These countries are being forced to implement structural adjustment programs, which have had a devastating impact on the citizens of these countries, especially on poor women and their families.

4. Ask two volunteers to read the following:

First Reader

The **debt crisis** originated in the late 1970s when transnational banks sought to invest funds deposited in their accounts after the OPEC oil price increases. These banks encouraged many Southern governments to take out loans that were used to benefit the elite in these countries. In the late 1970s and early 80s, because of high inflation, the Federal Reserve raised interest rates to unprecedented levels. This had a devastating impact on many countries in the South that had taken out loans from U.S. banks.

Second Reader

This is when **structural adjustment programs** were developed by the World Bank and the International Monetary Fund as a way to gain a stronger influence over the economies of debt-strapped nations that were having trouble meeting their loan payments. Essentially, loans are given only if the debtor nations implement free-market oriented reforms that are designed to give them less control over their economies and make them more open to international trade.

Facilitator's Note: Prepare a flip chart in advance that lists the following "Results of Structural Adjustment Programs."

5. Explain the following:

Results of Structural Adjustment Programs

For at least 80 indebted governments these changes have meant:

Cutting social spending, especially for education and health care

Reducing the state's role in the economy

Privatizing government services and assets

Lowering tariff barriers to imports

Removing restrictions on foreign investments

Cutting wages

Removing subsidies for food, fuel and public transportation

Devaluing the currency

Promoting crops for export, not for local consumption

The impact of structural adjustment programs, called SAPs, is so severe that UNICEF estimates that 6 million children have died each year since 1980 as a direct result of SAPs.

6. Discuss:

Social program cutbacks have a **disproportionate impact** on the poor, particularly poor women who rely on these services for their families' well-being. The consequences of **health care cuts** include deteriorating women's and children's health. **Cutbacks in education** often results in increased fees for tuition, uniforms, books, and meals, which place burdens on poor families and cause many of them to keep their children out of school.

Ongoing efforts exist around the world to expose the realities of structural adjustment policies. One of the main efforts in the U.S. to make the public aware of economic policies that adversely affect huge segments of the population, especially women and children, is the **50 Years is Enough Campaign**. This campaign is a broad-based, national coalition of more than 130 U.S. organizations, including the Unitarian Universalist Service Committee. Similar campaigns are going on in many other countries to raise awareness of the unjust and ultimately economically unwise projects mandated by the World Bank and the IMF. See the background and resource section for details about this campaign.

The past 50 years have provided ample evidence that instead of helping Third World nations, the World Bank and the IMF have underwritten projects and imposed policies that have drastically increased global poverty.[8]

Linda Gray MacKay

8 MacKay, Linda Gray. "World Bank and IMF Have Failed, and the Poor Pay the Price," *The Boston Globe*, July 14, 1994.

Facilitator's Note: In order to help participants understand the impact of structural adjustment programs, show the fourth video segment on the video tape entitled "A Matter of Interest" (13 minutes), which describes the role of international banks and businesses in creating the debt crisis that began in the 1980s. If time is short, show the shorter video segment entitled "Structural Adjustment in Nicaragua" (6 minutes). For the three-hour session, show both video segments.

7. After watching the video, discuss the following question:

> Do you see any similarities between the situation of poor people, particularly poor women and children in the U.S. and in the Global South, as a result of government cutbacks in social programs?

Platform for Action Positions on Poverty and Economics

(5 minutes)

Objective

To become acquainted with Platform for Action positions on poverty and economic issues.

Three-hour session: Add five minutes to this discussion for a total of 10 minutes.

Process

1. Introduce the following points:

> Two of the Critical Areas of Concern that are closely linked in the platform are **poverty** and the **economy**. The platform promotes women's economic rights and independence, including access to employment and appropriate working conditions and control over economic resources. In the section dealing with the economy, it proposes action to:
>
> - **Provide** business services, training and access to markets, information and technology, particularly to low-income women
>
> - **Eliminate** occupational segregation and all forms of employment discrimination
>
> - **Strengthen** women's access to credit and capital
>
> The Platform for Action recognizes (although not strongly enough according to most Southern activists) that **poverty** is directly related to the **absence** of economic **opportunities** and

Governments are not solely responsible for women's economic plight. We must lobby [transnational] corporations with the same intensity that we lobby our governments — and with greater intensity than corporations lobby our governments.

Laurel Parrott, president of Minnesota NOW

autonomy for women. Also noted was a lack of recognition of significant economic contributions by women, both remunerated and unremunerated. The platform proposes to:

- **Analyze,** from a gender perspective, policies and programs including those related to structural adjustment with respect to their impact on poverty

- **Ensure** that structural adjustment programs are designed to minimize their negative effects on vulnerable and disadvantaged groups

- **Create** an enabling environment that allows women to build and maintain sustainable livelihoods

This is one area of the platform that has received substantial criticism. According to the Center for Women's Global Leadership:

Despite documentation on the **harmful effects** of economic globalization on women, governments were **not willing** to address this topic substantially. The Beijing platform does acknowledge the negative impact of structural adjustment and calls for recognition that women's unwaged work constitutes a large percentage of national economies. But no effort was made **to address** the **causes** of these problems and governments remain engaged in practices that perpetuate them.

Brainstorming for Action
(5 minutes)

Objective
To collect ideas that can be used to formulate a local plan of action.

Three-hour session: Add five minutes to the discussion for a total of 10 minutes.

Process
1. To begin to formulate a local plan for action, use two flip charts or two flip chart pages posted on the wall.

2. Ask participants to make a theoretical list of possible activities they would like to undertake that relate to the topics of this workshop. Encourage participants to mention whatever comes to mind, regardless of their ability to perform the action.

3. On the second flip chart, list any organizations that participants know about that are addressing these issues.

Facilitator's Note: Attach lists from previous brainstorming sessions to the walls and encourage participants to add ideas or resources to any of the lists. All the lists will be used in the last session when the group develops a viable action plan.

4. Summarize the boxed information. Remind participants that more information about these programs that could be helpful for local action planning is included in the background and resource section.

Successful Strategies For Action

The International Forum on Globalization (IFG) is an alliance of 50 leading activists, economists, researchers and writers representing 19 countries. The IFG organized a public teach-in in New York on economic globalization, which was a stunning success and catalyzed many new organizing efforts. The San Francisco Bay Area 50 Years is Enough Campaign joined with IFG to sponsor a presentation in the Bay Area. Organizing forums and teach-ins on economic issues is an important way to educate and mobilize citizens to grapple with these critical matters.

Journal Writing

(5 minutes)

Objective

To give participants an opportunity to record items they wish to remember or process.

Process

1. Ask participants to take a few minutes to write down on the journal page for this session any reactions, additional areas they wish to pursue, questions they want to research, or additional action ideas or possible contacts they can think of. If time is short, ask the group to write between sessions and, when appropriate, to add them to the flip chart pages that will be posted at each session.

Assignments for Next Week
(3 minutes)

Process

1. Review information on other organizations working on corporate responsibility issues listed in the resource section.

2. Pay particular attention to the information on the impact of assembly plants on the lives of those who work in them; in particular those who work in the "maquiladoras" located in Central America, the Caribbean and Mexico.

3. Think about possible actions the group could take to address economic issues that are affecting the lives of women in the U.S. and around the globe.

4. Refer participants to the background and resource section for more specific details about the platform.

Closing Circle
(2 minutes)

Objective

To provide an opportunity to connect symbolically with others before separating.

Process

1. Encourage participants to gather in a circle around the centerpiece, holding hands. Ask someone to share a phrase summarizing their experience of the session. Invite participants to bring items to future sessions that remind them of women's lives or that honor women.

2. Ask for volunteers to read the section of the poem "Let Us Hold Hands" by Pat Mora or sing the song, "Come Sing a Song with Me" by Carolyn McDade.

Let us hold hands

with the woman who seasoned soups with pepper and hope
as her days took her further from sighs of trees she loved,

with the woman who parted her parched lips and sang
for her mother when they staggered onto these shores in chains,

with the woman who trained her stubborn tongue to wrap
around that spiny language, English, to place her child in school.

Let us now hold hands with the woman
who croons to the newborn left amid orange rinds and newspaper,
who teaches grandmothers to link letters into a word, a word,
who whispers to the woman dying with one breast,
who holds a wife whose face is more broken than any bone,
who bathes the woman found sleeping in black snow.

Excerpt from the poem *Let Us Hold Hands* by Pat Mora

Come Sing a Song With Me

Years ago I wrote this song and dropped it by the way because it so easily became sentimentally sweet. Last year it was one included in a singing circle at MCI, Framingham, Massachusetts' only prison for women. As we sang, women found the meaning of the song. They unlocked some door that had caged the song and set it free. Since that time, everytime I sing this song I hear their voices. I dedicate this song to their liberating action.

Words and Music by Carolyn McDade

Come dream a dream with me
Come dream a dream with me
Come dream a dream with me
  that I might know your mind

Come walk in rain with me
Come walk in rain with me
Come walk in rain with me
  that I might know your mind.

ADDITIONAL ACTIVITIES FOR THREE HOUR SESSIONS

Exploration of a Central Issue:
Economic Independence
(20 minutes)

Objective

To explore key aspects of economic independence for women.

Process

Facilitator's Note: This exercise was used in session two. If participants need to be reminded of the procedure, go over the following instructions with them.

1. To demonstrate the following activity, write the phrase "women's work" in a circle in the middle of a flip chart page. Write several words you associate with "women's work" in circles around the central circle and connect all the circles with lines. Then write a sentence that contains the words in your diagram. After demonstrating this technique, invite participants to write the words "economic independence" in the middle of a page and complete the exercise as demonstrated.

2. Refer participants to the "Diagram of a Mind Map" on page 28.

3. Tell participants that once they have free associated for several minutes, to then write a sentence that represents selected words or ideas from their matrix.

Facilitator's Note: Invite participants to read their sentence aloud. As they speak, pick out key words in their sentences and make a list on the flip chart of words that describe what women need to attain economic independence.

4. Reveal the following list of requirements for economic independence and compare it to the group's list.

Facilitator's Note: Prepare a flip chart in advance which lists the following requirements for economic independence for women.

Economic Independence for Women Requires
Access to credit and capital

Equal educational opportunities

Control of earnings

Equal pay for equal work

Appropriate working conditions

Child care resources

Right to inheritance

Journal Page

Background and Resources
on Women's Work and Global Economics

Women and Work

- About half the world's food is grown by women. In Africa, women produce roughly 80 percent of the food for local consumption and about 40 percent of rural women work without wages on family farms.[9]

- In developing countries, because of deforestation, gathering wood for cooking fuel — traditionally a task for girls and women — grows ever more difficult. In Bangladesh, girls spend more than six hours a day collecting fuel; in Nepal and Java the task takes three hours; in Tanzania it takes 1.9 hours.

- Women work an average of 13 percent more hours than men in every country. The difference ranges from as little as eight minutes a day in the Republic of Korea to almost three hours a day in rural Kenya — the equivalent of more than 45 round-the-clock days every year.[10]

- Close to 60 percent of all women worldwide over the age of 16 participate in the labor force outside the home. Including unpaid work done in the home, women perform more than two-thirds of the world's work, yet receive less than one-tenth of its income.[11]

- In the U.S., women earn an average of $.70 for every $1.00 earned by men who hold the same positions. The figure is even lower for minority women. While the gender wage gap is presently the smallest it has ever been, the remaining discrepancy shows that the national Pay Equity Act, passed more than 30 years ago, has not yet reached its goal.

- Women's salaries are often less than men's in the same profession. Female lawyers earn 78 percent of males' income; computer programmers 84 percent; machine operators and assemblers 68 percent.[12]

- Women now earn 40 percent of law degrees and one-third of M.D. degrees.[13]

- Women earn less than men in certain categories of jobs requiring comparable levels of training, skill and responsibility. Secretaries and telephone operators earn an average of $3,000 a year less than truck drivers or carpenters.

continued on next page

9 International Fund for Agricultural Development cited in "Women and the Global Economy," Global Exchange.
10 Women's Feature Service.
11 Global Exchange, "Women and the Global Economy."
12 Folbre, Nancy. *New Field Guide to the U.S. Economy*, New York: New Press, 1995.
13 Naisbett, John and Patricia Aburdene. *Megatrends 2000*, NY: Morrow, 1990.

Women and Work *(continued)*

- Women receive only 5 percent of multilateral banks' rural credit.[14]

- Employed women average 38 hours of housework per week; employed men average 22 hours. An employed woman with two children performs about 51 hours of housework per week.

- Globally, women account for less than 20 percent of managers and 6 percent of senior management positions.[15]

UUSC Partners Past and Present: Working Women

FUMEDI

FUMEDI, a Guatemalan organization that has been supported by the Unitarian Universalist Service Committee, is an example of a nongovernmental organization that works with indigenous women to help them develop a viable economic base.

This organization works with people in an area of Guatemala that has been engaged in civil war for the past 40 years. During the 1980s, the repression by the Guatemalan military was particularly vicious in this area, with many well documented massacres of whole villages taking place.

FUMEDI supports indigenous Guatemalan women's efforts to organize craft cooperatives, develop community stores and raise animals.

FUMEDI has formed groups of women, many of whom were widowed during the 1980s when indigenous men suspected of supporting the guerrilla forces were disappeared or summarily executed.

The women with whom FUMEDI works have been doubly exploited both because they are women and because they are indigenous. The women get together to discuss their needs and problems. Projects undertaken include handicraft cooperatives, the development of community stores, the setting up of corn grinding mills, pig raising and vegetable production. The women themselves design and manage these activities.

---

14 *Human Development Report*, United Nations Development Program, 1995.
15 U.N. Dept. of Public Information: Focus on Women. "Women and Economic Decision Making."

Sahanivasa

Sahanivasa is a UUSC partner organization in the Chittoor region of India that works with Dalit bonded and landless agricultural laborers who are among the most oppressed class of people in India. Dalits are the lowest rung of the unjust caste system, which although outlawed, still persists. Dalits are treated as "untouchables" by upper castes and are denied access to many public places in a kind of social apartheid. Most agricultural workers are Dalit, and most live well below the poverty line. Women agricultural laborers often suffer the most. Their employment is only seasonal and unstable. Wages are incredibly low. Because there is so much unemployment, the landlords are able to exploit the poor who are desperate for work. Sahanivasa has undertaken a number of activities to help the agricultural laborers, both men and women, to gain economic justice. Here are a few examples:

- Sahanivasa lobbied the state government to provide house plots and land titles for women in their own name — as result of this lobbying effort 600 plots were provided.

- Women laborers protested at harvest season for fair wages. After a strike, they managed to get a small pay increase.

- Sahanivasa demands that widow and old age pensions be provided for women. As a result, 170 such pensions have been authorized.

- Sahanivasa has provided poor women with access to credit. Women join the program and through it save a certain sum each month. After six months they are eligible for credit. All of the loan transactions take place at the village level. More than 1,000 women have joined such savings groups. Women are using the credit to start businesses such as selling groundnuts, tamarind, jaggery (unrefined sugar), raising animals and so on. Access to such credit spares poor families from the mercy of unscrupulous money lenders who charge exorbitant interest rates.

Dalit women use song and dance to protest abuses by upper caste people against them and their communities. Sahanivasa works to raise Dalit women's awareness of their rights.

Credit for Women

In many African countries, women account for more than 60 percent of the agricultural labor force and contribute up to 80 percent of the total food production. This work is in addition to their domestic responsibilities. Yet, they receive less than 10 percent of the credit to small farmers and one percent of the total credit to agriculture in general. Governments should enact laws to give property rights to women. Finance ministries and central banks should encourage organizational as well as structural changes in financial systems, including reallocation of government and external funds for women entrepreneurs, and encourage setting up small- and micro-enterprise financing. Commercial banks should recognize the market potential of women in the small- and micro-enterprise sector and structure their services to reach women entrepreneurs.[16]

Women are often denied credit, even though "microlending" banks, such as the Grameen Bank of Bangladesh, have discovered what excellent clients poor women make. With a payback rate of 98 percent, these small loans enable women (who statistically spend a higher percentage of their salaries than men directly on family maintenance) to significantly improve their families' standard of living.[17]

16 U.N. Dept. of Public Information: Focus on Women. "Women and Economic Decision Making."
17 *Washington Post*, February 2, 1995.

Women and Children in Poverty

- More than one billion people in the world today, the great majority of whom are women, live in unacceptable conditions of poverty.[18]

- Women constitute 57.7 percent of United States citizens who are living in poverty.[19]

- Women do 67 percent of the world's work but earn only 10 percent of the world's income.[20]

- Nearly 60 percent of the rural poor in less developed countries — 550 million people — are women. This is a 50 percent increase over the 1970 level (compared to a 30 percent increase for male rural poverty during the same period).[21]

- From 1960 to 1989, the percentage of global income claimed by the richest 20 percent grew from 70 percent to 83 percent. The poorest 20 percent saw their share fall from 2.3 percent to just 1.4 percent.[22]

- In the U.S., the wealthiest 20 percent have incomes over $180,000/year and own 80 percent of the nation's wealth. The poorest 20 percent own six percent of the wealth. The U.S. has the worst income gap among industrialized nations.

- Two-thirds of single mothers with children under age six in the U.S. live below the federal poverty line.[23]

- One-fifth of all people today suffer from hunger.

- Thirty-nine percent of children under age five in the least developed countries are underweight.[24]

- Currently, 20 percent of children in the United States grow up in poverty; in 1970 it was 15 percent. To reverse this trend, a broad group of professionals relying on convincing statistics are working to maintain and expand government programs for the poor, even during this time of economic adjustment. In the United States it has been found that:

continued on next page

18 Platform for Action.
19 U.S. Department of Labor.
20 Global Exchange: "Women and the Global Economy."
21 International Fund for Agricultural Development.
22 PEW Global Stewardship Initiative.
23 Stebbins, Susal. "Women and the Global Economy," Minnesota NOW, 1996.
24 *Human Development Report*, U.N. Development Program, 1995.

Women and Children in Poverty *(continued)*

Every dollar spent on supplemental food for pregnant women at nutritional risk saves three dollars in future short-term hospital costs.

Investing one dollar in prenatal services saves more than three dollars in caring for low birthweight infants.

Every dollar spent on immunizing children saves $10 in later medical costs enriched preschool programs increase performance and success of students in school later on.[25]

Glossary of Economic Terms

Balance of Payments: A country is said to have a balance of payments deficit when its income (credits from exports, cash inflows, loans, etc.) is less than its payments (debits such as imports, cash outflows, debt payments). A balance of payments surplus occurs when income is greater than payments.

Corporations: Firms which raise money to buy capital goods by selling shares of stock. The owners of the stock shares earn dividends, which are shares of the corporation's profit.

Debt Service: Payments on outstanding loans to cover interest or reduce principal.

Devaluation: National currency is priced according to how much of another currency it can buy or how much gold or other standard of value it is worth. This is the exchange rate. A country with a trade imbalance or balance of payments problems may devalue its currency. When a currency is devalued, its value declines relative to other currencies. For example, in 1982 one U.S. dollar could buy 28 Mexican pesos. In 1988 the peso had been devalued so that one dollar was the equivalent of 2,300 pesos.

Export Crops: Goods which are raised domestically and sold abroad rather than used to feed a country's population. For instance, much agricultural land in parts of Central and South America is used for growing coffee as an export crop.

Export Processing Zones (EPZ): Special areas created by some governments in the South to attract foreign investment in industry. Corporations operating in these zones typically import components for assembly in their factories in the EPZs. The finished or semi-finished goods are then exported to the United States or another foreign market. EPZ regulations generally include tax breaks for transnational corporations and a weakening of environmental restrictions and labor rights.

25 Folbre, Nancy. *New Field Guide to the U.S. Economy*, New York: New Press, 1995.

Free Market: This term is often used to describe capitalism in general, referring to the fact that goods, services and labor are bought and sold in an open market. The reality is that capitalism operates within a spectrum of more or less "freedom." Markets can be controlled through government regulation, through the concentration of industry in a few hands (monopolies, cartels), and through such illegal activities as price-fixing and discrimination.

Gender Division of Labor: Refers to occupational segregation in the labor market and to the unpaid and disproportionate contribution women make to maintaining the household such as cooking, cleaning and childcare.

Globalization: A term used to refer to the expansion of economies beyond national borders, in particular, the expansion of production by a firm to many countries around the world (globalization of production, or the "global assembly line"). This has given transnational corporations power beyond nation-states, and has weakened nation's abilities to control corporate practices and flows of capital, set regulations, control balances of trade and exchange rates, or manage their own economic policy.

Gross National Product (GNP): The total value of goods and services produced in a country in a year, including domestic goods and services and income earned abroad.

Inflation: An increase in prices, which lowers the purchasing power of money.

International Monetary Fund (IMF): Founded in 1944 at the Bretton Woods Conference by the Western industrial powers. It administers and coordinates exchange rate policies and provides member states with financing to enable them to balance their trade payments. Today, the IMF acts as a financial policeman in the developing world, pushing for trade liberalization, debt payments and privatization.

Maquiladoras: A Spanish word for foreign-owned plants that operate in Mexico, Central America and the Caribbean using local labor to assemble goods sold in the U.S. or other foreign countries. The policies of both the U.S. and Mexican governments encourage U.S. businesses to transfer parts of their operations to Mexican subsidiaries or subcontractors.

Nongovernmental Organizations (NGOs): A U.N. term for organizations involved in service provision and/or advocacy in the U.S. and abroad. In the U.S., NGOs operating in international development are often known as private voluntary organizations (PVOs).

Restructuring: The process of reorganizing government bureaucracies, firms, and sectors of the economy to lower costs and make them more competitive. This includes a move to free market policies and a decline in regulation. Key aspects of business restructuring include layoffs, use of overtime and temporary workers, contracting out, mergers, faster production, and cuts in wages and benefits among others. On the national level, this has included deregulation, privatization of government services, public sector layoffs, and an opening of the economy to foreign investment and trade.

Tariff: A government tax on imports or exports usually either to raise revenue or to protect domestic firms from import competition. A tariff may also be designed to correct an imbalance of payments. The money collected under a tariff is called a duty.

Transnational Corporation (TNC): A corporation that operates in more than one country. In the post-World War II era, TNCs have come to dominate the global economy, and some TNCs are richer and more powerful than many national governments.

World Bank: Founded in 1944 at the Bretton Woods Conference, also known as the International Bank for Reconstruction and Development. Established to coordinate with several regional banks in the development of nations, it provides long-term development loans. In recent years it has joined with the International Monetary Fund in implementing loan conditions that promote "free market" policies and restructuring.[26]

Structural Adjustment Programs (SAPs)

Impact of SAPs on Women

When we speak of the "poorest of the poor," we are almost always speaking about women. Poor men in the developing world have even poorer wives and children. And there is no doubt that recession, the debt crisis and structural adjustment policies have placed the heaviest burden on poor women, who earn less, own less and control less.[27]

Under the structural adjustment programs designed by the IMF and World Bank, the burdens of women increase because state spending in the social sector has been cut back. For example, women have to become both doctor and nurse to their families.[28]

Underlying these [structural adjustment] policies is a set of assumptions about women's work: that women are housewives, do not work and, therefore, that women can fill the gap created by cuts in social services. Of course, [the policy is] labeled "privatization." The governments must not

---

26 These definitions have been taken from "Women Crossing Boundaries: Fighting Back, the Fourth Women's Gathering in McAllen", Texas, December, 1993, *Analysis and Action for a New Economic Era: The Global Factory*, American Friends Service Committee and The United Methodist Study Guide on *Global Economics: Seeking a Christian Ethic* by Pamela Sparr.
27 Vickers, Jeanne. *Women and the World Economic Crisis*, New Jersey: Zed Books Ltd.
28 Women, Structural Adjustment and Empowerment: An interview with Merle Hodge, professor at the University of the West Indies in Trinidad and Tobago in *50 Years Is Enough: The Case Against The World Bank and the International Monetary Fund*, A Project of Global Exchange.

spend money on education, health and human infrastructure. They must be left to the private sector or to the household, meaning to women. The assumption is that women's time and labor can be exploited.[29]

Export-Oriented Economics Versus Human Rights

Protests erupted in Jamaica in 1984 against inflated fuel prices, raised in accordance with economic restructuring measures designed and financed by the World Bank. Non-unionized women earn as little as 50 cents per hour in export-oriented factories. A former World Bank Caribbean program director asserts, "The World Bank knows the needs of the Jamaican economy better than some local women's association. We can't direct the development of the Jamaican economy on the basis of the needs of these women in Kingston."[30]

A gynecologist and leading women's health rights activist, Dr. Ana Maria Pizarro is director of Si Mujer. Si Mujer is a Nicaraguan women's health organization that provides direct care and education and advocates for government policies that serve the interests of women's health.

The export-oriented model for economic growth based on foreign investment has jeopardized the gains in socioeconomic development achieved in the 1970s. We seem to have set back the clock in support of a model of development that places the interests of international capital before those of the majority of Caribbean people.[31]

Impact of Structural Adjustment in Nicaragua

The U.S.-supported World Bank and IMF imposed economic stabilization and structural adjustment programs (SAPs) on Nicaragua. In order to get badly needed international financing, Nicaragua had to comply. The World Bank and IMF programs prescribed drastic cuts in health care. In 1991 the Nicaraguan government spent 68 percent less on public health care than in 1988. In conjunction, the U.S. Agency for International Development financed an Occupational Conversion Plan that resulted in the loss of 500 nurses and 500 doctors from the public health care system. Now there are long waits, overworked personnel and 24,000 fewer medical consultations per day.

SAPs have detrimentally affected the health of Nicaraguans, especially women and children. The infant mortality rate has increased to 72 per 1000, up from 61 per 1000 in the 1980s. Maternal mortality now exceeds

29 Peggy Antrobus, Barbados, Founder and Tutor-Coordinator of the Women and Development Institute.
30 50 Years Is Enough! Pictorial History Facts supplied by the Environmental Defense Fund.
31 Antrobus, Peggy. "Structural Adjustment: Cure or Curse? Implications for Caribbean Development," in *Women and Economic Policy*, Ed Evers, Oxfam U.K., Focus on Gender Series, 1994.

15.9 per 10,000 live births, more than double the death rate in the '80s. Huge layoffs in the public sector mandated by World Bank and IMF stabilization program and SAPs have led to massive unemployment, which in turn has contributed to increasing malnutrition. The average Nicaraguan consumed 25 percent fewer grains and meat in 1992 than during any year between 1982 and 1989.

The Nicaraguan Women's Health Network points out that the deterioration of women's health did not begin with this government, but rather with the first structural adjustment measures, implemented in 1988. In 1988, the per-capita health budget was about US$36. Between 1988 and 1995, it has been reduced to $16, and 80 percent of that goes to cover salaries of health personnel, leaving only five dollars per person, per year, to fund actual health services.[32]

The International Gender Division of Labor

In the last two decades women around the world have become the majority workforce in low-paid, labor-intensive jobs. This is seen as part of the gender division of labor, a term that refers to how working roles and responsibilities are assigned to women and men on the basis of assumptions about gender. These assumptions (e.g., that women are "docile, passive workers who won't cause trouble") are based not on innate biological differences, but rather on historically and culturally assigned characteristics. They serve to reinforce the ghettoization of women in low-wage, insecure employment. Class, race, ethnicity and the level of development of a society are also factors that intersect with gender to define who is recruited for these jobs.

As waged work is being restructured globally, we find that core workers (i.e., those with full-time secure employment) are largely middle/upper class men, usually white, in the North; and we find that periphery workers (i.e., part-time temporary workers) are largely poor women, many of whom are women of color in the North, or members of ethnic or racial minorities in the South. Poor men and increasing numbers of youth are also in this peripheral labor force.

This division of labor is not just between sexes, but also between countries of the North (once colonial powers) and the Southern ex-colonies. For example, many of the goods we consume in the North are produced for export by women in the South. To make more profits, transnational corporations have moved their labor-intensive operations to the South where, in turn, local economies are losing all self-sufficiency in order to produce goods and food for export.[33]

Multinational corporations are increasing their profits by doing business where they can pay the lowest wages, maintain the poorest working con-

32 Pizarro, Ana Maria, MD, quoted in, "A High Price to Pay: Structural Adjustment in Nicaragua," Witness for Peace, 1995.
33 Culbertson, Debbie. *Doing the Gender Boogie*, Ten Days for World Development, Toronto, Canada, 1995.

ditions, and avoid environmental regulations. Free trade agreements have allowed them to use this strategy unhampered by international law and to eliminate or subvert national laws that interfere. In the North, new technologies have allowed an explosion in subcontracting. As a result, women face declining wages and lose jobs as companies downsize or relocate. Others turn to work in sweatshops and find contractual employment.[34]

The World Bank and the International Monetary Fund

The World Bank and International Monetary Fund were established in 1944 at a meeting in Bretton Woods, New Hampshire. Originally designed to finance the reconstruction of Europe after World War II, the Bank was also mandated to promote international trade and foreign investment. In the 1950s, the Bank shifted to funding long-term development projects in the Third World. After the debt crisis broke in the early 1980s, the Bank began to grant an increasing number of loans conditioned upon the recipient countries' adoptions of structural adjustment programs. Currently, policy-reform loans comprise a fourth of the Bank's lending portfolio. The Bank, based in Washington, D.C., has more than 170 member countries, most of them from the Third World. However, the U.S. and other industrialized countries dominate decision making at the World Bank. The United States holds the largest voting share (17.6 percent) and appoints the Bank's president.

The International Monetary Fund was established to facilitate world commerce by overseeing the currency exchange rates and by reducing foreign exchange restrictions of member nations. It also created a reserve of funds to be made available to countries experiencing temporary balance of payments problems so that they could continue trading without interruption. In 1982, the IMF began to issue loans with increased conditionality, requiring that recipient countries commit to the adoption of structural adjustment programs.

The IMF is also headquartered in Washington, D.C. Voting power in the IMF is based on the size of a country's financial contribution. Consequently, five industrialized countries control more than 40 percent of the votes. The United States alone holds 17 percent of the votes on the executive board.[35]

The Origins and Result of the Debt Crisis

Loans to Southern nations rose significantly in the 1980s for many reasons. One reason was that OPEC oil countries surpluses wound up in Northern banks that were anxious to put these funds into circulation. Another, according to UUSC International Programs Director George Ann Potter, author of *Dialogue on Debt*, was the fact that after President

---

34 Stebbins, Susal. "Women and the Global Economy," Minnesota NOW, 1996.
35 "A High Price to Pay," Witness for Peace, 1995.

Nixon's decision to remove the U.S. dollar from the gold standard and to devalue it, "the international system of fixed exchange rates was replaced by floating ones, leading to rampant speculation." This was also a time when banking regulations were eased and the U.S. dominance of international banking decreased dramatically. "As U.S. banks began to face strong competition from Europe and Japan, they abandoned their traditional conservatism, opting instead for high risk/profit loans to the Third World."*

The debt situation for the countries of the South was also directly affected by changes going on in this country. Reagan's tight money policy led to soaring interest rates because of Federal Reserve policies to lower inflation. As stated by Potter, "In the mid-1970s the median real interest rate averaged 1.6 percent, but in the early 1980s, due to the Reagan Administration's tight money, "monetarist" policies, interest rates exploded to an average 11 percent with some rates as high as 22 percent. No wonder U.S. bank lending to Third World countries increased more than 300 percent between 1978-82!"[36]

By the 1990s, debt had become a major constraint on the ability of indebted nations to meet the most pressing needs of their people. Instead, these nations now had to use their scarce resources to keep up with interest payments on old debts that had far surpassed the original loans that were made to them, as was pointed out in the United Nation's *Human Development Report* of 1994: "For developing countries, debt is a major constraint on economic growth and on investment in human development. In 1992 alone, developing nations paid $160 billion in debt service charges— more than two and a half times the amount of official development assistance they received and $60 billion more than total private flows to developing countries in the same year. The total external debt of developing countries grew fifteen-fold over the past two decades: in 1970, it was $100 billion, in 1980, around $650 billion and in 1992, more than $1,500 billion. Because of the service charges [interest costs], developing countries now pay more than they receive. In the past decade, net financial transfers on long-term lending to developing countries have been negative, with the industrial world receiving net transfers of $147 billion."[37] A slogan that is frequently used by activists in both the global South and North to describe these transfers is: "The debt has already been paid!"

Furthermore, between 1982 and 1990, $418 billion, the equivalent of six Marshall Plans, was removed from low-income countries in the South to the industrialized North. This occurred through multinational corporations taking profits out of the countries they operate in, loan payments,

---

36 Potter, George Ann. *Dialogue on Debt*, Center of Concern, Washington, D.C., 1988.
37 Human Development Report, United Nations Development Program, 1994.

*In 1970 six of the world's top 10 banks were U.S. owned, but by 1988 all of the top 10 banks were Japanese, with the highest-ranking U.S. bank, Citicorp, placing only 28th.

wealthy citizen investment and deposits outside the country and military spending.

Exploitation of Women in Maquiladoras

Maquiladoras (maquilas) are assembly plants based in the global South, especially in Mexico, Central America and the Caribbean, where goods are produced for export. Governments see maquilas as offering miracle answers to the economic crisis resulting from a decade of structural adjustment policies. Yet while governments and domestic capital rush to compete for foreign investors willing to set up maquilas in exchange for low wages, non-existent health and/or environmental conditions, and special tax and infrastructure incentives, unions have been slow to develop a response. With unemployment running between 30 and 60 percent, opposition to maquila investment would be unacceptable. At the same time, hostility to any kind of labor law protection or union organization leaves workers at the mercy of employers who seem intent on imposing turn of the century working conditions.

Mexico's border maquila program has been in place for close to 30 years. NAFTA has paved the way for the extension of maquilas throughout the country. There are even suggestions that installation of maquilas could "answer" the economic crisis of states such as Chiapas. Yet the vast majority of maquiladoras are still located along the Mexican/U.S. border. And the majority of the workforce continues to be female. Of the close to 500,000 workers that labor in Mexico's 2,000 maquila factories, about 70 percent are women. Weekly salaries average about $US50, plus productivity bonuses (exchanged for food at designated grocery stores). With this, women workers must support themselves and, in many cases, their children, with costs as high or higher than on the U.S. side of the border.

Exposing Human Rights Violations

Factor X, Casa de la Mujer (Women's House) in Tijuana has recently started a campaign to expose human rights violations in the maquilas — particularly the right to reproductive health and to a clean and healthy environment. Women are more attractive to employers because they believe the myth that women are naturally submissive, and will patiently accept the monotony of the assembly work, the speed-ups, and long days. But that doesn't mean they respect women's basic rights. Women must present a doctor's certificate to show that they are not pregnant before they are considered for employment. To make sure that their workers don't get pregnant and that employers don't have to pay maternity benefits, employers regularly distribute birth control pills or provide monthly birth control injections. Some government controlled unions have signed agreements obliging workers to notify employers as soon as they are pregnant. This violates women's right to maternity that the labor code is supposed to protect.

Organizing in the Maquilas

Attempts at organizing have been met with repression and, for the most part, failure. Governments are keen to protect the "economic viability" of maquila factories. In the few instances where unions have succeeded, companies often respond by closing down and relocating elsewhere. In Central America, as in Canada and the U.S., the threat of closure is an effective anti-union tactic. According to some activists, another reason for the lack of organization is that unions have not prioritized the maquila sector, perhaps because women make up the vast majority of the maquila workforce.

In some factories, workers are attempting to win the right to independent unions. In a few instances, they have succeeded. In other factories organization is more indirect, often starting with workshops on health and safety concerns, the national labor code or community campaigns to stop the chemical dumping by companies that is causing birth defects. Factor X, for example, is currently training 10 maquila workers to be health promoters.

There is a growing recognition among maquila organizers that the old union strategies need to be revamped to include a deeper understanding of gender and the day-to-day realities of the women who make up the bulk of the workforce. "Because we can't pretend women and men are the same," one organizer said. "It's the women who get up at 4 or 5 a.m. to get the food prepared. It's the women who are being forced to show their soiled sanitary pad to prove they aren't pregnant. It's the women who have to fight off sexual advances. It's the women who have to keep the family together and are leading the fight for healthy communities."[38]

---

38 Adapted from an article reprinted in Culbertson, Debbie. *Doing the Gender Boogie*, Ten Days for World Development, Toronto, Canada, 1995, which appeared in *Correspondencia*, à magazine of Mujer a Mujer, a collective of women based in Canada, the U.S. and Mexico.

The Platform for Action

Women's Equal Economic Participation
(Section F of Chapter IV)

Strategic Objective

To promote women's economic self-reliance and control over economic resources.

Actions by governments:

- Enact and enforce legislation to guarantee the rights of women and men to equal pay for equal work, or work of equal value.
- Adopt and implement laws against gender-based discrimination in employment.
- Devise mechanisms and apply positive action to enable women full and equal participation in economic decision making.
- Promote and support businesses run by women and strengthen their access to credit and capital.

Actions by governments and financial institutions:

- Increase women's participation on advisory boards.
- Mobilize the banking sector to increase lending to women.

Actions by national and international funding and development agencies:

- Implement policies to provide more resources to rural women.
- Support initiatives to provide resources to small-scale women entrepreneurs.

Poverty (Section A of Chapter IV)

Strategic Objective

To enable women to overcome poverty.

Actions by governments:

- Analyze, from a gender perspective, the impact of national programs and policies.
- Develop policies and programs to promote equitable distribution of resources within a household.
- Restructure and target the allocation of public expenditures to promote women's equal and more equitable access to productive resources.
- Revise laws and administrative practices to give women full and equal access to economic resources.
- Strengthen links between the formal banks and non-formal lending institutions to enhance women's access to credit.

Actions by multilateral financial institutions and bilateral donors:

- Review the impact of structural adjustment programs for reducing negative impact on women.

Actions by NGOs:

- Mobilize to improve effectiveness of government anti-poverty programs and monitor their implementation.
- Develop national strategies for improving women's health, education and social services.

NGO Beijing Declaration

Despite the fact that the Platform for Action and the Beijing Declaration which highlights the platform's major points included several important breakthroughs, many nongovernmental agency representatives, especially those from the South, felt that social and economic justice issues were largely ignored in the documents. The day before the end of the conference, a group of nongovernmental organizations released an alternative statement called the NGO Declaration to present their concerns. This statement focuses on the globalization of market economics as "a root cause of the increasing feminization of poverty." It denounces the "intersection of gender, race and poverty which creates multiple burdens of discrimination for many women of color." The group asserted that the imposition of structural adjustment programs on the countries of the South and economic restructuring in the countries of the North has resulted in "increasing poverty, debt and unemployment." The declaration calls on governments to urge action to cancel multilateral debt and to force international financial institutions to become accountable. The NGOs call for alternative development models that are economically and socially equitable and environmentally sound. They expressed concern about cutbacks — made necessary to cover debts or deficits— in government social programs such as income subsidies, health care, food, housing and education, which have a devastating impact on poor women and their children in both the North and the South. Another issue about which they expressed concern was the disproportionate share of public funds allocated to the military.

U.S. Commitments to the Platform for Action

Working Women, the Women's Bureau at the Department of Labor, has followed up its survey on working women by responding to the three areas that matter most to working American women: pay and benefits, work and family responsibilities, and valuing of women's work through job training and career advancement. The department is developing an

"Honor Roll" of organizations and companies that have pledged to improve the lives of women in any of these areas.[39]

The Department of the Treasury, through the Community Development Financial Institutions (CDFI) Fund, has established a presidential awards program to honor outstanding micro-lending organizations. The awards will help publicize the importance of microenterprises and micro-lending organizations, and will provide benchmarks for organizations to use in assessing their own efforts. The CDFI Fund will also coordinate a new Federal Microenterprise Initiative to ensure that funding by federal agencies effectively supports the growth and development of the U.S. microenterprise field.

The U.S. Agency for International Development's (U.S. AID) Office of Microenterprise Development has agreed to launch new microenterprise programs in more than 15 countries, which will enable low-income women entrepreneurs to gain access to credit, often for the first time. U.S. AID will work with local implementing organizations to enable them to expand their outreach and become financially sustainable. U.S. AID will also promote microenterprise through the World Bank's new Consultative Group to Assist the Poorest.

The Interagency Committee on Women's Business Enterprise (ICWBE) in conjunction with the National Women's Business Council (NWBC), works to secure economic self-sufficiency for women through entrepreneurship.[40]

Call for Corporate Responsibility in the Maquiladoras

Many maquilas are owned by U.S. corporations and a majority of the production of these plants are exported for sale in the United States. The arrival of U.S. companies along the U.S./Mexican border created staggering social and environmental consequences on both sides of the border. These consequences include various unrestrained waste discharges, air pollution emissions and improper toxic waste disposal that jeopardizes the health of citizens in U.S. and Mexican border towns.

The Coalition for Justice in the Maquiladoras is a tri-national alliance of religious, environmental, labor, Latino and women's organizations that seeks to pressure U.S. transnational corporations to adopt socially responsible practices within the maquiladora industry. The coalition is working to ensure a safe environment along the U.S./Mexican border, safe working conditions inside the maquila plants and a fair standard of living for the industry's workers.

39 For more information contact the Department of Labor, at (202) 219-6611.
40 For more information contact the Interagency Committee on Women's Business Enterprises, at (202) 622-8232.

For more information contact: The Coalition for Justice, 3120 West Ashby, San Antonio, Texas 78228, (210) 732-8957, Fax: (210) 732-8324.

Advocacy Campaign Against the GAP in El Salvador

Due to pressure from a U.S. and Canadian grassroots campaign, the GAP signed an unprecedented agreement to allow third-party monitoring of its supplier factories in El Salvador. The December 1995 agreement is the first of its kind to be signed by a retailer.

According to the provisions, the GAP will support efforts to clean up factory conditions in El Salvador. The retailer responded to the firing by its supplier, Mandarin International, of 350 workers for forming a union by applying pressure to the company to rehire the employees or face harsh penalties. The GAP plans to require all of its supplier plants in Central America to allow local human rights officials access to the plants to monitor compliance with GAP's code of conduct.

The GAP campaign was spearheaded by the National Labor Committee, a coalition effort of 23 U.S. unions as well as the Union of Needletrades, Industrial and Textile Employees (UNITE), and many local groups throughout Canada and the United States. The campaign received public support by presenting documented cases of labor abuse in the Central American maquiladora factories where GAP clothing is produced. The campaign views the GAP agreement as the initial step in affecting positive changes throughout the global garment industry.[41]

Women's Eyes on the Bank Campaign

At the U.N. Fourth World Conference on Women, women from Africa, Asia, Latin America, the Caribbean, the Pacific, Europe (East and West) and North America met to discuss their common economic problems — poverty, rising unemployment, cutbacks in public services, increased tensions at home, rising food costs, and their difficulties supporting themselves and their families. A common goal was to increase women's control over their lives and improve their economic well-being. One of the key strategies they developed was a campaign to urge changes in the World Bank, whose policies directly affect the lives of more than a billion women.

About 1,000 women and women's organizations from around the world signed a petition to James Wolfensohn, president of the World Bank, call-

---

41 "GAP Pact a Major Step for Retailer Campaign," *Working Together: Labor Report on the Americas*, No. 16, Jan.-Feb., 1996.

ing for major reforms. Wolfensohn met with women at the conference and pledged to begin implementing the campaign demands to:

- Increase participation of local women in Bank policy making. When Wolfensohn became Bank president in 1995 he ordered the Bank's offices in Africa to begin consultations with grassroots groups about economic problems in their countries. Women want the Bank to ensure that all field offices set up such consultations that include women and representatives of women's organizations.

- Change the way the Bank develops policies and programs so they will automatically look at their impact on family life and women's and children's needs. The campaign calls for gender needs assessments in the poverty studies the Bank does in preparation of their financing plans. The campaign calls on the Bank to determine the impact that certain policy goals and economic targets will have on countries, especially on the women in those countries, before it finances projects designed to reach those goals and targets. It also urges that information from these studies be made available to the public.

- Allocate more funds to projects designed to improve women's health, education, access to land and credit.

- Increase the number and racial diversity of women in senior management positions at the Bank.

Women in the U.S. have a particularly important role to play in this campaign since the bank is located here, and because the U.S. plays such a dominant role in the Bank.

For more information contact: U.S. Committee, Women's Eyes on the Bank Campaign, Nancy Forsythe, Department of Sociology, Art-Sociology Building, University of Maryland, College Park, MD 20742, Tel: (301) 405-6420, Fax: (301) 314-6892, E-mail: af55@Umail.umd.edu

50 Years Is Enough Campaign

The 50 Years Is Enough Campaign is a national broad-based coalition of more than 130 U.S. social justice, religious, development, student and environmental organizations, including the Unitarian Universalist Service Committee (UUSC), who share a common critique of the World Bank and the International Monetary Fund (IMF) and the economic model they promote. The campaign is committed to broad mobilization of the U.S. public for international and domestic economic justice. Similar campaigns are going on in many other countries. The objective of these campaigns is to raise the awareness of both policy makers and the general public regarding the unsustainable, unjust and ultimately economically unwise projects and policies that have been promoted by the World Bank and the IMF.

The campaign is working to force the World Bank and the IMF to adopt a set of criteria that will take into account a wide range of factors, including true project costs, sustainable development implications, community needs and community involvement in decision making.

The campaign calls for fundamental reform of the World Bank and the IMF or their replacement by democratic alternative institutions and seeks to create support for development policies that are economically, socially and environmentally just and sustainable.

For more information contact: Fifty Years Is Enough, 1025 Vermont Ave., N.W., Suite 300, Washington, DC 20005, Tel: (202) 463-2265 (campaign), (202) 879-3187 (media), Fax: (202) 879-386, E-mail: wb50years@igc.apc.org

The U.S./Guatemala Labor Education Project

The U.S./Guatemala Labor Education Project (U.S./GLEP) educates people in the U.S. about the denial of basic worker rights in Guatemala and provides ways in which people in the U.S. can respond effectively to the efforts of Guatemalan workers to achieve economic justice. U.S./GLEP believes that in a global economy it is in the interests of U.S. as well as Guatemalan workers that basic worker rights are respected everywhere. Denial of basic rights is an unfair trade advantage that hurts workers here and abroad.

U.S./GLEP campaigns are conducted only at the request of Guatemalan workers and trade unions. Two of their specific program areas include:

- Ensuring that U.S. companies respect the basic rights of Guatemalan workers and
- Enforcing U.S. trade laws that condition Guatemala's exports to the U.S. on the observance of basic worker rights

For more information contact: Steve Coats at: U.S./GLEP c/o ACTWU-Chicago Joint Board, 333 South Ashland Avenue, Chicago, IL 60607, Tel: (312) 262-6502, Fax: (312) 262-6602.

The Interfaith Center on Corporate Responsibility

The Interfaith Center on Corporate Responsibility (ICCR) is an international coalition of more than 275 Protestant, Roman Catholic and Jewish institutional investors including denominations, orders, pension funds, health care corporations and dioceses with combined portfolios worth an estimated $45 billion. They are committed to merging social values with investment decisions. ICCR members believe that they must achieve more than an acceptable financial return. They utilize religious investments and other resources to challenge unjust or harmful corporate policies and to work for peace, economic justice and stewardship of the earth. In 1994 ICCR-member alternative investments surpassed $300 million. Religious shareholder activism began in 1971 when the Episcopal Church submitted a shareholder resolution calling on General Motors to withdraw from South Africa.

Religious investors have negotiated with corporations and have addressed shareholders at dozens of annual meetings. They use their power and influence to bring about change. For example, in April 1995, a delegation of religious stockholders went to Kimberly-Clark's annual meeting in Dallas to urge the company to spin-off its tobacco business. Known for its health and hygiene products, Kimberly-Clark has also been a major player in the tobacco industry worldwide. Religious investors argued that the tobacco interest was contradictory to the company's principal business. Though the resolution achieved an impressive shareholder vote with more than 22 percent abstaining or in favor of spinning off tobacco, the proponents left the meeting thinking that the company had not been persuaded to divest. However, three weeks later, in a surprising reversal, Kimberly-Clark announced it would spin-off its $404 million tobacco business because of its "incompatibility with the company's strategic direction." Pressure from ICCR and institutional purchasers working with others in the anti-tobacco movement made a crucial difference.

For more information on many resources and publications, including its newsletter, *The Corporate Examiner*, published 10 times annually, contact: ICCR, 475 Riverside Drive, Room 566, New York, NY 10115, Tel: (212) 870-2295.

Session 4

Access to Education, the Media and Communications

Critical areas of the platform covered in this session:

Education and Training of Women (Section IV.B)

Women and the Media (Section IV.J)

The Girl Child (Section IV.L)

Two-Hour Workshop

Activities	Minutes
Opening Circle	15
Exploration of a Central Issue: Education and Women Worldwide	20
Exploration of a Central Issue: Media Images of Women (includes video)	25
Break	10
Exploration of a Central Issue: Women's Access to the Media	15
Alternative Media: Women in Black	15
Platform for Action Positions	5
Brainstorming for Action	5
Journal Writing	5
Closing Circle	5
Total Time:	120

Materials

Two flip charts

Centerpiece — Pictures and colorful multicultural objects

Magazines

Preparation

Write on flip chart pages:

Blank page: Benefits of education for women and girls

Benefits of education for women and girls (page 183)

Ways to improve literacy for girls (page 184)

What is implied by advertising images of women? (page 185)

Countering dominant media images (page 186)

Ask for:

Two volunteers to read education gap facts

Five volunteers to read Women in Black segment

Three-Hour Workshop

Activities	Minutes
Opening Circle	15
Exploration of a Central Issue: Education and Women Worldwide	20
Storytelling *	30
Exploration of a Central Issue: Media Images of Women (includes video)	25
Break	10
Exploration of a Central Issue: Women's Access to Media	15
Assessing the News *	25
Alternative Media: Women in Black	15
Platform for Action Positions*	10
Brainstorming for Action	5
Journal Writing	5
Closing Circle	5
Total Time:	180

Materials

Two flip charts

Centerpiece — Pictures and colorful multicultural objects

Magazines

Front sections of a local and a national newspaper

Preparation

Write on flip chart pages:

Blank page: Benefits of education for women and girls

Benefits of education for women and girls (page 183)

Ways to improve literacy for girls (page 184)

What is implied by advertising images of women? (page 185)

Countering dominant media images (page 186)

Ways U.N. organizations are working to reverse gender bias in education (page 201)

Teenage motherhood (page 201)

Blank page: Assessing the news (page 202)

Ask for:

Two volunteers to read education gap facts

Five volunteers to read in Women in Black segment

*exercises and/or time added

Opening Circle
(15 minutes)

Objective

To focus the group and allow for brief personal sharing.

Process

1. Light the candle and read this excerpt from the NGO vision statement:

   > Visualize nations where girls are educated and valued as much as boys, and all people are free to develop their full potential.

2. Explain:

   > This workshop focuses on education, mass media and communications. Educational opportunities are often tied to gender and economic status. Reflect briefly on how your own educational opportunities were shaped by your gender and class.

   Facilitator's Note: Model this sharing by being the first to speak.

Exploration of a Central Issue: Education and Women Worldwide
(20 minutes)

Objective

To consider the level of educational opportunities for women around the globe.

Process

1. Explain:

   > Education is a fundamental right and will lead to a more equitable society — a goal set by the countries of the world in the Universal Declaration of Human Rights adopted in 1948. Consider what the current educational situation is for women around the world.

2. Invite two participants to read aloud the following points on the education gap.

First Reader

Since 1970, as primary education improved worldwide, female adult literacy in the South has increased by two-thirds, but illiterate women still outnumber illiterate men.

On average, only 55 percent of the women in developing nations are literate. Improving this rate would boost economic output and personal growth. A study of 88 nations showed that literacy gains of 20-30 percent boosted the gross domestic product by eight to 16 percent.

School curricula often exclude female contributions and perspectives.

Second Reader

The most frequent action for girl characters in primary school books is watching boys.

In university classes, males speak twice as often as females; women are more likely to begin with a "self put-down," such as, "I don't know if this is right but..."

Only 18 percent of girls compared to 60 percent of boys have computers at home.[1]

3. Brainstorm on how the education of girls and women has positive effects on participants' lives. (5 minutes) Write answers on a flip chart.

Facilitator's Note: Review the "Benefits of Education for Women and Girls" on a pre-prepared flip chart.

Benefits of Education for Women and Girls

Better health

Smaller families

Greater productivity

Improved status and self esteem

Better educated children

Facilitator's Note: Read the flip chart above. When reviewing it, verbally share the entire explanation of the shortened phrase.

- **Better health:** An educated mother can raise a healthier family. In Peru, educated women were found to have **healthier children** regardless of whether there was a clinic

---

1 Based on information appearing in the United Nations Development Program *Human Development Report*, 1995, and *Failing at Fairness* by Myra and David Sadker, Simon and Schuster, 1994.

or hospital nearby. Another study shows that a **one percent** rise in women's **literacy** has **three times** the effect of a one percent rise in the number of **doctors**.

- **Smaller families:** Educated women tend to have fewer children, slowing population growth. According to a 1993 report of the Population Action Council, average family

Girls forum at Huairou

size and child death rates are lowest when **family planning** and **health programs** are combined with high levels of **education** for women. In Brazil, uneducated mothers have an average of 6.5 children each, but those with secondary education have only 2.5 children. Worldwide, **fertility rates are reduced 5 to 10 percent for each year a girl goes to school.**

- **Greater productivity:** Educated women are more **economically** productive. Each additional year of schooling raises a woman's wages by **15-20 percent**, compared to an 11 percent increase for men.

- **Improved status:** Educated women tend to make more **independent decisions** and stand up for themselves. According to a UNFPA report, educated women believe they have a right to good health care.

- **Effect on children:** Women, when educated, tend to **encourage** their children to become educated.[2]

Facilitator's Note: Review pre-prepared flip chart that lists the following "Ways to Improve Literacy for Girls."

Ways to Improve Literacy for Girls

Ensure girls' access to education
Eliminate gender stereotyping in curricula
Set specific time-frames to reduce gender gap
Elicit parental support for education
Enroll adolescent mothers in programs
Provide day care facilities[3]

Three-hour session: Add the exercise "Storytelling" presented in the section entitled "Additional Activities" for a total of 30 minutes.

2 *Literacy: A Key to Women's Empowerment*, United Nations.
3 Ibid.

Exploration of a Central Issue: Media Images of Women

(25 minutes)

Objective

To explore the range and effects of media images on women.

Process

1. Describe the video:

    > What is produced in the media about women presents certain assumptions about the roles women can play in society. The following video called "Still Killing Us Softly" explores the images of women found in advertisements.

    Facilitator's Note: Show the 10-minute video clip excerpted from "Still Killing Us Softly."[4] The material in this clip is quite powerful.

2. After sharing participants' responses to the video, ask the following questions:

    -   What assumptions about women are implied in media messages?

    -   What do you think should be done about them?

    Facilitator's Note: Prepare a flip chart in advance which highlights the implications of advertising images of women.

3. Review the points from the video you have listed on the flip charts.

What Is Implied by Advertising Images of Women?

Women are never okay as they are

Women must make themselves over

Dismembering makes women less than human

Women become objects

Violence against women is justified

Masculine = dominant and brutal

Feminine = passive and submissive

---

4 The 35-minute version of this film, produced by Jean Kilbourn, is available for rental from Cambridge Documentary Films, P.O. Box 385, Cambridge, MA 02139.

Countering Dominant Media Images [5]

Stop talking about your weight (especially in front of young girls)

Make a list of women you admire

Concentrate on things you do well

Question the motives of the fashion industry

Write companies that impress or offend you

Stop fighting your body

4. If the video is not available, ask participants to turn to the journal page for this session and write down the positive and negative images of women they have seen in the visual, print and/or audio media. Ask participants to list images from different cultures if they have had an opportunity to be exposed to media in countries other than the U.S. (5 minutes).

Facilitator's Note: Supply magazines for participants to flip through while they are thinking.

5. Ask the group to break into pairs and share their examples with someone else (10 minutes).

6. Share the following points:

> Through the lens of the media, social and occupational roles are **strictly divided** along gender lines. When women appear at all — and numerous studies around the world document their dramatic under-representation in almost all kinds of media content — they tend to be depicted within the home and are **rarely portrayed** as **rational, active** or **decisive**.[6]

> Studies worldwide show there is a relationship between **viewing violence** in the media and subsequent **violent actions** by men against women and children. Consider the combination of violence and "soft" pornography that has permeated our society in the past decades.

Break

(10 minutes)

5 About-Face: About Time, San Francisco.
6 Gallager, Margaret. "Women in the Media," in *Women: Looking Beyond 2000*. United Nations, 1995.

Exploration of a Central Issue: Women's Access to the Media

(15 minutes)

Objective

To become aware of the power women are denied in the mainstream media.

Process

1. Discuss the following:

    > U.N. data show that women have pursued higher-level **mass communication education** in increasing numbers during the past 15 years. Yet the media employment gap persists. Administration, production and editorial posts within the media remain largely a **male monopoly**. In the majority of cases, women's share of media jobs is well **below 30 percent**. Women are almost invisible (averaging from four to eight percent) in the technical area. These jobs are highly skilled and highly paid and often lead to careers in program production or senior management. **Print journalism** offers better prospects but there are seldom women bureau chiefs. In radio and television there is considerable gender segregation, with women tending to be concentrated in occupations as announcers, presenters and production assistants that may sometimes be well-paid but may not lead to further career development.[7]

    > It is no wonder that women are almost invisible in both the print and electronic media. Review the graphic: "Face of the News, January 1995" to illustrate this reality.

7 Ibid.

The Face of the News – January 1995

Newspaper: Front Page Averages*

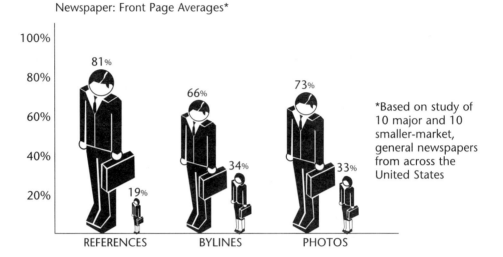

*Based on study of 10 major and 10 smaller-market, general newspapers from across the United States

REFERENCES   BYLINES   PHOTOS

Television: News Show Averages for ABC, CBS and NBC

Television: News Show Averages for ABC, CBS, NBC, CNN and PBS

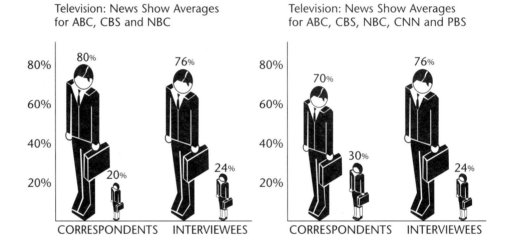

CORRESPONDENTS   INTERVIEWEES

CORRESPONDENTS   INTERVIEWEES

2. Ask the group to consider how to increase women's access to positions of power in the media. Briefly discuss ways to put pressure on media institutions to use more women-affirming material.

Three-hour session: Add the exercise "Assessing the News" presented in the section entitled "Additional Activities" for a total of 25 minutes.

Alternative Media: Women in Black

(15 minutes)

Objective

To consider creative ways to communicate women's issues.

Process

1. Suggest:

> An effective way to get the attention of the media and the public is to use artistic, creative methods. An example of this was an hour long vigil by Women in Black at the Fourth World Conference on Women.

2. Request five volunteers to read:

First Reader

Women in Black is a movement that has inspired groups of women in different parts of the world to stand in their own towns and cities, on street corners, in market squares and in other public places for one hour a week dressed in black. They protest silently the many forms of violence that are increasingly a part of everyday life around the world.

Second Reader

We are Women in Black and we are part of "A Gathering of Spirit," an international spontaneous worldwide grassroots movement.

> Black is the color that we wear;
> Black, the color that speaks our anger.
> Silence is the language that we speak;
> Silence, a language that voices our anguish.

Everywhere, women are breaking the silence; women are naming the violence. They are making public the many forms of "personal" violence against women. The issues have been many. The form in which protests have been expressed also vary: silence, posters, placards, pamphlets and sometimes even lamps, have been an expression of this collective rebellion and resistance.

Third Reader

Women in Black vigils began in Tel-Aviv, Haifa and Jerusalem where together, Palestinian and Israeli women spoke in favor of a homeland for the Palestinians and protested the politics of hatred that was destroying their homes and lives.

- Mothers have walked to the market squares with photos of their disappeared and dead children in Chile, Argentina, El Salvador and Guatemala.

- Women in Bangalore, India, protested the razing of the mosque in Ayodhya.

- Women demonstrated on the streets of Belgrade every Wednesday from the beginning of the war there in 1991.
- Women have demanded that rape in war be treated as a war crime.

Fourth Reader

At the NGO conference, hundreds of women stood together, holding placards some of which read:

- "We are the miracles by which we survive."
- "Our vision: respect for human rights is the foundation of peace."
- "Bosnia is bleeding."
- "We have suffered immeasurable pains."
- "Reverse structural adjustment."
- "Women for environmental and social justice."
- "Stop poisoning poor communities."
- "Stop coercion and violence against women for population control."
- "Women are not for bashing."

Fifth Reader

After an hour of silent vigil, candles are lit and testimony offered. Women stand, protest and remember in silence innocent victims. They refuse to let the politics of hatred and intolerance destroy the humanity that binds and lives within all faiths. Will you stand with them?[8]

A Women in Black demonstration at the NGO forum.

8 Text for this reading was adapted from a brochure produced by Vimochana and the Asian Women's Human Rights Council and distributed at the Fourth World Conference on Women. See resource section for additional suggestions on signs that could be used in local vigils.

Platform for Action Positions on Education, Mass Media and Communication, and the Girl Child

(5 minutes)

Objective

To become acquainted with platform positions on issues covered in this session.

Process

1. Explain the following points from the platform:

The platform states that **non-discriminatory education** benefits both girls and boys, and thus ultimately contributes to more equal relationships between women and men. Investing in formal and non-formal education and training for girls and women has resulted in an exceptionally high social and economic return and has proved to be one of the best means of achieving economic growth and development. It proposes action to:

- Ensure **equal access** to education

- Eradicate **illiteracy** among women

- Improve women's access to vocational **training**, science and **technology**, and continuing **education**

The platform states also that the continued projection of negative and **degrading images** of women in media communications of all types **must be changed**. Women should be empowered by improving their skills, knowledge and access to information technology. This will strengthen their ability to combat negative portrayals of women internationally and to challenge instances of abuse of power within this increasingly important industry.

Women's overall **share of media jobs** is low. In Africa, Asia and Latin America the average female staff percentage is below **25 percent** for broadcasting and the press. In Europe it reaches 30 percent for the press and 36 percent for broadcasting and print journalism. Even where more women are employed, few make **policy decisions**. The platform proposes action to:

- Promote a balanced and **non-stereotypical** portrayal of women in the media.

- **Guarantee access** by women to information and participation in all forms and levels of the media.

Because of the importance of focusing on the treatment of the girl child a special platform section was created entitled "The Girl Child" which focuses on issues relating to girls' education, health and welfare.

Facilitator's Note: Refer participants to the Platform for Action in the background and resource section for more detail.

Brainstorming for Action
(5 minutes)

Objective
To collect ideas that can be used to formulate a local plan of action.

Process

1. To begin to formulate a local plan of action, use two flip charts or two flip chart pages posted on the wall.

2. Ask participants to make a **theoretical list** of possible activities they would like to undertake that relate to the topics of this workshop. Encourage participants to mention whatever comes to mind, regardless of their ability to perform the action.

3. On the second flip chart, list any **organizations** that participants know about that are addressing these issues.

Facilitator's Note: Attach lists from previous brainstorming sessions to the walls and encourage participants to add ideas or resources to any of the lists. All the lists will be used in the last session when the group develops an action plan.

4. Summarize the boxed information. Remind participants that more information about these programs that could be helpful for local action planning is included in the background and resource section.

Successful Strategies for Action

Women Are Good News (WAGN) is a national media-watch organization, based in San Francisco, which monitors and advocates for increased representation of women in public affairs programs and news commentary. In 1991, WAGN waged a public education campaign to increase the number of women guests on PBS news programs. Their efforts paid off. Women guests on Washington Week in Review and on public affairs programs in the San Francisco Bay Area have substantially increased.

"Slipping from the Scene," the seventh annual **Women, Men and Media** survey of news coverage of and by females, shows a significant drop in front-page references to and photos of females. The survey, undertaken annually since 1989, was co-chaired by Betty Friedan, internationally known author and visiting distinguished professor at the University of Southern California and George Mason University, and Nancy Woodhull, a founding editor of USA TODAY, who is president of Nancy Woodhull & Associates, Inc., a media research and management consulting firm. Initially, the survey examined 10 major-market newspapers. It has been expanded since to include 10 additional newspapers from smaller markets as well as television news shows. The findings and methodology tell a lot about how people can monitor the media, analyze current trends and develop future possibilities.

Recommended Actions [9]

- Look and listen to the locally produced public affairs programs carried by your network and PBS affiliate. Conduct a one-month tally of how many women and men appear on these programs. If women are not equally represented, call and make an appointment to meet with the program producers as well as the executives of the station and demand equal representation by women. Ask the station to give you a copy of the male-female representation for the year to date.

- Take the front page of your daily newspapers and monitor the number of male-female bylines and male-female sources used in each story. Tally for one month and meet with newspaper executives to discuss ideas for improvement.

- Listen to the political talk shows on your local radio stations. If men predominate, start advocating for an equal number of women talk show hosts. Studies show that male dominated talk shows receive mostly call-ins from other men. Women do not call in to these shows because they feel their opinion will be dismissed or discounted.

9 DeStefanis, Nancy. Executive Director of Women Are Good News.

Journal Writing

(5 minutes)

Objective

To give participants an opportunity to record items they wish to remember or process.

Process

1. Ask participants to take a few minutes to write down on the journal page for this session any reactions, additional areas they wish to pursue, questions they want to research, or additional action ideas or possible contacts they can think of. If time is short, encourage them to write these down between sessions and, when appropriate, add them to the flip chart pages that will be posted at each session.

Closing Circle

(5 minutes)

Objective

To provide an opportunity to connect symbolically with others before separating.

Process

1. Encourage participants to gather in a circle around the centerpiece, holding hands. Ask someone to share a phrase summarizing their experience of the session. Invite participants to bring items to future sessions that remind them of women's lives or that honor women.

2. Ask for volunteers to read the section of the poem "Let Us Hold Hands" or sing "Woman to Woman."

Let us hold hands
with the woman who holds her sister in Bosnia, Detroit, Somalia,
Jacksonville, Guatemala, Burma, Juarez and Cincinnati,
with the woman who confronts the glare of eyes and gunbarrels,
yet rises to protest in Yoruba, English, Polish, Spanish, Chinese,
Urdu.

Let us hold hands
with the woman whocooks, with the woman who laughs,
with the women who heals, with the women who prays,
with the women who plants, with the women who harvests,
with the women who sings, with the women whose spirits rise.

Excerpt from the poem *Let Us Hold Hands* by Pat Mora.

Woman to Woman

Words by Rabbi Sofer and Carolyn McDade
Music by Carolyn McDade

To act in submission increases domination
To act with integrity increases equality
To know our anger frees our love
To free our love reveals our rage

To act in hate increases hate
To act in love increases love
To act in despair increases despair
To act in hope increases hope

ADDITIONAL ACTIVITIES FOR THREE HOUR SESSIONS

Storytelling

(30 minutes)

Objective

To explore the conditions of girls and consider what happens to prevent girls from getting the education they deserve.

Process

1. Ask the group to break up into pairs. Each person in the pair should read one of the stories included here and then tell that story to their partner. (15 minutes)

First Story: Why has Wanjiku dropped out of school? (from Kenya)

As Nyambura lowered her pail into the sun-dappled stream from which she fetched her family's water each morning, she heard a pure, high voice singing the old song about the maize flowers blooming all over Kenya. It was Wanjiku; the voice was unmistakable — and much missed in class now that her parents had pulled her out of school to help her mother at home after the birth of her latest brother. Nyambura didn't quite understand why they had done that; her own mother had just as much work as Wanjiku's. And it made her uncomfortable that she was still in school when Wanjiku wasn't. She set her pail down and ran up the path to greet her former classmate; she didn't want Wanjiku to feel they weren't close friends just because they no longer saw each other daily.

"We got a new goat to go with my new brother," said Wanjiku as Nyambura took her hand.

"Which one is more trouble?" asked Nyambura, smiling.

"It's hard to tell. The goat, I guess. Yesterday it ate the sleeve of my red blouse."

They laughed together and, at the stream's edge, kicked off their sandals to cool their feet in the water.

"It's my little sister who's exciting," said Wanjiku. "She's beginning to talk. She still stumbles when she walks, but she chatters away. Just like me at her age, Mamma says."

Nyambura wondered if Wanjiku's baby sister would ever go to school. She tried to remember the proverb her mother had learned at the dressmaking center where she had also learned to read a few years before. All the eight-year-old girl could recall, though, was that when she had asked if she should stay at home like Wanjiku, to help with the younger children and the other household chores, her mother had pulled her ears gently and said, "Not you, honeypot. With that head of yours, you're going to write the kind of books that taught me how to read."

"And your father thinks the same," his voice had boomed suddenly in the doorway, "so don't go asking him such foolish things." He had entered the house, smiling, and threatened to tickle her to death if she raised the question again. That had closed the matter — for her at least... The problem, thought Nyambura, as she looked at her friend's rippled reflection in the water, was that Wanjiku's head was just as good as hers — different, but every bit as good. One of the reasons that she missed Wanjiku so much in class was that her friend's answers to their teacher's questions often set off new thoughts in her own head. Had each made the other's head better? And now Wanjiku was asking just the question Nyambura had been dreading: "What's going on at school?"

"We're learning division," she replied. "It's easy," she added, remembering how good Wanjiku had been at math. "I could teach it to you if you like." Suddenly she realized that she'd said something wrong.

"Of course it's easy," Wanjiku retorted. "Just the opposite of the times tables we were doing when I left. If five times two is ten, then two goes into ten five times." She stood up and filled her pail. "You know," she said, "I bet I can get my older brother to teach me everything he's learned in school. I don't really need to go myself."

Nyambura wondered, but said nothing. That brother wasn't very interested in school — and he never seemed to have time for anyone but his friends. Then her mother's proverb came back to her: "Educate a boy and you educate one person; educate a girl and you educate a nation."[10]

Second Story: What will Jenny do with her baby? (from Los Angeles)

"So you don't even want to think about giving up this baby for adoption, Jenny?"

Jenny fought back her tears. It was bad enough that the smog in Los Angeles was so thick that you could hardly breathe, but this question brought tears to her eyes. Why was it wrong to want to have or keep your own baby just because you were young and unmarried? She had agreed to see Lucy at the teen counseling center only to please her aunt. So what if Lucy had given her own kid up and had gone back to school? They were different people. Very different people. And so what if she was only 16? Her mother had been even younger when she'd had her first kid.

"I ran into Mrs. Eliot the other day. She said that you were her best student in biology," said Lucy.

Jenny knew that ploy for what it was. Butter her up, then get her to say "yes" to exactly what she didn't want to do. It wasn't that she disliked Lucy — even if the counselor was a prude. Only 17 and already a prude. "You wouldn't understand," she said at last.

---

10 *Girls: Challenging the World*, United Nations.

"Try me."

"This baby is the most gorgeous thing I'll ever make. You should see its father. And this kid will love me. It will really love me." The way no one ever had, she thought, except maybe her aunt and grandmother. Jenny's mother had left her with them when she was only three, and had died in an accident soon afterwards. But her aunt had four other kids. And counting herself, her grandmother had five all in the same house...That was why she needed someone all her own.

"Have you seen a doctor?" Lucy asked.

"Sure. At the beginning."

"But not since?"

Jenny shook her head. "Gran's better than any doctor."

"Probably," said Lucy. "But you could help by getting yourself checked out each month. For the baby's sake as much as yours — so that this kid will be healthy as well as gorgeous." Ah, yes, Jenny remembered. Pregnancy could make both you and your kid anemic. That was lack of iron. Or was it iodine? No, iodine was for the baby's nervous system and its brain. She could almost hear Mrs. Eliot stressing that point when they'd been doing human biology. "I've cut down on junk food," she replied, her voice betraying her pride at being so organized. "I also got some mineral supplements to take. And I'll be going back to the clinic after final exams next month... And when I realized I was pregnant, I got myself checked for AIDS. I'm okay for that, too. And I also got lots of stuff about safe sex."

There was a poster over the counselor's desk depicting a rooster in sneakers and sloppy socks. Above his head was a question: "What do you call a guy who flies the coop when a baby shows up?" Jenny laughed. That was what had happened to Lucy. Her own boyfriend, Bob, was sometimes a jerk, but he would stick around for his own kid.

"Does Bob know about the baby?" Lucy was asking.

Actually, he didn't. The baby wasn't showing yet — and Jenny had decided to put off telling him until after his exams the following month.

"Jenny, do you know much a baby costs each month — especially in a town like this?"

"I make good money at the nail shop. Especially with the tips." She put on her sexiest drawl and flashed the smile everyone talked about. "All the customers ask for me — and they know I don't do no one unless they tip me good... And Bob's boss says he's a great mechanic, the best he's ever had. So after his exams, when he can work full time and go to night school like he says —"

"Jenny," Lucy interrupted softly, "a baby costs hundreds of dollars a month."

She could stay with the baby at her aunt's, but just the cost of diapers... Would Bob spend his money on a baby? And would he be a good father — playing with the baby, singing to it, changing its diapers, taking it out in the stroller...?

Who knew? Jenny dropped her gaze to the worn linoleum on the floor. Bob liked cool clothes. And cool cars. And who knew how he'd behave with a baby? She'd never really thought about that sort of thing. Suddenly it occurred to her that she might have to leave school to work full-time. But she was smart. She could always go back. She could also go to night school. She could work at The Nail during the day and finish school at night. And her grandmother, and aunt and cousins could take care of the baby and play with it...Only then...whose baby would it be?[11]

2. Paraphrase the following while displaying the flip chart below:

> Around the world there are about 100 million children between the ages of six and 11 who are not in school; **more than 60 percent are girls.** Two-thirds of the world's 948 million adults who cannot read and write are women. For those women who have been unable to learn to read and write during their childhood, the U.N. Educational, Scientific and Cultural Organization (UNESCO), the U.N. Children's Fund (UNICEF) and the U.N. Development Fund for Women (UNIFEM) have set up **adult literacy projects**, like the center which Nyambura's mother attended. In addition, UNESCO and UNICEF are working to promote images of **dynamic, resourceful** girls, some of whom also excel at math and science and other activities usually associated with boys, in textbooks and the media.

UNESCO and UNICEF are working to promote images of dynamic resourceful girls.

11 Ibid.

Ways U.N. Organizations Are Working to Reverse Gender Bias in Education

Advocating for high school education for all

Promoting adult literacy programs

Promoting images of dynamic, resourceful girls

Showing girls excelling in math and science

3. Share this information while displaying the flip chart below:

> Thirty percent of the 500,000 women who die in childbirth every year are teenage girls; a major cause of these deaths is anemia, which is due to iron deficiency. UNICEF is fighting to eliminate this pernicious disease, as well as iodine deficiency problems. The babies of teenage mothers are often underweight and twice as likely to die as babies born to women in their twenties or above. In part because a child's health depends, to a great extent, on the amount of education its mother has received, the United Nations Population Fund (UNFPA), UNICEF and the World Health Organization (WHO) have urged governments to experiment with ways to keep pregnant girls in school. Brainstorm about reasons why pregnant girls should continue their education.

Teenage Motherhood

Thirty-five percent of the 500,000 women who die in childbirth are teenagers

Babies of teenagers are often underweight — twice as likely to die as those born to women 20 years of age or older

U.N. organizations urge governments to experiment with ways to keep pregnant girls in school

Assessing the News

(25 minutes)

Objective

To become aware of the role women play in all aspects of the media.

Facilitator's Note: Bring several front sections of the local paper and a national newspaper to the session.

Process

1. Give each participant one section of the newspaper and ask them to:

    - Count the number of bylines by men and by women on the front page and throughout the front section.

    - Note the content of the stories written by women.

    - Count all photos.

    - Count the number of stories in which women appear in photos but not in the content of the story.

2. Ask participants to report their findings as you record them on a flip chart.

3. Share the following statistics of average female: [12]

    - Bylines on front page 34%

    - Bylines on local page 41%

    - Bylines on op-ed page 27%

    - References on front page 19%

    - References on local page 26%

    - Appearance in photos on front page . 33%

    - Appearance in photos on local page . 39%

12 Women Are Good News, San Francisco, 1995.

Journal Page

Journal Page

Session 4

Background and Resources
on the Education and Media Coverage of Women

The Education Gap

- 905 million men and women — almost a quarter of the world's adult population — are illiterate. Sixty-five percent of illiterate adults are women.[13]

- In some South Asian and African countries, the illiteracy rate for adult women is more than 80 percent. According to the United Nations, the illiteracy rates for women 30 years and over are: 93.4 percent in Nepal, 89.2 percent in Pakistan, 98.2 percent in Burkina Faso, 97.9 percent in Mali and 90.4 percent in Togo.

- From 1970 to 1992, worldwide primary and secondary school female enrollment increased from 38 percent to 68 percent, reflecting the growing commitment to universal primary education. Still, 130 million children don't have access to primary education; two-thirds of these children are girls.[14]

- Half as many women as men in developing nations are enrolled in tertiary (higher) education. Around the world, women continue to represent only a small proportion of math and science students.[15]

- Studies in Malaysia show a 20 percent greater return on investment in the education of girls — including improved nutrition and family health, lower birth and infant mortality rates — but global education investments tend to favor boys.

- School curricula often exclude female contributions and perspectives.

- Educated women are more likely to delay marriage and plan their families. They have fewer children who receive better health care and are more likely to succeed in school.

- In the United States, according to a recent study by the American Association of University Women, girls are systematically excluded from equal education through stereotyping and prejudice. Boys are preferred over girls in subjects such as math, science and technology.[16]

13   World Education Report, United Nations Educational, Scientific and Cultural Organization (UNESCO), 1993.
14 Human Development Report, United Nations Development Program, 1995.
15 Ibid.
16 Human Development Report, United Nations Development Program, 1995, American Association of University Women, 1995, and *Failing at Fairness* by Myra and David Sadker, Simon and Schuster, 1994.

UUSC Partners Past and Present: Promoting Women's and Girls' Access to Education

The Rural Women's Social Education Center: Literacy Training

The Rural Women's Social Education Center (RuWSEC), a former UUSC project partner organization, works in the Madras region of India to empower rural women from the lowest strata of society to realize their potential, actively participate in improving their own status, and contribute constructively in social change activities.

The Rural Women's Social Education Center uses role play and skills training to help Dalit women realize their potential and

act to improve their status.

One component of RuWSEC's program has been literacy and assertiveness training for girls and young women. In a six month survey of 2,000 households in 28 villages, RuWSEC researchers found that 50 percent of girls aged six to 10 and 75 percent of girls aged 11 to 14 were not in school. All were functionally illiterate. The principal reason for girls staying home was that their mothers worked long hours as day-laborers and depended on their daughters to manage domestic tasks, such as caring for younger children and helping with the evening meal. Because daughters were needed at home both mornings and evenings they missed the opportunity to attend any kind of school.

In the fall of 1990, RuWSEC initiated a literacy project specifically designed to reach these girls. Flexibility was the key to RuWSEC's strategy. Where possible, literate adolescents or young women were recruited to be trained as literacy educators. Where no literate women or girls could be identified, two or three 15 to 18 year old girls were selected to receive intensive literacy training along with basic teaching skills. Each instructor was then assigned a group of 10 learners in her village, with the expectation that instructors would meet with them in their own homes if necessary.

By June 1992, classes were being held in 23 villages with 320 learners participating. Students have been highly motivated and stayed with these classes. RuWSEC also developed reading materials for these students, since so few books are suitable for semi-literate adolescents and adults. In addition to basic reading skills, participants learned speaking skills, body awareness and numeric skills. One literacy worker described the program this way: "We are not just teaching literacy, we are teaching self-confidence and self-respect."

Vimochana Forum for Women's Rights: Grassroots Media

Women's words for centuries have rarely ever been heard, nor even read. They have never found their way into the language and thinking that has structured our history, our politics, our culture. But today the woman's word cannot be so easily written off, nor can her song be stilled.

Excerpt from a Streelekha pamphlet

Vimochana Forum for Women's Rights, located in Bangalore, India, uses various strategies to educate and empower women to celebrate their creativity, protest injustices and put pressure on authorities to bring about positive changes in Indian society. The group helps women who are victims of harassment, sexual violence and wife beating bring complaints to police stations and follow up their cases in the courts. They work in the poor neighborhoods to fight for housing rights for women. They also hold meetings where small groups of women in schools, workplaces, poor neighborhoods and other places can talk about the problems that confront them. Among the creative activities that Vimochana has undertaken are:

- Poetry in the Park: Group members meet each year on International Women's Day (March 8th) in a park to tell stories, read their poetry, sing and celebrate who they are.

- The Women's Wall: Wanting to claim a physical space in the city for women to express themselves, they chose a wall facing one of the main bus terminals and began to write messages and poems for women there.

- Street Utsav: This is a day of painting and street theater.

- Streelekha Women's Bookplace: The first feminist bookstore in India, this meeting place for women also includes a lending library.

In addition to these activities Vimochana holds seminars, makes posters, performs street theater, songs, holds film screenings, and produces publications in both Kannada and English.

Haitian Women in Solidarity: Video Project

Haitian Women in Solidarity (SOFA) is a national women's organization formed in 1986. Its objective is the liberation of Haitian women from exploitation and oppression. SOFA has worked with victims of violence in a neighborhood of the capital, Port-au-Prince. The organization videotapes testimonies from human rights victims as part of its effort to press charges against the perpetrators through the Inter-American Commission on Human Rights of the Organization of American States. As a result of this work, women began to organize a clinic for victims of rape and other violence against women to provide comprehensive, respectful health care, therapy, human rights advocacy and health education. SOFA has tapes of its health education sessions and its Victims of Violence Counseling Training Course for use by other women's groups. It has also produced a tape about the development of the clinic so that others communities can organize their own.[17]

17 UUSC Project Partner Data Sheet, 1996.

Delhi Community Health Workers: Working with Girls

Twenty girls, ages nine to 12, sit in a circle and sing a song while two of them mime the words. The song is about a girl who tells her family, naming each member in successive verses, that she will go out on her own, they cannot imprison her any more.

Girl children face discrimination within their own homes where boys are given better education, food and medical treatment. They are often held back from school, do all the household chores, suffer restricted mobility and lack freedom of expression and control over all aspects of their lives. In India, discrimination against girls takes severe forms ranging from the selective abortion of female fetuses and female infanticide to neglect, denial of rights, physical abuse and even the murder of wives.

Olga Benoit (right), representative of Haitian Women in Solidarity, speaks with Heather Foote, Director of UUSC's Washington office at the NGO forum in Huairou.

With songs, role-play, discussion groups, games and street theater, the Delhi Community Health Workers Program works with young girls to empower them, and to give them the support, knowledge and skills they need to challenge their subordinate status within Indian society. The girls also learn about their rights as women and how to develop their leadership potential. The program with young girls evolved when these children demanded to have their own group modeled after the women's groups that had been organized for women in their reproductive years. This program operates in four large urban slums on the outskirts of New Delhi.

Sexist Media Images and Violence

Studies worldwide show that there is a relationship between viewing violence in the media and subsequent violent action by men against women and children. Consider the combination of violence and "soft" pornography that has permeated our society in the past decades. Husbands rape their wives in TV soap operas; products from liquor to facial soap are sold with women's bodies; products in our country are advertised with near naked women; songs emphasize women's bodies as objects to be used and abused. These negative images have contributed to a society where sexual violence is an everyday occurrence, and on the increase. We are in danger of accepting violence against women as a normal way of life. The problem concerns us all. Following are some misconceptions about violence against women that are often supported by media imagery, contrasted with true descriptions of what is actually happening.

The following list was developed by Women's Media Watch, an organization based in Kingston, Jamaica.

FALSE	TRUE
Accepting violence against women. If a man beats his wife it is a sign physically that he loves her.	The problem concerns us all. Women do not enjoy being abused. It's a sign he wants to control her.
Women are sexually abused or raped because of how they dress or behave.	Rape is never the woman's "fault." It doesn't matter what she wears or where she goes, a woman does not cause rape. The rapist is the one who has committed a crime.
Only certain types of women get sexually abused.	Old women, little girls, disabled women, married women, are all sexually abused — ANY woman can be sexually abused or raped.
Women want to be raped.	Rape is a crime of violence, aggression and power. Women do not enjoy nor ask for rape.

The Platform for Action

Women's Education
(Section B of Chapter IV — Strategic Objectives and Actions)

Strategic Objective
To ensure women's access to quality education and training.

Actions to be taken by governments:

- Provide, by the year 2000, universal access to basic education and completion of primary education by at least 80 percent of primary-school-age children.
- Close the gender gap in primary and secondary education by the year 2005 and achieve universal primary education in all countries before the year 2015.
- Reduce the female illiteracy rate, especially among rural, migrant, refugee, internally displaced and disabled women, to at least half the 1990 level.
- Develop non-discriminatory education and training, including vocational training, especially in science and technology.

Actions to be taken by international organizations and donors:

- Maintain or increase funding levels for education in structural adjustment and economic recovery programs.

Actions to be taken by governments, educational institutions and communities:

- Provide support for child care and services to mothers.
- Create flexible education, training and programs for lifelong learning.

Women and Mass Media

(Section J of Chapter IV — Strategic Objectives and Actions)

Strategic Objective

Enhance the role of traditional and modern communications media to promote awareness of equality between women and men.

Actions to be taken by governments:

- Promote women's equal participation in the media.
- Encourage and recognize women's media networks.
- Promote research and implementation of an information strategy for ensuring a balanced portrayal of women.

Actions to be taken by national and international media systems and NGOs:

- Develop balanced and diverse portrayals of women by the media.
- Encourage the establishment of media watch-groups to monitor the media.
- Train women to make greater use of information technology.

Human Rights for the Girl Child
(Section L of Chapter IV — Strategic Objectives and Actions)

Strategic Objective

Promote the survival, development, and protection of the girl child.

The Rural Women's Social Education Center provides education to girls who must work during the day.

Actions to be taken by governments:

- Ensure girls universal access to and completion of primary education.

- Pass and strictly enforce laws on minimum legal age at marriage.

- Develop and implement policies to protect the rights of girls and ensure equal opportunities for them.

- Encourage efforts to promote changes in negative attitudes and practices toward girls.

- Develop and adopt curricula to improve opportunities for girls in such areas as math, science and technology.

- Protect girl children from economic exploitation; define a minimum age for admission to work.

Actions to be taken by governments, international organizations and NGOs:

- Promote an educational setting without barriers.
- Develop policies and programs giving priority to formal and informal education for girl children.
- Provide public information on removing discriminatory practices against girls in food allocation, nutrition and access to health services.
- Protect the safety and security of girls from all forms of violence, including in the workplace.
- Take appropriate measures, including legislative and administrative, to protect the girl child at home and outside.

The U.S. Commitments to the Platform for Action

Education

The Department of Education will take action on a range of issues to remove barriers facing girls and women with disabilities, those with low incomes, and those from ethnic and racial minorities. Priority initiatives are to:

- Convene a national assembly on girls' and women's education and launch a public awareness campaign to change gender discriminatory policies and practices.

- Convene a leadership forum dedicated to nurturing a new generation of women leaders.

- Intensify efforts to raise the number of family-friendly employers who encourage family involvement in learning.

- Intensify efforts and collaborate with other agencies to promote girls and women in science, mathematics and technology, and combat violence against girls and women.[18]

Note: No commitments were made regarding access to mass media or images of women in the media.

Women Are Good News Campaign[19]

Women Are Good News (WAGN) is a national media watch organization that monitors and advocates for in-creased representation of women on public affairs programs and news commentary. WAGN began in 1991 by conducting a study of the number of male and female commentators on public affairs programs carried by KQED, the San Francisco affiliate of PBS. WAGN found that only 15 percent of the commentators on shows like *Inside Washington*,

Members of Women Are Good News in front of the PBS affiliate in San Francisco protest the under-representation of women on news programs.[20]

18 Contact: Department of Education at (202) 401-1000.
19 For more information contact: Nancy DeStefanis, Executive Director, Women Are Good News, 1550 California Street, Suite 6318, San Francisco, CA 94109
20 Ibid. Photo by Bobby Law.

Washington Week in Review, *The McLaughlin Group*, and *The MacNeil-Lehrer News Hour* were women. In addition, WAGN monitored the local public affairs show produced by KQED, *This Week in Northern California*, and found that KQED's record was equally dismal — only 27 percent of the guests were women.

To dramatize the point that PBS, as a public broadcasting system, had failed to meet its mandate of reflecting the diversity of the American community, a demonstration was held in front of KQED headquarters in San Francisco.

These demonstrations paid off. KQED signed an agreement with WAGN to substantially increase the number of women appearing on their public affairs programs. *Washington Week in Review* has made the most progress; nearly 50 percent of its guests are now women. WAGN continues to monitor local and national public affairs programming because much remains to be done to reach parity. In 1992, WAGN expanded its studies to include the commentary on the networks following the three Presidential debates; not surprisingly, women accounted for only 25 percent of the commentators.

National Media Monitoring Project

Betty Friedan, co-chair of the National Media Monitoring Project remarked, "The drop in news coverage is part of a backlash against women across the country. Coupled with the dismantling of programs designed to reduce or eliminate sex discrimination and the scapegoating of welfare mothers, the decline in news coverage is another sign of the heightened symbolic annihilation of females."

- Front-page female references slid an average of 25 percent in 1994 (the highest since the survey began) to 19 percent in 1996.

- The number of front-page photos containing one or more females dropped from 39 percent in 1994 to 33 percent in 1995.

- Front-page female bylines went up slightly, from an average 33 percent in 1994 to 34 percent in 1995. However, the average has remained somewhat static since 1992 (34 percent; the same in 1993).

- As in previous years, female journalists did not appear to seek out female sources any more often than males.

- The average percentage of stories reported by female correspondents on the nightly news shows on ABC, CBS and NBC dropped from 21 percent in 1994 to 20 percent in 1995.[21]

---

21 Copies of the report are available by calling the president of Unabridged Communications, Junior Bridge, who designed and conducted the survey, at (703) 671-5883.

Women in Black Vigils: Poster Ideas

A very useful and effective education and organizing event is a Women in Black Vigil. It doesn't take much effort or many people to focus public attention on women's rights issues in this very effective way, which has been modeled for us by women from around the world.

Here are a few ideas for posters:

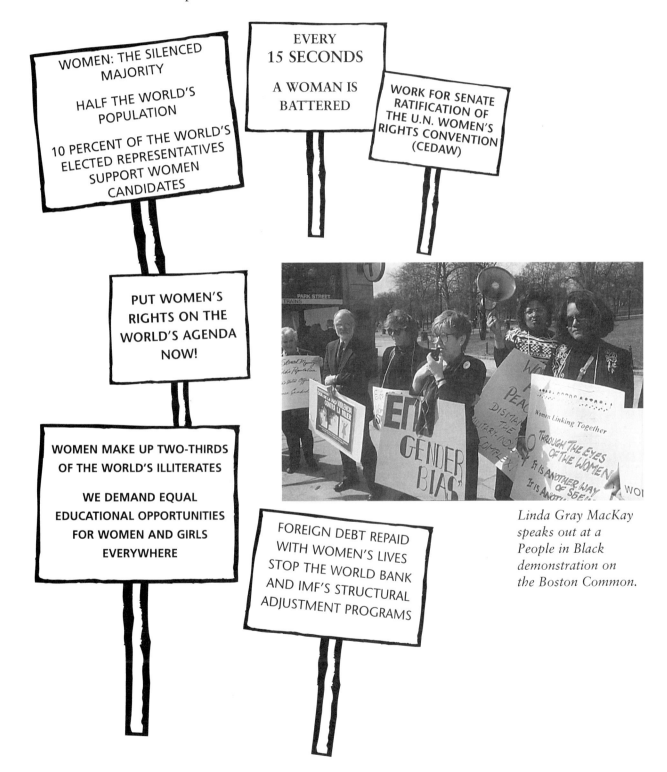

WOMEN: THE SILENCED MAJORITY

HALF THE WORLD'S POPULATION

10 PERCENT OF THE WORLD'S ELECTED REPRESENTATIVES SUPPORT WOMEN CANDIDATES

EVERY 15 SECONDS

A WOMAN IS BATTERED

WORK FOR SENATE RATIFICATION OF THE U.N. WOMEN'S RIGHTS CONVENTION (CEDAW)

PUT WOMEN'S RIGHTS ON THE WORLD'S AGENDA NOW!

WOMEN MAKE UP TWO-THIRDS OF THE WORLD'S ILLITERATES

WE DEMAND EQUAL EDUCATIONAL OPPORTUNITIES FOR WOMEN AND GIRLS EVERYWHERE

FOREIGN DEBT REPAID WITH WOMEN'S LIVES STOP THE WORLD BANK AND IMF'S STRUCTURAL ADJUSTMENT PROGRAMS

Linda Gray MacKay speaks out at a People in Black demonstration on the Boston Common.

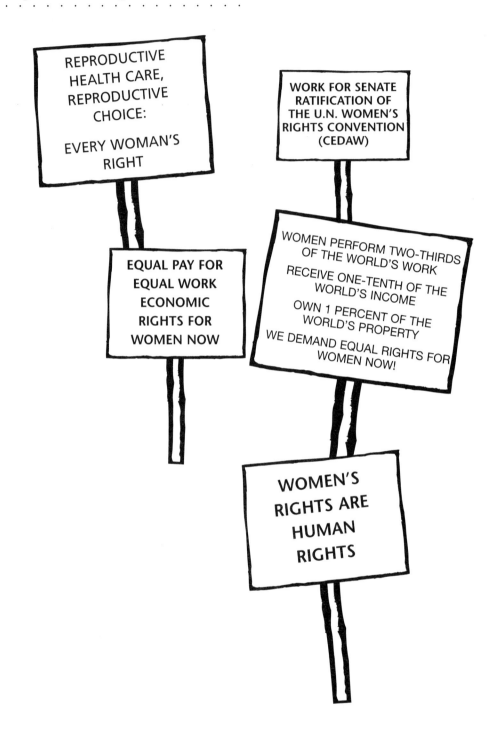

Environmental Sustainability

Critical areas of the platform covered in this session:

Women and the Environment (Section IV.K)

Two-Hour Workshop

Activities	Minutes
Opening Circle	15
Exploration of a Central Issue: Consumption	20
Exploration of a Central Issue: Environmental Justice	25
Break	10
Global Environmental Issues Role Play	30
Platform for Action Positions	5
Brainstorming for Action	5
Journal	5
Assignments for Next Week	3
Closing Circle	2
Total Time:	**120**

Materials

Opening circle centerpiece

Two flip charts

Preparation

Write on flip chart pages:

Consumption (page 221)

Ways to conserve (page 222)

Approaches to coalition building (page 223)

Major causes of global environmental degradation (page 225)

Three-Hour Workshop

Activities	Minutes
Opening Circle	15
Exploration of a Central Issue: Consumption*	35
Exploration of a Central Issue: Environmental Justice*	35
Break	10
Global Environmental Issues Role Play	60
Platform for Action Positions*	10
Brainstorming for Action	5
Journal	5
Assignments for Next Week	3
Closing Circle	2
Total Time:	180

Materials

Opening circle centerpiece

Two flip charts

Preparation

Write on separate flip chart pages:

Consumption (page 221)

Ways to conserve (page 222)

Approaches to coalition building (page 223)

Major causes of global environmental degradation (page 225)

*exercises and/or time added

Opening Circle

(15 minutes)

Objective

To focus the group and to allow for brief personal sharing.

Process

1. Light the candle and read this excerpt from the NGO vision statement:

    > Visualize a world where clean water, food and housing are priorities for each citizen in every village, town and city.

    > Visualize the globe where the massive amounts of money spent on guns and weapons is used instead to end poverty, preserve health and well-being and create sustainable human development.

2. Introduce the following:

    > Since this workshop focuses on environmental sustainability, let's reflect briefly on what **concerns** we have about **environmental degradation** as it affects us **personally**. Share ideas about how lifestyle decisions may contribute to environmental degradation.

Facilitator's Note: Model this sharing by being the first to speak.

Exploration of a Central Issue: Consumption

(20 minutes)

Objective

To consider consumption patterns in the U.S. and how they might change.

Three-hour session: Add 15 minutes to this discussion for a total of 35 minutes.

Process

1. Discuss the following information on consumption:

    > **Consumption patterns** in industrial countries are big contributors to global environmental degradation.

    > Ninety-three million people — roughly the population of Mexico — are added to the world's population each year, and the current total of 5.6 billion could double by the year 2050. About 95 percent of the future population increase will be in the developing world. At the same time, citizens in **industrialized** nations — **one fifth** of the global population — use **two-**

thirds of all **resources** and generate **75 percent** of all **wastes** and pollution.[1]

Facilitator's Note: Prepare the information below on a flip chart in advance.

Consumption

Industrial countries

15-25% of the population consume:

65-75% of resources

85% of all forest products

72% of steel products

75% of energy sources

U.S. Citizens

Represent: 4.6% of world's population

The **Pentagon** generates a **ton of toxic waste per minute,** more than the five largest U.S. chemical companies combined, making it the **largest polluter in the U.S.**

The Pentagon is the **largest sole consumer** of energy in the U.S.[2]

2. Ask the group to break into small groups and discuss:

    - How to change personal consumption patterns

    - How social organization in your communities would have to change (such as better public transportation) to help reduce environmental damage

    - How you could encourage your communities to bring about such changes

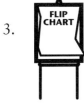

3. After about 10 minutes, bring the groups back together to share ideas with one another. Write the ideas on a flip chart. Once the group has recorded its own ideas, reveal the following list, already written on the flip chart, and highlight any additional ideas the group may not have suggested.

Facilitator's Note: Prepare the following on a chart in advance and add any other ideas you have.

1 Pew Global Leadership.
2 H. Patricia Hynes. *Taking Population out of the Equation,* Amherst, MA.

Ways to Conserve

Bicycling

Public transit use

Car pooling

Composting

Recycling

Food collectives

Flushing less

Taking fewer showers

Exploration of a Central Issue: Environmental Justice

(25 minutes)

Objective

To become aware of inequities surrounding environmental degradation.

Three-hour session: Add 10 minutes to this discussion for a total of 35 minutes.

Process

1. Explain the following:

> The **effects** of a degraded environment are **distributed unequally** throughout the U.S. and the world. Because of a lack of economic resources and political power, **the poor** are more likely to **suffer the adverse effects of exhausted resources and pollution** than the wealthy. The environmental justice movement, which is concerned about this inequity, recognizes that community empowerment and democratic accountability must be part of the solutions to ecological problems.
>
> Women bring an important perspective to the environmental justice movement. The **majority** of the **world's poor** are **female**. In addition, women in the South are more involved in food production and hence they are more immediately affected by decreased productivity of the land. Therefore, these women have both an intimate knowledge and understanding of the local conditions of the land and the link between economic, political and social structures and the environment.[3]

3 Wiltshare, R. *Environment and Development: A Grassroots Women's Perspective*, University of the West Indies, Barbados, 1993.

2. Discuss the following questions:

    Who are the chief polluters in this state?

    If we don't know, how can we find out?

    Where are the most polluted areas located?

    Who lives there?

    How can we help solve environmental problems?

    If you don't live in a neighborhood where there is a toxic waste dump, how could you help support those who do to get it cleaned up?

    What organizations could you contact for information?

3. Review the following material on the flip chart.

Facilitator's Note: Write only the bold-face words on a flip chart before the session begins.

Approaches to Coalition Building

Contact state and regional governmental offices such as the Environmental Protection Agency for information on problem areas and names of local organizations

Contact local grassroots environmental organizations in toxic dump areas

Set up a focused activity with a **limited timeframe** to be undertaken by a diverse group from affected area/non-affected area

4. Explain:

    By forming a coalition around a focused project with a limited timeframe, people from various cultural and income groups are more likely to **take the risk** of working together. Once individuals have an opportunity to work together successfully, future actions may be possible but future action is not the goal. Groups that undertake this type of coalition work are usually successful and provide a positive climate for future undertakings by other similar groups.

    Since the World Conference on Women held in Nairobi in 1985, a dynamic global grassroots movement for environmental justice has emerged, with many women as its leaders. These women met in Beijing to assess further progress made at the 1992 Earth Summit and the 1994 International Conference on Population and Development. The World Conference on Women sought to close the data gap on women's susceptibilities and exposures to environmental hazards, enhance women's knowledge of sound resource use practices, and involve women in environmental decision making.

Break
(10 minutes)

Global Environmental Issues Role Play
(30 minutes)

Objective

To become familiar with issues and strategies from various regions of the globe that relate to the critical area of "Women and the Environment."

Three-hour session: Add 30 minutes to this session for a total of 60 minutes.

Process

1. Discuss the environment as an aspect of the Fourth World Conference on Women.

   As individuals and in thousands of new as well as long-established women's organizations, ranging from community groups to international networks, **women are bringing their unique life experiences,** concerns, perspectives and holistic analyses into the processes through which the United Nations, governments, international financial institutions, transnational corporations and public and private institutions shape policies that effect their lives. **Many of these concerns are environmental.**[5]

2. Ask participants to divide into groups of four, and then count off by four. Ask each person to read the material below associated with her or his number.

   1. Environmental Justice (page 234) and Sustainable Communities (page 235)

   2. The Green Belt Movement (page 237) and Wangari Maathai's story (page 238)

   3. Women and the Environment (page 239) and Winona Laduke's speech (page 241)

   4. The Way Forward (page 243)

Women have moved into the forefront of environmental initiatives because they are typically the first to recognize environmental problems and are most directly affected by them. In Africa, Asia, Latin America and other developing regions, women are often the primary users and managers of land, forests, water and other natural resources.[4]

Bella Abzug

4 "Women and the Environment," in *Women: Looking Beyond 2000*, United Nations, 1995.
5 Bella Abzug, co-founder of the Women's Environment and Development Organization, made this comment in a publication written for the United Nations which was published in preparation for the Beijing conference.

3. Each person will assume the role of a person involved in the issue who wants to inform others, share common concerns and discuss possible solutions to environmental problems.

4. Begin the role play. (20 minutes, or about four minutes for each person)

Facilitator's Note: If one person is dominating a discussion, invite others in the group to share their perspectives. Encouragement from the facilitator can keep discussions more balanced.

5. Review with the entire group the major causes of global environmental degradation.

Facilitator's Note: Write the following on a flip chart prior to the session:

Major Causes of Global Environmental Degradation

Short-term/short-sighted economic approaches

Migration from rural to urban areas

Inadequate planning and resource allocation

Displacement of people

Technologies and development strategies that exploit resources

Militarization

6. While displaying the above causes on the flip chart, paraphrase the following.
    - Economic systems that exploit and misuse nature and people in the drive for short-term and short-sighted gains and profits
    - Urbanization resulting from rural to urban migration and inadequate planning and resource allocation in towns and cities cause degradation of the urban environment
    - The displacement of small farmers and indigenous peoples by agribusiness, timber, mining, and energy corporations, often with encouragement and assistance of international financial institutions, and with the complicity of national governments
    - Technologies designed to exploit, not preserve natural resources (fossil fuel technology, mineral extraction, unsustainable forest harvesting)
    - Militarization including war, military bases, arms production and nuclear testing divert resources from human

needs, poison the natural environment and perpetuate the militarization of culture, encouraging violence against women and men

7. Summarize the information in the box that follows:

The rapid pace of environmental degradation is a growing concern for communities around the globe. Listed below are a few facts that illustrate the severity of the situation.

State of the Environment

Per capita water supply is a third lower than it was in 1970 due to the addition of 1.8 billion people to the population. Twenty-six countries, with a combined population of 230 million, face water shortages. Many of those countries have high population growth rates.

Eleven percent of the planet's soils have been severely degraded in the last 45 years, a total area of nearly three billion acres, the size of India and China combined.

During the 1980s, tropical forests were lost at a rate of almost 42 million acres a year. At this rate, tropical forests, which are home to 50 percent of all plant and animal species as well as people, will be gone in 115 years.[6]

Platform for Action Positions on the Environment

(5 minutes)

Objective

To become acquainted with the platform's position on the environment.

Three-hour session: Add five minutes to this session for a total of 10 minutes.

Process

1. Discuss women's role in environmental policy making:

In most developing countries, women are responsible for **obtaining water and fuel** and **managing household** consumption. As a result, they are especially concerned with the quality and sustainability of the **environment**. Yet, because women are largely absent from **decision making**, environmental policies often do not take into account the close links between their daily lives and the environment.

6 PEW Global Stewardship Initiative.

All regions of the world are affected by accelerated resource depletion and environmental degradation, due to drought, desertification, deforestation, natural disasters and polluting substances. Awareness of these disasters has increased markedly in the past decade. However, **women** are still largely absent from public decision making in environmental management, protection and conservation although they are among **critical actors at the grassroots level**.

The Platform for Action argues that **women**, particularly indigenous women, hold **pivotal roles** in **environmental conservation**. It states that the strategic actions needed for sound environmental management require a **holistic and multidisciplinary** approach.

Former UUSC project partner, Long Live the Peasant Association in Burkina Faso, Africa bought carts to help women transport water to their homes more efficiently.

The platform seeks to remedy this situation by advocating for:

- Increasing the proportion of **women at all levels of decision making**, planning and technical management, and control environmental degradation

- Ensuring the **integration of women's needs, concerns and perspectives** in policies and programs for environmentally sound and sustainable development

- Developing **environmentally-sound technology in consultation with women**

- Expanding **consumer awareness**, which will lead to more sustainable patterns of consumption

Facilitator's Note: Refer participants to the background and resource section, which highlights some of the specific recommendations of the platform in these areas.

Brainstorming for Action

(5 minutes)

Objective

To collect ideas that can be used to formulate a local plan of action.

Process

1. To begin to formulate a local plan for action, use two flip charts.

2. Ask participants to make a **theoretical list** of possible activities they would like to undertake that relate to the topics of this workshop. Encourage them to mention whatever comes to mind, regardless of their ability to perform the action.

3. On the second flip chart, list **organizations** that participants know about which are addressing these issues.

Facilitator's Note: Attach lists from previous brainstorming sessions to the walls and encourage participants to add ideas or resources to any of the lists. All the lists will be used in the last session when the group develops a viable action plan.

4. Summarize the information in the box that follows. Remind participants that more information about these programs that could be helpful for local action planning is included in the background and resource section.

Successful Strategies for Action

The Action for Cancer Prevention Campaign is an effort being organized by the Women's Environment and Development Organization (WEDO) to take action to prevent cancer, particularly breast cancer, as well as other diseases caused or triggered by preventable environmental factors. In addition to organizing regional conferences and a worldwide conference, WEDO supports local efforts to educate and act around this issue.

Licking River Roundup is an effort organized by the City of Newark, Ohio, in close collaboration with numerous community organizations and citizens, to involve the public in cleaning up litter and toxic substances that are polluting their local river and destroying wildlife habitat.

Journal Writing

(5 minutes)

Objective

To give participants an opportunity to record items they wish to remember or process.

Process

1. Ask participants to take a few minutes to write down on the journal page for this session any reactions, additional areas they wish to pursue, questions they want to research or action ideas and possible contacts they can think of. If time is short, encourage them to write these down between sessions and, when appropriate, add them to the flip chart pages that will be posted at each session.

Assignments for Next Week

(2 minutes)

Process

1. Urge participants to read "A Guide to Corporate Welfare" and the "Foreign Policy Fact Sheet."

2. Ask participants to do the "Let Us Slice the Pie!" exercise and bring it back next week to compare with other participants' responses.

3. Review action ideas suggested throughout the series and keep budget issues in mind as you contemplate possible group action strategies, which will be decided in the last session.

Closing Circle

(2 minutes)

Objective

To provide an opportunity to connect symbolically with others before separating.

Process

1. Encourage participants to gather in a circle around the centerpiece, holding hands. Ask someone to share a phrase summarizing their experience of the session.

2. Ask for volunteers to read part of the poem "Let Us Hold Hands" by Pat Mora or suggest that the group sing the song "Sister Carry On" by Carolyn McDade.

Women are presenting themselves... as dynamic forces and potential agents of progress and change. This new brand of women's politics no longer presents the perspective of victims, but rather the assumption that women possess rights and can enforce legal claims. We support the process of worldwide action for women with a view to achieving sustainable and just development.[7]

**Rita Griebhaber,
Green Party Member
of Parliament, Germany**

In this time that fears faith, let us hold hands.
In this time that fears the unwashed, let us hold hands.
In this time that fears age, let us hold hands.
In this time that fears touch, let us hold hands,
brown hands, trembling hands, callused hands, frail
hands, white hands, tired hands, angry hands, new
hands, cold hands, black hands, bold hands.

In towns and cities and villages, mano a mano, hand in hand,
in mountains and valleys and plains, a ring of women circling
the world, the ring strong in our joining,
around our petaled home, this earth, let us join hands.

Excerpt from the poem *Let Us Hold Hands* by Pat Mora

7 Griebhaber, Rita. "Making Human Rights and Democracy a Reality for Women."

Sister, Carry On

With spirit

Words and Music by Carolyn McDade

Sis-ter, car-ry on — Sis-ter, car-ry on — It

may be rock-y and it may be rough, but sis-ter, car-ry on - -

Sister, don't lose the dream
Sister, don't lose the dream
Don't sell out for no short time gain
Sister, don't lose the dream

Sister, don't settle too soon
Sister, don't settle too soon
Til everybody's got their rights
Sister, don't settle too soon

Sister, we share the way
Sister, we share the way
Heart to heart and hand to hand
Sister, we share the way

Stand in solidarity
Stand in solidarity
Together bring a brand new day
Stand in solidarity

Sister, carry on
Sister, carry on
May be rocky and it may be rough
But, Sister, carry on.

Journal Page

Session 5

Background
and Resources
on Women and the Environment

Notes on the Environment

- During the 1980s, tropical forests were lost at a rate of almost 42 million acres a year. At this rate, tropical forests, which are home to 50 percent of the world's population of all plant and animal species as well as to people, will no longer be in existence in 115 years.[8]

- Overpackaging of products is particularly prevalent in the countries of the North and produces mounds of unrecycled, non-biodegradable waste.

- American women, who do 73 percent of U.S. household shopping and make the health care decisions in 71 percent of all households, repeatedly tell pollsters they look for "green" products. Of 37 million Americans classed as "strongly environmentalist," 60 percent are women.[9]

- Some environmental pollutants — especially pesticides — mimic the effects of the hormone estrogen in the body, and may cause breast cancer and endometriosis. There were only 21 reported cases of endometriosis in the world 70 years ago; today there are 5 million cases in the U.S. alone.[10]

Environmental Justice

The developed world, despite its stable population levels, threatens the resource base and biospheric system much more than the developing world with its rising population. The example of deforestation is instructive. While local populations can nibble around the edges of rain forests, it takes enormous capital investments to deforest on a major scale. The massive highway project that opened up the Brazilian rain forest to grand-scale exploitation could not have been built by the local peasants; it was financed by the World Bank. As a U.S. official described the situation, "Yes, rapidly growing numbers of peasants contribute to tropical deforestation, but on a global scale their activities are probably more akin to picking up branches and twigs after commercial chain saws have done their work."[11]

The effects of a degraded environment are distributed unequally throughout the U.S. and the world. Because the poor lack economic resources and political power, they are more likely to suffer the adverse effects of exhausted resources and pollution than the wealthy. In many countries, particularly in the South, livelihood becomes for the poor a question not of profit, but of survival. Pressed by such urgent conditions in the short

8 *1993 Information Please Environmental Almanac*, NY: Houghton Mifflin Co., 1993.
9 Ottman, Jacuelyn A., *Green Marketing*.
10 U.S. National Report.
11 Sagoff, Mark. "Population, Nature, and the Environment" in *Beyond the Numbers: A Reader on Population, Consumption and the Environment*. Laurie Ann Mazur, ed., Washington, DC, Island Press, 1994.

run, the poor must often resort to practices that will be environmentally detrimental in the long run. When this happens, not only does the environment suffer, but the poor further limit the resources available to them. For example, the governments of many South American countries, such as Brazil, actively encourage resettlement, farming and ranching (and hence destruction) of their rain forests. This is in part designed to relieve the pressures of the urban poor on the infrastructure. However, the nutrient-poor soil of the rain forests is ill-suited for such development; low productivity turns these settlements into new areas where the poor struggle.

The environmental justice movement recognizes that distributive justice, community empowerment, and democratic accountability must be part of the solutions to ecological problems. Women bring a vital perspective to the environmental justice movement and women in low-income communities of color often face the worst environmental hazards. In the U.S., a recent study showed that people of color were more likely to work in or live near landfills, incinerators, hazardous waste and other polluting industries. Housing in these communities often contains lead-based paint and asbestos.[12] Because the urban crisis threatens personal health, family, and the neighborhood community, women of color have frequently found themselves in leadership roles. Women lead and make up the majority of membership of the groups Native Americans for a Clean Environment, Mothers of East Los Angeles, and Concerned Citizens of South Central Los Angeles. The organized environmental efforts by women of color have great potential and are seen as a threat by corporate elites.[13]

Sustainable Communities[14]

"Sustainability" in its contemporary use means maintaining a lifestyle that will meet the needs of the present life on earth without compromising the ability of future generations to meet its needs. The elements necessary to create a sustainable community include:

- Respecting, protecting, and restoring the natural environment

- Using no more than we truly need

- Sharing equitably with others living with us on our planet

- Leaving our children at least as much as we have enjoyed in the way of possibilities, opportunities, and quality of life

12 International Institute for Environment and Development.
13 Bullard, Robert D. *Confronting Environmental Racism*, Boston: South End Press, 1993.
14 Based on findings at the U.N. Conference on Environment and Development (also known as the Earth Summit) held in Rio de Janeiro, 1992.

Earth Friendly Living

Select three practices from the following lists that you are not currently doing and begin to add them to your habits.

Recycling

- Separate aluminum, glass, newspaper, cardboard, white paper and colored paper before recycling.
- Buy products in recyclable containers.
- Avoid plastics.
- Avoid disposable plates, cups and utensils.
- Use cloth diapers rather than disposable diapers.
- Use rags instead of paper towels.
- Use coffee mugs instead of disposable cups.
- Use both sides of sheets of paper.
- Recycle used motor oil.
- Compost food wastes and yard debris.
- Mend and repair rather than discard and replace.
- Buy packaged goods in bulk.
- Buy used goods (from thrift stores and garage sales).
- Take your grocery bags back to the store for reuse or use a permanent bag.

Transportation

- Use public transportation, carpool, bike or walk.
- Drive a fuel efficient car.
- Keep your car well-tuned.
- Live close to your place of work.
- Call ahead before you shop and consolidate your errands.

Trees

- Plant trees in your community.
- Plant fruit & nut trees in your backyard.
- Do not buy products made from tropical hardwoods.

Hazardous Products

- Use biodegradable soaps and detergents.
- Use alternatives to toxic household products.
- Dispose of household hazardous wastes properly.
- Use rechargeable batteries.
- Purchase appliances with alternatives to ozone-damaging chlorofluoro-carbons.[15]
- Think about purchasing a car without air conditioning to avoid using CFCs.
- Purchase a halon-free fire extinguisher.

Home Energy Use

- Insulate, caulk and weather-strip your home.
- Install a timer on your thermostat.
- Insulate floors with carpeting
- Install double-paned windows.
- Wear a sweater rather than turn up the thermostat.
- Install a solar water heater.
- Insulate your water heater and storage tank.
- Keep your water heater at 120 degrees.
- Use energy efficient appliances
- Use florescent in place of incandescent light bulbs.
- Turn off lights and appliances when not in use.
- Plant trees to shade your house in the summer.
- Hang your clothes in the sun to dry.
- Keep lint screen and outside exhaust on dryer clean.

15 Chlorine is the common link in many of the world's most notorious environmental poisons — dioxin, DDT, Agent Orange, PCBs and the ozone-destroying chlorofluorocarbons (CFCs) are all based on chlorine. These and other chlorine-containing substances dominate government lists of "priority pollutants" that threaten health and environment. Pulp and paper companies use chlorine and chlorine dioxide to bleach woodpulp bright white, producing and discharging thousands of organichlorides- including dioxins, furans, and other highly toxic, persistent substances — into the environment and into the paper products themselves. Pulp mill discharges have caused severe damage to fish and ecosystem balance in lakes, rivers and seas across the world, and people who eat fish caught downstream from chlorine-bleached pulp mills are at cancer risks as high as one in 50, according to U.S. EPA. Chlorine can be replaced with oxygen-based bleaches, including hydrogen peroxide, chlorine-free white pulp and paper that is suitable for the most damaging applications. By 1996, chlorine-free paper will account for 70 percent of all printing and writing paper in Germany and Scandinavia.

Water Conservation

- Install a water-saving showerhead.
- Take showers rather than baths.
- Install a space-occupier in your toilet.
- Install sink faucet aerators.
- Turn off the water between rinses when shaving or brushing teeth.
- Use a broom rather than hose to wash walkways.
- Do not let the hose run when you wash your car.
- Wash your car with a bucket of soapy water.
- Water plants and lawn in the morning to minimize evaporation.
- Install a drip-irrigation watering system.
- Plant drought-tolerant plants.

Pesticides/Eating Habits

- Buy organic foods to discourage pesticide use.
- Grow your own food using alternatives to pesticides.
- Buy foods without additives and preservatives.
- Avoid highly processed foods.
- Support food co-ops and farmers' markets.
- Buy foods grown or produced locally.
- Be creative with leftover food.

Activism

- Educate yourself and others on environmental issues.
- Purchase from environmentally responsible businesses.
- Know the voting records of your elected officials.
- Write letters to your representatives supporting environmental action.
- Get involved in local politics to influence local environmental policy decisions.
- Take time to learn about and enjoy nature.

The Green Belt Movement

The Green Belt Movement, organized by Wangari Maathai, addresses the need of rural people and the urban poor for wood fuel, fencing and building materials, forest preservation, water catchment and green spaces in urban centers. In addition, the movement addresses the issues of malnutrition and hunger and the low economic status of women. To enhance leadership skills, the movement informs and educates participants about the linkages between degradation of the environment and development policies. The organization tries to empower women in particular and the civil society in general so that individuals can take action and break the vicious circle of poverty and under-development. It encourages women to create jobs, prevent soil loss, slow the processes of desertification and loss of biodiversity and plant indigenous food crops. In the process the women learn new farming techniques. Thus far, women have planted 10 million trees.[16]

16 From a monograph distributed by Wangari Maathai at the Beijing conference.

Wangari Maathai's Story

Wangari Maathai was present, outspoken and circulating her latest ideas in a self-published pamphlet at the Fourth World Conference on Women in Beijing in September 1995. Wangari Maathai is not one to mince words. She recently addressed a meeting packed with distinguished Africans, diplomats and international development experts. "Many leaders have been unaccountable to their people, have stolen from their people by diverting aid loans and other resources into personal fortunes," said Wangari Maathai. Such boldness has earned her a reputation as a troublemaker at home in Kenya. She was the first woman in black Africa to gain a Ph.D. and the first Kenyan woman professor at the University of Nairobi. But when she tried to run for political office the ruling party would not accept her as a candidate. Then the university would not have her back — and nor would anyone else. Living on her savings, she worked as a volunteer for the National Council of Women in Kenya, encouraging professional women to work with rural women. It was then that the link between women and environment became apparent to her.

Rural women spend most of their time traveling long distances to fetch increasingly scarce water and firewood. Their land is poor and they grow crops like tea and coffee to sell on international markets, rather than food. Prices are so low they cannot feed their families. Wangari Maathai organized women to plant trees for firewood. She paid them for each tree that survived — personal income for them, when traditionally only men touched the family's money.

That was in 1977, and it was the beginning of the Green Belt Movement, which has so far planted 10 million trees. Now she devotes all her time to it and aims to start a Pan-African movement. Maathai has also been active in the urban environment. When the city commission in Nairobi proposed to allow construction on the site of Jeevanjee Gardens she encouraged people to speak out against it and organized a meeting between the public and developers. The project was eventually canceled.

She has also campaigned to save Uhuru Park — the most important open space in downtown Nairobi — from being turned into an office complex, conference center and shopping mall. "I'm not opposed to development, but development that plunders resources like forest, land, air and food, oblivious of the needs of tomorrow, is short-sighted and self-defeating," said Maathai. Some politicians said it was "un-African" for a woman to stand up and answer back when men spoke. She was detained, then released on bail, and charged with 'publishing false rumors." But Wangari Maathai has never stopped talking and writing. She asserts, "Unless people speak out and demand environmental sustainability, our children will be condemned to the concrete, unhealthy jungles typical of many unplanned, overcrowded and polluted cities of other countries." There has been a price to pay for the Uhuru project controversy. Developers closed the Green Belt offices. Wangari Maathai now works out of her home. Apart from two rooms where she and her youngest son live, the house has been given over to office space. "People in the North who give aid don't know when the aid is not reaching the people." says Maathai. "And the working people don't know aid borrowed in their name is stolen by their leaders and that they are paying for it."

Unfairness and hypocrisy anger her, as when the North pays next to nothing for crops but charges high prices for the pesticides to grow them. Maathai says that people love to blame the victims, accusing Africans of not working hard enough and not knowing what they are doing. "But those people are working," she argues, "they get up at five in the morning and work till late at night and they don't know why things are so bad." Maathai said, "At 50, I know I have maybe another 20 active years. Before anything happens to me I want to know that the seeds have really been planted, that things will carry on changing."

Her ideas are being put to the test more quickly than she may have feared. An active member of the Opposition Forum Group, she went on a hunger strike with other women in Uhuru Park, pressing for the release of political prisoners. On March 4, 1992, she was clubbed unconscious by police and taken to a hospital in Nairobi and listed in critical condition.[17]

Women and the Environment

Women's Role in Environmental Sustainability

All over the world women contribute substantially to food production, processing and preparation. Their agricultural work often provides women with valuable knowledge about local ecosystems, including soil features, multiple uses of crops, and health care for small livestock. Their experience is vital to maintaining crop diversity.[18]

In rural Botswana, frequent drought has threatened local livelihoods that depend on agriculture and livestock raising. The leaders of a local NGO, Thusano Lefatsheng, realized that indigenous food and medicinal plants, already well adapted to periodic drought, could provide an important alternative source of income for local women. The group researches, purchases, processes, and markets indigenous products and promotes new cash crops. The group has also developed a profitable, sustainable farming system that includes traditional and new crops, trees, medicinal plants and livestock. over 1,500 people were working on this project by 1989, mostly poor women from drought stricken areas.[19]

17 Williamson-Fien, Jane. "Women's Voices - Teaching Resources on Women and Development," Windsor: Global Learning Centre Incorporated, 1993, in *Doing the Gender Boogie*, Ten Days for World Development, Debbie Culbertson, Toronto, Canada, 1995.
18 World Resources Institute, "World Resources 1994-95."
19 Ibid.

For city planners, bureaucrats, politicians, developers and loggers, the very word "land" conjures up grandiose plans leaving them wide-eyed and excited about the profits to come. However, if you have lived and worked on the land for generations then land is a source of livelihood and spirituality, establishing links with the past, present and future. Many villages are threatened by outside encroachments. Their indigenous knowledge is subdued by dominant cultures. In the shift from subsistence farming to cash crops, rural women have been relegated from having equal access or possession of customary lands to being landless or waged laborers due to resettlement and plantation schemes.[20]

The Delhi Community Health Workers help foster the use of traditional herbal remedies passed down from mother to daughter.

The Green Revolution: Women-Centered Principles

The Green Revolution encouraged Third-World farmers to plant high-yielding varieties of crops, often hybrids, which require pesticides and expensive fertilizers. Insects develop resistance to pesticides and new ones must be developed to eradicate them. In addition, the pesticides have negative health effects on farmers.

Vandana Shiva, a physicist and director of the Foundation for Science, Technology, and Natural Resource Policy in Dehrahun, India, makes an elegant and compelling defense of the regenerative capacity of life, which she terms the "feminine principle." She links women's age-old roles in growing food, storing grain, and selecting seed with their roles in human reproduction, that is, the conservation and reproduction of genetic potential through the generations as creative and evolutionary processes of self-renewal.

Shiva has launched an international campaign against genetic engineering of seeds and food by transnational corporations, a practice that she charges deprives local food growers of their property rights and sustainable approach to agriculture and exposes consumers to health risks. The sterile hybrid seeds, which cannot reproduce themselves, and industrialized agriculture, which is endlessly repetitive and uniform, supplying processing factories and mass markets intolerant of diversity, are far removed from the power of self-renewal.

20 All Women's Action Society.

Local Women Lead

In the Comas District in Lima, Peru, most residents are extremely poor and lack access to health care, education and employment. In January 1991, a cholera epidemic broke out that could have been devastating. Garbage had accumulated in many areas, attracting large rodents and insects; latrines were poorly maintained; and water was often stored in unsanitary conditions. More than half the residents did not have potable water or adequate sewage.

In response, a Peruvian NGO obtained commitments from 200 women coordinators and approximately 1,500 mothers on its grassroots committees to start a public clean-up campaign. They removed the garbage, fumigated 5,000 centers where milk was prepared and distributed, and cleaned 3,000 latrines. Notices about the epidemic were placed in public places and 10,000 pamphlets were distributed describing how to prevent the disease from spreading. Another NGO supported the effort by giving weekly training on hygiene and environmental sanitation to 100 women coordinators. As a result of all these efforts, the epidemic was contained.[21]

Winona Laduke, Director of the Indigenous Women's Network

Excerpted from her address to the NGO Forum on Women, Huairou, China

Nations of indigenous peoples are not, by and large represented at the United Nations. Most decisions today are made by the 180 or so member states to the United Nations. Those states, by and large, have been in existence for only 200 years or less, while most nations of indigenous peoples, with few exceptions, have been in existence for thousands of years. Ironically, there would likely be little argument in this room, that most decisions made in the world today are actually made by some of the 47 transnational corporations and their international financiers whose annual income is larger than the gross national product for many countries of the world.

This is a centerpiece of the problem. Decision making is not made by those who are affected by those decisions, people who live on the land, but corporations, with an interest which is entirely different than that of the land, and the people, or the women of the land. This brings forth a fundamental question, What gives these corporations like CONOCO, SHELL, EXXON, DIASHAWA, ITT, RIO TINTO ZINC, and the WORLD BANK, a right which supersedes or is superior to my human right to live on my land, or that of my family, my community, my nation, our nation, and to us as women? What law gives that right to them, not any law of the creator or Mother Earth. Is that right contained within their wealth that which is historically acquired immorally, unethically,

21 World Resources Institute.

through colonialism, imperialism, and paid for with the lives of millions of people, or species of plants and entire ecosystems. They should have no such right. And we clearly, as women, and as indigenous peoples demand and will recover that right, that right of self-determination and to determine our destiny and that of our future generations.

The origins of this problem lie with the predator/prey relationship industrial society has developed with the Earth, and subsequently, the people of the Earth. This same relationship exists vis-à-vis women. We, collectively find that we are often in the role of the prey, to a predator society, whether for sexual discrimination, exploitation, sterilization, absence of control over our bodies, or being the subjects of repressive laws and legislation in which we have no voice. This occurs on an individual level, but, equally, and more significantly on a societal level. It is also critical to point out at this time, that most matrilineal societies, in which governance and decision making are largely controlled by women have been obliterated from the face of the Earth by colonialism, and subsequently industrialism. The only matrilineal societies which exist in the world today are those of Indigenous nations. We are the remaining matrilineal societies, yet we also face obliteration.

Finally, while we may, here in the commonness of this forum, speak of the common rights of all women, and those fundamental human rights to self determination, it is incumbent upon me to point out the fundamental inequalities of this situation, so long as the predator continues, so long as the middle, the temperate countries of the world continue to drive an increasing level of consumption, and, frankly continue to export both the technologies and drive for this level of consumption to other countries of the world — there will be no safety for the human rights of women, rights of indigenous peoples, and to the basic protection for the Earth, from which we get our life. Consumption causes the commodification of the sacred, the natural world, cultures, and the commodification of children and women.

From the United States position, consider the following points: The U.S. is the largest energy market in the world. The average American consumes seven times as many wood products per capita as anywhere else in the industrialized world, and overall that country consumes one third of the world's natural resources. In Canada, by comparison, per capita energy consumption is the highest in the world. Levels of consumption in the industrial world drive destruction of the world's rain forests, drive production of nuclear wastes, and production of PCBs, dioxin and other lethal chemicals, which devastate the body of our Mother earth, and our own bodies. Unless we speak, and take meaningful action to address these levels of consumption, and subsequently, the exports of these technologies, and levels of consumption to other countries (like the international market for nuclear reactors), we will never have any security for our individual human rights as Indigenous women, and for our security as women.

If we are to seek and struggle for common ground for all women, it is essential to struggle for this issue. For, it is not, frankly, that the women of the dominant society in so called first world countries should have equal pay, and equal status, if that pay and status continues to be based on a consumption model which is not only unsustainable, but causes constant violation of the human rights of women and nations elsewhere in the world. It is essential to collectively struggle to recover our status as Daughters of the Earth. In that is our strength, and security, not in the predator, but in the security of our Mother for our future generations. In that, we can ensure our security as the Mothers of our Nations.

The Way Forward

This statement was adapted from a paper prepared by Development Alternatives with Women for a New Era (DAWN) for the 1992 UNCED Earth Summit. DAWN is a network of women from the South involved in research, action and policy making concerning environment and development issues. The paper draws on the perspectives of poor women and their experiences in defining, coping with and challenging environmental degradation. DAWN proposes that the women's and environmental movements work together to encourage recognition of the need for the following steps necessary for human development and the sound management of the environment.

First, it is imperative that arrangements for natural resource management be pivoted on people and the community.

Second, present trends lead to more external control and market decisions. The indication is for greater community control.

Third, food is produced by those who cannot afford to consume it and consumed by those who do not produce it. Inappropriate technology and the ever-increasing consumption levels of a minority of the world's population is putting severe stress on natural environments. At the same time, quick-fix solutions, which focus on symptoms of poverty and imbalance identify local populations as the source of their poverty and environmental degradation. Population control has therefore become a major theme within the environmental debate. The focus on population per se has gathered great currency in spite of the fact that:

a) The data have repeatedly demonstrated that population size decreases where women are educated and their economic and social status is improved.

b) There is no demonstrated relationship at the micro level between population size and environmental degradation.

c) Empowering women and providing women with reproductive health care is essential to giving them control over their bodies.

Sustainable livelihoods must be the foundation of sustainable development. The carrying capacity of the earth cannot sustain present levels of material resource consumption of the industrialized world, however, this carrying capacity is not limited to sustaining the well being of people. Research has indicated that for every major resource, including energy, food and minerals, the wealthy industrialized states, which have least of the world's population, consume the greatest portion of the earth's resources and generate the most waste. A global and national policy thrust — which provides the basis for material as well as spiritual well being, cultural integrity and basic human rights — will yield more effective and long-term results for balanced population growth and sustainable development.

Fourth, the international community has to address the new international economic order as one involving mutual responsibilities and requiring justice with equity as a matter of priority. International financial institutions must identify human development and sustainable livelihoods as primary objectives of development. These institutions must be more gender balanced, more democratic and be made accountable to communities.

Fifth, it is imperative to alter affluent lifestyles and eliminate over-consumption.[22]

The Platform for Action
Environment
(Section K of Chapter IV)

Strategic Objective
Promote women's contribution to managing and safeguarding the environment.

Actions to be taken by governments include:
- Ensuring opportunities for women to participate in environmental decision-making at all levels
- Reducing risks to women from known environmental hazards
- Facilitating and increasing women's access to information and education

22 Wiltshire, Rosa. Environment and Development: Grassroots Women's Perspectives, 1992.

- Promoting research on women and the environment

Actions to be taken by governments, international organizations and the private sector:

- Considering gender impact in the work of the appropriate U.N. bodies and encourage design of projects that benefit women

- Developing gender-sensitive database and support research on women and sustainable development

U.S. Commitments to the Platform for Action

While the U.S. Commitments to the Platform for Action do not contain any specific actions to be taken on behalf of the environment, Jean Nelson, counselor to the administrator of the U.S. Environmental Protection Agency and member of the U.S. Delegation to the Fourth World Conference on Women, made this statement during the conference in Beijing:

> "The protection of the public health and its environment — our air, land and water — is critical to the economic security and the well-being of the people of our country — and all countries. It is important to every woman in the world."

Why do we think it is important for women's lives that environmental issues are fully integrated into the agenda for the next century? The statistics are startling.

- Two Americans out of every five live in areas where the air is too polluted to meet national health standards.

- Asthma is on the rise, especially among women. Thirty million Americans get their drinking water from systems that have violated our public health standards. Thousands of people in Wisconsin fell ill from contaminated drinking water in 1993; 100 died.

- Millions of American children — including 50 percent of poor black children — have toxic levels of lead in their blood.

- The incidence of breast cancer is soaring. One American woman in eight will contract the disease.

The United States sought to assure equal access for women to education — including the information they need on environmental hazards and actions they can take to protect the environment. The platform is clear. Access to education, information and resources to further environmental protection and natural resource management are critical to achieving a world of equality, development and peace.

The U.S. took a leadership role in pursuing the incorporation of all of these issues into the Platform for Action. In our country there is a tradition within Native American culture of making decisions for the seventh generation. We are confident that this document will affect the future for women and men, girls and boys, to the seventh generation.

Contacting the Environmental Protection Agency to find out what actions they are taking to implement this statement is a first step toward determining how we can hold the U.S. government accountable to the Platform for Action on this issue.

Cancer Prevention Campaign

Lung, cervical and breast cancer are the leading cause of cancer deaths worldwide. Breast cancer is by far the most prevalent type of cancer in women worldwide. Over the past few years, the incidence of breast cancer has reached epidemic proportion. Each year, it is responsible for 161,000 deaths in industrialized countries and 147,000 deaths in developing countries. In the past two decades, rates of breast cancer deaths have increased much more rapidly in developing nations than in industrial ones. Worldwide, breast cancer rates have increased 26 percent since 1980. One in eight women in industrialized countries is expected to develop breast cancer over an 85-year life span; 30 years ago this number was one in 20.

The Women, Health and the Environment Action for Cancer Prevention Campaign is a follow-up activity to the Women's Agenda 21 demands from WEDO's World Women's Congress, which was held in preparation for the U.N. Conference on Environment and Development in 1992. The campaign seeks to promote women as participants in the development and implementation of sustainable and equitable policy.

Since 1993, WEDO has worked with women's groups and public agencies across the United States and internationally to co-convene public hearings and educational conferences to foster Action for Cancer Prevention. The public hearings and conferences inform, link and mobilize the public to act on the preventable links to cancer. WEDO's "Guide to Holding a Public Hearing" is available on request.[23]

Licking River Roundup

For the past seven years, on the first Saturday after Labor Day, hundreds of volunteers from Licking County and beyond have gathered to help clean and beautify the river. Canoeists scour the bed and banks pulling out tires and trash. The River Roundup has been successful in keeping the river cleaner than it has been in years, providing habitat for herons and ducks, a life for fish and fishermen. It has inspired like efforts on other waterways in the area. The Licking River Roundup is sponsored by the City of Newark Division of Recycling and Litter Prevention.[24]

23 To order the Guide or obtain more information about the campaign, please contact: WEDO, 355 Lexington Avenue, 3rd Floor, New York, NY 10017-6603, (212) 973-0325; E-mail: wedo@igc.apc.org.
24 For more information about the project, including a booklet on how to undertake your own cleanup effort, contact: Marti Kolb, Coordinator, Tel: (614) 349-6699.

Cooking Co-op

Those of us living in the United States need to reduce our consumption. One innovative way to share resources is to form a cooking cooperative. As many families as are interested in being a part of the cooperative would take turns cooking for all of the members of the cooperative. People in the cooperative do not usually reside at the same location. Whomever cooks the food for a given evening would deliver it to the homes of others in the cooperative. The rest of the evenings, dinner would be delivered to them by the other members of the co-op. A good way to organize such a cooperative would be to appeal to people in the same church or community organization.[25]

25 Provided by Vail Weller, a student at Starr King School for the Ministry.

Assignments for
Session Six

In order to become more familiar with the way that the U.S. government divides up its scarce resources, and in preparation for the final session when the group will make action plans, read "A Guide to Corporate Welfare" and the "Foreign Policy Fact Sheet" and do the "Federal Budget Pie Chart Exercise" developed by the Women's Action for A New Direction (WAND). Bring the chart back next week to compare it with other participants' responses. In the next session, we will take a budget test to see how much we know about the federal budget. Keep budget issues in mind as you contemplate possible action strategies.

A Guide to Corporate Welfare[26]
Adapted from the *Corporate Welfare Guidebook*

The average taxpayer pays $415 a year for families on welfare, while paying three times that much to subsidize corporate profits. Most taxpayers understand that the government spends money on social welfare. Few pay attention to the ways in which government spends much more money on corporate welfare through preferential tax breaks, tax credits and tax loopholes.

Through the details in the tax code, favored corporations and businesses receive generous and unfair shares of federal support, amounting to $70 billion a year according to a recent Congressional Budget Office report.[27]

While American taxpayers complain that their hard-earned tax dollars are wasted on welfare programs, few realize that the most expensive federal "welfare" clients are not teenage moms, but wealthy multinational corporations.

Entitlement Spending
Entitlement status means a guaranteed benefit. Entitlement spending refers to programs that make payments to any person, business or government entity that matches eligibility criteria established by Congress. At over $840 billion, this is the largest and fastest growing part of the federal budget. Once enacted into law, entitlement programs are permanent and categorized as "mandatory spending."

For example, entitlement programs have constituted the vast majority of programs that serve as the social safety net, including Medicaid, Medicare, Social Security, Aid to Families with Dependent Children (AFDC), food stamps and veterans' benefits. Medicare (health care for the elderly) and Medicaid (health care for the poor and disabled) are the fastest growing entitlements.

26 Adapted from the *Corporate Welfare Guidebook*, Tax Watch, 910 17th St. N.W., Suite 413, Washington, DC, 20006, Tel: (202) 776-0595.
27 CBO July 1995.

Discretionary Spending

Discretionary spending is regularly reviewed, unlike tax expenditures. Discretionary spending is the part of the budget that Congress has the greatest control over. Congress annually decides how to spend approximately $500 billion by cutting, expanding or maintaining certain programs. Discretionary spending decisions are reviewed in the annual Congressional process of negotiating and debating the federal budget and passing appropriations bills.

For example, discretionary spending pays for such programs as Pell Grants for student aid, job training and the Job Corps, Head Start, low-income housing vouchers and federal aid to education. Discretionary spending also covers defense spending, business and agricultural subsidies, environmental protection programs, federal construction projects, law enforcement and other federal programs.

Tax Expenditures

The largest businesses and corporations, which can afford full-time lobbyists and generous campaign contributions to elected officials, may benefit the most from these manipulations of the tax code. Corporate interests can get special treatment because their contributions earn them influence over members of Congress. This influence and access is used to convince legislators to enact tax provisions in their favor.

Corporate Tax Handouts

Corporate tax handouts amount to half the federal deficit. While discretionary spending undergoes public scrutiny and the rigors of public debate in the annual budget negotiations in Congress, [the tax expenditure budget negotiations in Congress], the tax expenditure budget receives minimal public attention and no public annual review and debate. Only when the tax expenditure budget receives the same level of discussion will Congress do something to cut corporate welfare costs.

Over the past 50 years, the corporate tax burden has been steadily declining, shifting the federal tax burden from businesses to individual taxpayers. The proportion of federal taxes paid by corporate America has been cut in half since 1950. In 1952 corporate income taxes contributed 32 percent of federal revenues. By 1992 big business contributions had dropped to nine percent.

Federal spending for all social programs, particularly those benefiting poor children, was significantly reduced during the 1980s.[28]

Ralph DeCosta Nunez

---

28 Nunez, Ralph DeCosta. *Hopes Dreams, and Promises*, Institute for Children and Poverty, New York, 1994.

Rewarding Special Interests

Rewarding special interests with corporate tax breaks corrupts the political process. The rewards of corporate welfare open the door to corrupt relationships between policymakers and corporate lobbyists. Corporations subsidize political campaigns. In return, politicians create and protect corporate tax preferences that favor their contributors. Congressional hearings to reform corporate welfare are necessary for restoring credibility and integrity to the corporate tax code and the political process.

Tax Expenditures Take Many Forms

Tax expenditures include tax deductions, tax exclusion, tax credits, tax loopholes and tax deferrals. Tax deductions allow corporations and individuals to subtract a certain percentage of business expenses from their total taxable income.

WHERE YOUR FEDERAL TAX DOLLARS GO: "WELFARE" VS. "CORPORATE WELFARE"

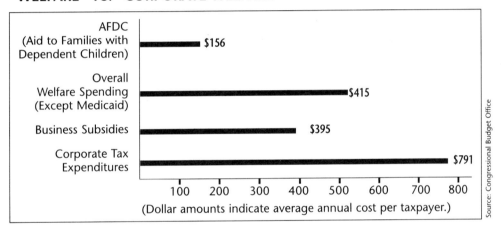

Source: Congressional Budget Office

(Dollar amounts indicate average annual cost per taxpayer.)

Corporate welfare is booming. At the federal level, it takes ... far more of your tax dollars than much maligned poverty welfare programs such as food stamps and children's assistance.[29]

Ralph Nader

Budget Decisions Are Policy Decisions

The federal government spends approximately $1.5 trillion each year. Budget decisions determine priorities; all budget decisions are in fact policy decisions.

The Real Money Is in the Tax Code

Many in Congress are demanding deficit reduction and a balanced budget. Most of the proposals thus far have focused on cutting programs that help the poorest Americans, while the programs that help the well-to-do remain relatively untouched.

29 Nader, Ralph, *Liberal Opinion Week*, 10/23/95.

Business Support Outweighs Federal Social Spending Three-to-One

Trying to balance the budget by cutting social spending is unfair and impractical, because federal spending on services for the poor represents only a tiny fraction of federal spending. If we are going to address the federal deficit, we must rein in federal spending on corporate support, which outweighs social spending three to one.

Corporate Tax Handouts Cost $791; AFDC Costs $156 per Taxpayer

Much of the current budget debate has focused on reducing "welfare" costs to cut the deficit. Total spending on the primary welfare program Aid to Families with Dependent Children (AFDC) has been about $14 billion a year, costing the average taxpayer $156. Adding in costs for food stamps, housing assistance and child nutrition increases the costs to $415 per taxpayer.

Corporate Tax Breaks Cost More Than Spending on Low-Income Families

In contrast, federal tax benefits for corporations cost almost $70 billion a year, or $791 per taxpayer. An identified 153 sources of FY 1995 federal business welfare totaled $167.2 billion, or $1,388 per individual taxpayer.

To be fair and effective in cutting the deficit, Congress must look at every part of the budget, including tax giveaways that award large corporations billions of dollars a year in corporate welfare.

CORPORATE WELFARE COSTS...HOW MUCH?

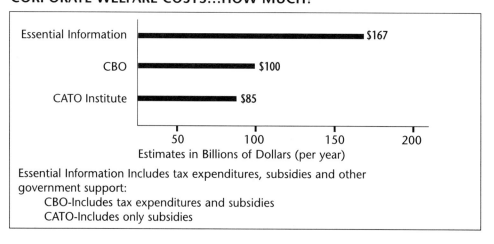

DECLINING CORPORATE INCOME TAX SHARE OF FEDERAL REVENUES: 1952-1992

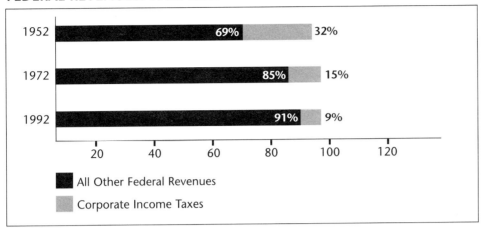

Congressional Hearings Are Needed

Congressional hearings to reform corporate welfare are necessary for restoring credibility and integrity to the corporate tax code and the political process.

Foreign Aid Facts

1. **What percentage of the federal budget goes to foreign aid?**
   A University of Maryland study revealed the American public's great misunderstanding of U.S. foreign aid spending. The common belief was that 15-20 percent of the U.S. budget was spent on foreign aid, and that a more appropriate figure would be around five percent. The surprising truth is that the U.S. actually spends less than one percent of its total budget on foreign aid.

2. **What percentage goes to support development?**
   The current foreign aid budget was approximately $13 billion, down from $19 billion in the mid-1980s; meanwhile, defense spending has been relatively immune from cuts. Only $6.5 billion, one half of one percent of the total budget, is spent on humanitarian and development programs.

3. **Relative to the GNP, how does the U.S. rank among the industrialized nations?**
   Only Japan gives more in aid than the U.S. However, as a percentage of GNP, U.S. foreign aid ranks last among 21 industrialized nations.

4. **Where does most of our foreign aid go?**
    The bulk of foreign aid goes to Israel, Egypt and Pakistan. This year the largest cuts in foreign aid have been in aid to the poorest nations, especially those in Africa.

5. **How does foreign aid help the U.S. economy?**
    In the last 30 years, more than two dozen countries have "graduated" from foreign aid and become U.S. trading partners. These partners now purchase more than 40 percent of total U.S. exports. Each $1 billion in exports creates roughly 20,000 new jobs at home and a large portion of the foreign aid budget is actually spent on goods and services produced in the U.S. and on programs that intentionally promote U.S. exports, businesses and investments.

6. **Does development assistance really help the people in the South?**
    Development assistance has helped make dramatic improvements in the South. Since 1960, infant mortality rates have fallen by half, life expectancy has increased from 46 to 63 years, and primary school enrollment has increased from 48 percent to 78 percent.

7. **What are some new approaches to development assistance?**
    Microlending — small loans to the very poor, especially women — has proven one of the most effective forms of "aid." With a payback rate of more than 95 percent, these loans have helped the poor in the South, and in this country, lift themselves out of poverty.

8. **How can foreign aid help the U.S. address global problems?**
    The major issues facing the U.S. today are global ones: an interdependent economy, the deteriorating condition of the earth's ecosystem, education levels, disease, drug trafficking and arms proliferation. More than ever before, solutions to U.S. problems will require partnership with others around the world.[30]

30 *Ten Myths and Realities of Foreign Aid*, InterAction, 1995

Federal Budget Pie Chart Exercise

The federal budget is not rocket science. But budget decisions determine the priorities of our country. With the Pentagon getting $7 billion more than it asked for in 1996, while programs for women and children are being slashed, many feel that federal priorities are out of alignment.

The distribution of the federal budget is heavily weighted toward military expenditures. The U.S. is number one in military spending compared to all other countries in the world. According to the U.N., we spend five percent of our $6.1 trillion gross national product on the military, far surpassing other Western industrial nations (France: two percent; United Kingdom: four percent; Sweden: two percent). At the same time, the U.S. lags far behind other countries on key socioeconomic indicators, which are measures of the well-being of the American people as a whole.[31]

Investments in programs that guarantee a social safety net for low-income people, fund vital local services, and enrich the infrastructure of the country are seriously underfunded. The "Let Us Slice the Pie" exercise was developed by Women's Action for New Directions to educate and mobilize women around federal budget issues. Use it as a tool to test your knowledge and to learn more about the federal budget.

31 "Women's Budget," Women's International League for Peace and Freedom, February 1996.

HOW DO YOU THINK THE FEDERAL BUDGET PIE WAS SLICED IN FY 1995?

Cover the next page before completing this page. Check your answers with the next page when you are done.

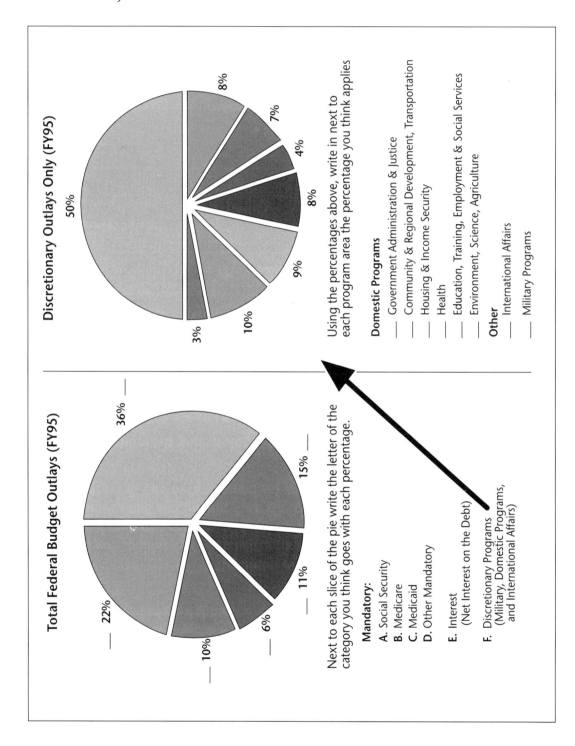

Discretionary Outlays Only (FY95)

50%
8%
7%
4%
8%
9%
10%
3%

Using the percentages above, write in next to each program area the percentage you think applies

Domestic Programs
___ Government Administration & Justice
___ Community & Regional Development, Transportation
___ Housing & Income Security
___ Health
___ Education, Training, Employment & Social Services
___ Environment, Science, Agriculture

Other
___ International Affairs
___ Military Programs

Total Federal Budget Outlays (FY95)

36%
22%
15%
10%
11%
6%

Next to each slice of the pie write the letter of the category you think goes with each percentage.

Mandatory:
A. Social Security
B. Medicare
C. Medicaid
D. Other Mandatory

E. Interest
(Net Interest on the Debt)

F. Discretionary Programs
(Military, Domestic Programs, and International Affairs)

THE FY95 BUDGET BREAKDOWN

Based on Office of Management and Budget estimated outlays/spring 1995
(percentages are rounded to nearest whole number; dollar figures reflect actual
OMB numbers in billions of dollars)

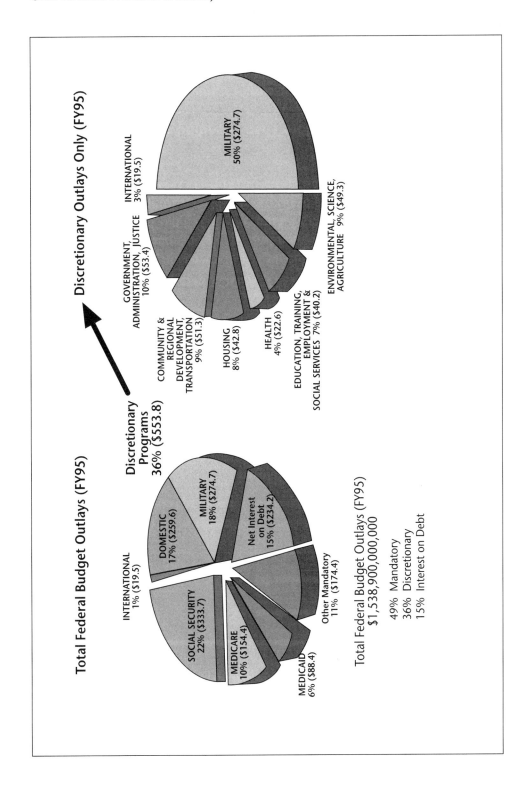

Discretionary Outlays Only (FY95)

INTERNATIONAL
3% ($19.5)

MILITARY
50% ($274.7)

GOVERNMENT,
ADMINISTRATION, JUSTICE
10% ($53.4)

COMMUNITY &
REGIONAL
DEVELOPMENT,
TRANSPORTATION
9% ($51.3)

HOUSING
8% ($42.8)

HEALTH
4% ($22.6)

EDUCATION, TRAINING,
EMPLOYMENT &
SOCIAL SERVICES 7% ($40.2)

ENVIRONMENTAL, SCIENCE,
AGRICULTURE 9% ($49.3)

Discretionary
Programs
36% ($553.8)

Total Federal Budget Outlays (FY95)

INTERNATIONAL
1% ($19.5)

DOMESTIC
17% ($259.6)

MILITARY
18% ($274.7)

Net Interest
on Debt
15% ($234.2)

Other Mandatory
11% ($174.4)

SOCIAL SECURITY
22% ($333.7)

MEDICARE
10% ($154.4)

MEDICAID
6% ($88.4)

Total Federal Budget Outlays (FY95)
$1,538,900,000,000

49% Mandatory
36% Discretionary
15% Interest on Debt

What do you think a woman's federal budget would look like?[32]

The federal government could enhance women's economic potential through policies such as full employment, a guaranteed adequate annual income, universal access to health care and the guarantee of child care for all who need it. In the circles and blanks below, record how you would like to see federal funds allocated.

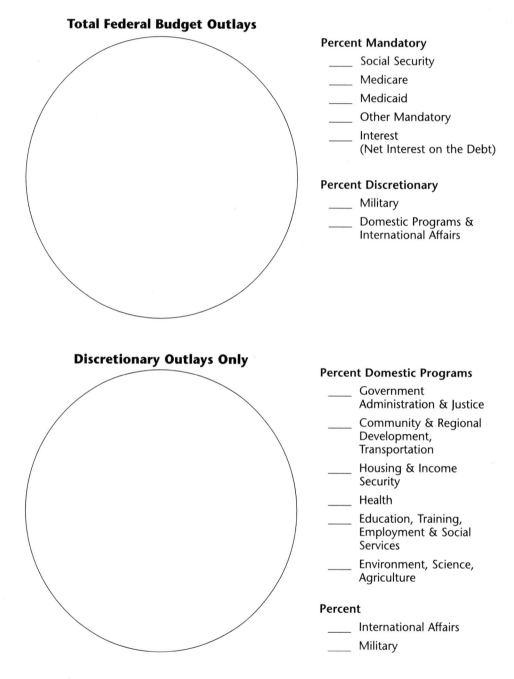

Total Federal Budget Outlays

Percent Mandatory

_____ Social Security

_____ Medicare

_____ Medicaid

_____ Other Mandatory

_____ Interest
       (Net Interest on the Debt)

Percent Discretionary

_____ Military

_____ Domestic Programs &
       International Affairs

Discretionary Outlays Only

Percent Domestic Programs

_____ Government
       Administration & Justice

_____ Community & Regional
       Development,
       Transportation

_____ Housing & Income
       Security

_____ Health

_____ Education, Training,
       Employment & Social
       Services

_____ Environment, Science,
       Agriculture

Percent

_____ International Affairs

_____ Military

32 For information on a woman-oriented approach to federal budgeting, write for a copy of the "Women's Budget," special edition, February 1996, written by Jane Midgley and produced by the Women's Budget Project of the Women's International League for Peace and Freedom in conjunction with: Women's International League for Peace and Freedom, The Feminist Majority Foundation, Women's Actions for New Directions (WAND), and the National Welfare Rights Union. (See the background and resource section for addresses.)

Developing Local Plans for Action

Critical areas of the platform covered in this session:

Women in Power and Decision-Making
(Section IV. G in Platform)

Institutional Mechanisms for the Advancement of Women
(Section IV. H in Platform)

Two-Hour Workshop

Activities	Minutes
Opening Circle	5
Exploration of a Central Issue: International Human Rights Law	10
Exploration of a Central Issue: The Federal Budget	20
Platform for Action Positions	5
Break	10
Plan for Action	60
Closing Circle	10
Total Time:	120

Materials

Opening circle centerpiece

Two flip charts

Preparation

Write on separate flip chart pages:

>Importance of international human rights law (page 263)

>CEDAW calls on governments to: (page 264)

>Power ratio/women in top decision-making positions (page 272)

>Advantages of women in political office (page 272)

>Options for action (page 276)

>Action plan questions (page 278)

>Blank pages for group action plans

Make copies of the:

>Commitment to Action sheet

>UUSC's International Human Rights Network sign-up sheet

>Evaluation form

Ask for six volunteers to read during the federal budget activity

Three-Hour Workshop

Activities	Minutes
Opening Circle	10
Exploration of a Central Issue: International Human Rights Law	25
Exploration of a Central Issue: The Federal Budget*	25
Platform for Action Positions*	20
Break	10
Plan for Action*	80
Closing Circle	10
Total Time:	**180**

Materials

Opening circle centerpiece

Two flip charts

Preparation

Write on separate flip chart pages:

Importance of international human rights law (page 263)

CEDAW calls on governments to: (page 264)

Power ratio/women in top decision-making positions (page 272)

Advantages of women in political office (page 272)

Options for action (page 276)

Action plan questions (page 278)

Blank pages for group action plans

Make copies of the:

Commitment to Action sheet

UUSC's International Human Rights Network sign-up sheet

Evaluation form

Ask for six volunteers to read during the federal budget activity

*exercises and/or time added

Opening Circle

(5 minutes)

Objective

To focus the group and allow for brief sharing.

Process

1. Light the candle, ask participants to read the NGO vision statement in the box below.

Look at the World Through Women's Eyes

Theme of the NGO Forum on Women '95 held in China, September 1995

Visualize a world where all conflicts — domestic violence, gun fights on the streets and civil wars — are solved through negotiation. When women and families feel safe in their homes, on the street and in their communities.

Visualize a society where clean water, food and housing are priorities for each citizen in every village, town and city. Where women can get credit and access to other resources they need to be fully economically productive.

Visualize nations where girls are educated and valued as much as boys, and all people are free to develop their full potential. Where men, too, are responsible for their fertility and sexuality, and family planning is transformed into comprehensive reproductive health care. Where women's knowledge and experience are integrated into every day decisions. And legislation is passed through Parliaments with a critical mass of women representatives.

Visualize the globe where the massive amounts of money spent on guns and weapons is used instead to end poverty, preserve health and well-being and create sustainable human development.

This is the kind of world women organizing for the NGO Forum on Women in Beijing want to build.

Look at the world through women's eyes.

---

2. Explain the following:

> Since this workshop focuses on developing a plan of action to translate the Platform for Action from words to deeds, share your feelings about the need to take action on the issues covered in the workshop series.

Exploration of a Central Issue: What Is International Human Rights Law?

(10 minutes)

Objective

To focus participants' attention on international human rights law, which contains the legal basis for significant protections for women.

Three-hour session: Add 15 minutes for a total of 25 minutes.

Process

1. Discuss international human rights law:

   > An important part of the international movement for human rights is international human rights law. Before considering the characteristics of specific international laws, consider this basic question:

   > What role do laws play in organizing and changing social interactions?

2. Ask participants to brainstorm on the above question and record a list of words or phrases on a flip chart. (5 minutes) After brainstorming, present the following phrases that were pre-written on a flip chart:

Importance of International Human Rights Law

Connecting law and morality at the global level

Human rights violations are no longer ignored

Publicly noting violations sometimes leads to policy change

Facilitator's Note: When reviewing this list, emphasize that making people aware of the existence of human rights laws (see background for list) and working to bring about their ratification by the Senate are important ways to build support for women's rights.

3. Discuss the following:

   > An important international law is the **Convention on the Elimination of All Forms of Discrimination Against Women (CEDAW)**, often called the women's convention. After being ratified by 20 member nations of the U.N., CEDAW became an international law in 1981. President Carter signed it in 1979, but it has yet to be ratified by the Senate, even though it has the support of most senators. The key to getting it ratified is to get it out of the Senate Foreign Relations Committee.[1] More than

---

1 Jesse Helms is currently the chair of the Senate Foreign Relations Committee and is an opponent of the treaty.

150 countries have ratified CEDAW; the United States is the only major industrialized country that has not.

Facilitator's Note: Review some of the key provisions of CEDAW listed on the flip chart (in bold-face). Share the longer phrases verbally.

CEDAW Calls on Governments to:

Acknowledge **women's contributions** to society

Recognize the **common responsibility of men and women** in the **upbringing** of **children**

Suppress forced prostitution and the **trafficking of women**

Grant women equal **access to credit and loans**

Modify traditions when necessary; for example, marital status should not abridge a woman's rights to child custody or to her own nationality

Ensure women **equal rights to conclude contracts and administer property**

Guarantee the **freedom to choose** one's **residence** and domicile

Ensure the **right to promotion, job security** and all job benefits including **maternity leave**

Guarantee **equal rights in education**

Ensure women's **eligibility for election to public bodies**

Provide access to **health care information** and services

Guarantee the right to **decide freely** on the **number** and spacing of one's **children**

UUSC-sponsored silent vigil to recognize International Women's Day.

Facilitator's Note: Tell the group that continuing efforts to lobby for CEDAW's ratification at the national level, as well as efforts to promote CEDAW resolutions at the local and state level, are important strategies for action. See the box below and the background and resource section for specific information on how to go about these lobbying efforts.

Successful Strategy for Action

Following an aggressive public awareness campaign, the **City Council of Iowa City, Iowa, unanimously ratified the CEDAW treaty** on August 5, 1995, becoming the first city to do so. Council members and activists say the ratification reflects the demand of the people of Iowa City and the people of the world for women's equality.

The National Committee on the United Nations Convention on the Elimination of Discrimination Against Women provides ongoing information that can be used in local efforts to lobby for CEDAW's ratification.

Exploration of a Central Issue: The Federal Budget

(20 minutes)

Objective

To become familiar with facts about the federal budget.

Three-hour session: Add 5 minutes to this discussion for a total of 25 minutes.

Process

1. Explain:

> For the past five sessions we have discussed some of the most **critical issues for women** today. During this session we will discuss **steps** that can be taken to address these issues. One of the most important steps is putting pressure on elected officials to support programs that are important to women. This involves learning more about the **federal budget**.

> At the end of the last session, you were encouraged to do the "Federal Budget Pie Chart Exercise" developed by Women's Action for A New Direction and to read the "Guide to Corporate Welfare," and the "Foreign Aid Fact Sheet." Take a federal budget quiz to see how much you learned. (5 minutes) Check your answers when you are finished.

Federal Budget Quiz

1. What portion of the $553 billion of the discretionary portion of the federal budget goes toward foreign aid?
    a. 30 percent
    b. 1 percent
    c. 15 percent

2. Which country provides the most foreign aid?
    a. Japan
    b. The United States
    c. Germany

3. Which country spends more on the military than any other country in the world?
    a. The United States
    b. North Korea
    c. Russia

4. Foreign aid provides no economic benefits to the United States.
    a. True
    b. False

5. What portion of the federal discretionary budget went to the military in Fiscal Year 1996?
    a. 20 percent
    b. 50 percent
    c. 15 percent

6. Where is most U.S. foreign aid spent?
    a. In the foreign nation to which it is sent
    b. In the U.S.

7. How much of the federal budget funds is used to fund so called entitlement programs such as Social Security, Medicare, or Medicaid?
    a. 3 percent
    b. 16 percent
    c. 38 percent

8. In Fiscal Year 1996 the Pentagon received:
    a. $ 2 billion less than it requested
    b. $ 7 billion more than it requested
    c. $200 million more than it requested

9. What percent of the federal budget has financed welfare through the Aid to Families with Dependent Children (AFDC) program?

    a. 15 percent

    b. 5 percent

    c. 1 percent

10. Corporate tax subsidies represent an amount equal to what percent of the federal deficit?

    a. 3 percent

    b. 30 percent

    c. 50 percent

11. Which of the following industrial nations has the largest gap between the rich and the poor?

    a. Canada

    b. England

    c. The United States

12. Some corporations are taxed at a lower tax rate than some low-income households.

    a. True

    b. False

13. The percent of federal tax revenues received from corporations (as opposed to individuals) has shrunk from 31 percent in the 1950s to ___ percent in the '90s.

    a. 25 percent

    b. 15 percent

    c. 10 percent

Answers:

1b, 2a, 3a, 4b, 5b, 6b, 7c, 8b, 9c, 10c, 11c, 12a, 13c

1. b. 1 percent
   Less than one percent of the federal budget is spent on foreign aid. Over the past decade, according to the U.S. Agency for International Development (U.S. AID), foreign assistance has been cut by a third, from more than $19 billion in the mid 1980s to less than $13 billion in FY 94. The current U.S. AID budget for humanitarian and development programs is $6.5 billion — or one half of one percent of the federal budget.

2. a. Japan
   In total dollars, the U.S. ranks second to Japan in foreign economic and development assistance. In terms of the percent of the Gross National Product (GNP) that is allocated towards foreign aid, the U.S. ranks last among 21 industrialized nations. The average American taxpayer spends less than 16 cents a day in federal taxes on humanitarian and development programs to foreign nations.

3. a. The United States
   The U.S. has paid a heavy price for making the military a national priority. U.S. spending on the military overshadows many other important federal priorities.

4. b. False
   Foreign aid does provide economic benefits to the United States. By promoting the economic growth of developing countries, foreign aid is an effective tool for increasing U.S. exports and creating jobs at home. During the past decade, U.S. exports to developing countries have more than doubled — from $71 billion in 1986 to $180 billion in 1993 and represent nearly 40 percent of total U.S. exports.

5. b. 50 percent
   50 percent of the federal discretionary budget was allotted for military spending during Fiscal Year 96.

6. b. In the United States
   Roughly 90 percent of food aid is spent on U.S. goods and services and millions of foreign aid dollars go to programs that specifically promote investment and export opportunities for U.S. businesses.

7. c. 38 percent

Social Security, Medicare and Medicaid together make up 38 percent of the Federal budget.

Social Security = $333.7   (22 percent)

Medicare   = $154.4   (10 percent)

Medicaid   = $ 88.4   (6 percent)

8. b. $7 billion more

The Pentagon received $7 billion more than it asked for in 1996. This comes at a time when programs for women and children in this country are being cut back.

9. c. 1 percent

10. c. 50 percent

The amount of funds lost to the Federal Treasury because of corporate tax breaks is 50 percent of the federal deficit.

11. c. The United States

The richest fifth of the U.S. population has increased its wealth steadily over the last 20 years, while the two-fifths at the bottom of the income scale have been steadily losing their economic footing. The richest 2.5 million Americans have nearly as much income as the roughly 100 million Americans with the lowest incomes. Inflated CEO salaries and benefit packages, paid for in part by special tax subsidies, contribute to this widening gap.

12. a. True

Some corporations are taxed at a lower rate than some low-income households. Within certain industries the effective corporate tax rate is quite low. For example, after calculating for corporate tax breaks and loopholes, the overall effective corporate tax rate for the life insurance industry is 22 percent, while the rate for the 18 largest mutual life insurance companies (like Prudential and Metlife) is only 10.8 percent.

13. c. 10 percent

Dips in corporate tax rates have led to a steady decline in the corporate share of income taxes collected since the 1940s to its lowest point ever.

2.   Ask volunteer readers to read the following information, which will help clear up some important misconceptions about the federal budget.

Reader 1

Although there is a great deal of focus on the amount of aid allocated to welfare through the Aid to Families with Dependent Children program, in fact the federal share of this program has represented less than one percent of the federal budget, and only three percent of most state budgets.

Reader 2

While many U.S. citizens complain about tax dollars being spent on welfare, few realize that the federal welfare recipients who cost the most are not teen mothers but wealthy corporations. Although federal spending on welfare for the Aid to Families with Dependent Children program (AFDC) has amounted to $14 billion a year, tax benefits to corporations amount to nearly $70 billion a year. In addition, few taxpayers are aware that the proportion of federal taxes paid by corporations as compared to that paid by individual taxpayers has dropped from 32 percent in 1952 to only nine percent in 1992.

Reader 3

There is also a great deal of misinformation about the amount of money that the U.S. government spends on foreign aid. A University of Maryland study found that the common belief is that 15 to 20 percent of the federal budget goes to foreign aid, whereas the surprising truth is that the U.S. actually spends less than one percent of its total budget on foreign aid and less than half of that aid is allocated to humanitarian or development programs.

Reader 4

In total aid, only Japan gives more foreign aid than the U.S., but when the amount of funds a nation allocates to foreign aid is compared to its Gross National Product (GNP), the U.S. ranks last among all industrialized nations. The bulk of foreign aid goes to only a few nations: Israel, Egypt and Pakistan, receive the majority of aid for political or foreign policy reasons, whereas the largest cuts in U.S. foreign aid have been suffered by the world's poorest nations, especially those in Africa.

Reader 5

It is critical that development assistance to the poorest nations be maintained or increased in order to support much needed childhood health and immunization programs, international family planning programs as well as programs to support the education and empowerment of women and girls as agreed to at the U.N. conferences held at Cairo and Beijing.

Reader 6

Many women at Beijing expressed the belief that they and their families would be better served if more government funds were directed to programs to meet human needs instead of funding bloated defense budgets. Fifty percent of the

U.S. discretionary budget, that portion of the budget decided on each year by the President and Congress, supports the military. In fact, in Fiscal Year 1996, Congress allocated $7 billion more to the military than had been requested by the Pentagon.

3. Ask participants to take out their "Let Us Slice the Pie" exercise and name areas where they would like to see more funds allocated to address some of the issues raised during the workshop series. List them on a flip chart.

4. Explain:

    > UUSC and many other NGOs concerned about global welfare have joined together to urge governments to support **social safety net programs** for women and children and **development assistance** to the **poorest nations**. Part of this effort involves contacting public officials to hold our government responsible for carrying through on the commitments made at Cairo and Beijing to support women's education, empowerment and health care.[2]

Platform for Action Position on Women in Power and Decision Making and Institutional Mechanisms for the Advancement of Women
(5 minutes)

Objective
To become acquainted with positions articulated in the Platform for Action.

Three-hour session: Add 15 minutes to this discussion for a total of 20 minutes.

Process
1. Note the following points concerning women in decision making positions:

    > The platform specifically calls on governments and the U.N. to create **mechanisms for women's advancement** at the highest possible levels and methods for collecting more **accurate data** relating to women and their contributions to society.

2. Take a few minutes to discuss why it is important to have more women in government. Share the material you have written on the flip chart with the group.

---

2 The section entitled "U.S. Commitments Made to the Platform for Action" in the background section provides a brief review of some of the commitments made by the U.S. government at Beijing.

Power Ratio: Women in Top Decision-Making Positions:

Governments Worldwide:
Legislatures and parliaments - 11 percent
Ministerial and cabinet positions - seven percent

U.S. Government:
House of Representatives - 11 percent
Senate - eight percent

Progress in U.S. State Legislatures:
1971 - eight percent
1991 - 18 percent

Business:
Directors in Fortune 500 companies - six percent
Minimum wage jobs held by women - 62 percent

Advantages of Women in Political Office:

Visibility of women in leadership roles helps reinforce the idea of women's equality

Increases the possibility of **greater attention to issues related to women and children**

Facilitator's Note: Refer participants to the background and resource section entitled, Platform for Action, which highlights the specific recommendations of the platform in these areas.

3. Distribute copies of the Commitment to Action sheet, the UUSC International Women's Rights Network sign-up sheet and the workshop evaluation form to each participant before the break. Ask participants to fill in the Commitment to Action sheet and the network sign-up sheets and pass them in during the "Closing Circle." Explain that the Commitment to Action sheet is designed to help groups that form out of the workshop to take action on women's rights.

Facilitator's Note: Be sure to mail in the network sign up sheets and evaluation forms to UUSC.

4. Remind the group that the goal of the series has been to get to the stage for action on women's rights. Ask participants to consider what they would be willing to contribute, in time or talent over the next three months, to make group action on women's rights possible.

Break

(10 minutes)

Facilitator's Note: During the break, post the flip charts that were made during previous brainstorming sessions. These can provide a reminder of ideas proposed by the group as they work on their action commitments.

Commitment to Action
What Will You Do to Bring Beijing Home?

☐ Join UUSC's International Human Rights Network: Focus on Women

☐ Become part of an ongoing women's rights taskforce

☐ Talk to friends and neighbors about these issues

☐ Help create and distribute information at church services or community events about women's rights

☐ Write a letter to local newspapers or to church/organization newsletters

☐ Write or call legislators about the need to support CEDAW and develop a U.S. National Plan of Action to implement the Beijing platform

☐ Participate in a delegation visit to a legislator

☐ Help organize a consciousness raising event

☐ Organize a Women in Black vigil on women's rights

☐ Become part of a local women's rights telephone tree for alerting people to important events or information

☐ Organize or participate in a media task force

☐ Organize or participate in a school outreach effort

☐ Make changes in your lifestyle to conserve the environment

☐ Contribute funds or organize a fundraiser for UUSC's women's rights projects

☐ Maintain a women's rights bulletin board in your community or congregation by reading and posting relevant material every few weeks

☐ Other _____

_____
NAME

_____
ADDRESS   CITY   STATE   ZIP

_____
PHONE (DAY)   (EVENING)

Please return to International Programs, UUSC, 130 Prospect St.,
Cambridge, MA 02139-1845
Group keeps one copy and sends photocopy to UUSC.

Plan For Action

(60 minutes)

Objective

To commit to at least two actions that are possible for the group to undertake during the next six months.

Three-hour session: Add 20 minutes to this discussion for a total of 80 minutes.

Process

1. Explain the following paragraph and the information in the box:

    > This workshop series was designed to educate participants on the issues addressed in the Platform for Action. Its primary goal was to move group members to act on what they have learned. UUSC hopes to interest participants in its newly formed International Human Rights Network. By joining the network, you will be connected to national and international efforts on behalf of women.

UUSC's International Human Rights Network: Focus on Women

What is UUSC's International Human Rights Network: Focus on Women?

Building on the momentum of the U.N. conferences at Cairo and Beijing, the Unitarian Universalist Service Committee has formed a network of women and men who are willing to join in efforts to advance justice, equality and women's rights around the world.

What will I get if I sign up to be part of the network?

You will receive background information and action alerts suggesting ideas for advocacy and action to influence public opinion and policy in support of women's rights. You will also receive materials to educate yourself and others about women's rights. Through the network you will also be connected to other national efforts such as WEDO's Contract with the Women of America, the 50 Years is Enough Campaign or efforts to ensure the continuation of income support programs for poor women and their children.

How much does it cost?

There is no membership fee.

Contact: Linda MacKay, International Programs, UUSC,
Tel: (617) 868-6600, Fax: (617) 868-7102,
E-mail: postmaster@uusc.org

Join UUSC's International Human Rights Network: Focus on Women

Act today to support human rights for women around the globe!

☐ Send me information and alerts on women's rights issues. I would like to become a member of UUSC's International Human Rights Network: Focus on Women.

☐ Call me so that we can discuss ideas or resources available from UUSC to plan a women's rights event or start a women's rights group in my congregation or community.

☐ I would like more information on how I can become a member of the Unitarian Universalist Service Committee.

☐ I am unable to join the network, but I would like to contribute $25, $50 or $100 to support the work of the Unitarian Universalist Service Committee's women's rights projects around the world.

_____
NAME

_____
ADDRESS   CITY   STATE   ZIP

_____
PHONE (DAY)   (EVENING)

_____
UU CONGREGATION

Are you affiliated with other women's organizations? Which ones?

_____

_____

_____

Please return to International Programs, UUSC, 130 Prospect St., Cambridge, MA 02139-1845

2. Outline the following proposals for local action on the flip chart and review the detailed list below with the group:

Options for Action

Congregational/Community Action

Legislative Advocacy

Media Outreach

Organizing for Local Action

Connecting with Other Campaigns

Becoming a Member of UUSC's International Human Rights Network: Focus on Women

Congregational/Community Action

- Plan a program or service to engage the members of your congregation/community in the struggle for women's rights.
    - Share the full-length version of one of the videos used in the series or other videos that are available from UUSC or other organizations.
    - Invite a person who attended the Beijing conference or a panel of speakers to discuss women's rights issues in your congregation or community.

- Organize a program on domestic violence. For resources, including a video, contact Jody Shipley and Marilyn Gentile at UU's Acting to Prevent Violence Against Women at 3221 Snyder Avenue, Modesto, CA 95356, Tel: (209) 545-1837) or Margi McCue at (503) 238-7973.

- Arrange for your religious education program to use the "No Punching Judy" program, a UUSC resource that deals with domestic violence, which was written by Margi McCue.

- Support UUSC's Promise the Children program, a national advocacy campaign to maintain economic support programs for poor children and their families. Contact: Kim McDonald or Jackie Ladd at UUSC, Tel: (800) 388-3920.

- Organize a Women in Black vigil.

- Contact local schools to assess how girls are treated at all levels of the educational system. Meet with your school committee or superintendent to urge them to do a gender equity assessment using the American Association of University Women Guide available from UUSC.

- Plan a fundraiser to support UUSC's women's human rights projects.

Legislative Advocacy Group

- Call, write, or visit your senators and representatives to educate and influence them on women's rights issues.

- Respond to action alerts from UUSC's International Human Rights Network: Focus on Women.

- Plan a state or local CEDAW resolution effort.

- Organize a candidate forum.

- Circulate the Contract with American Women petition.

- Organize a delegation to visit your representative or senator to discuss concerns such as the development of a U.S. National Plan of Action to implement the Beijing platform and the need to ratify CEDAW.

- Join voter registration efforts.

- Support women candidates for office.

Media Action Task Force

- Arrange to meet with the editorial board of your local newspaper and/or the managers of your TV and radio stations to urge an increase in coverage of women's issues.

- Write letters to the editor of your local newspaper on women's rights issues.

- Call in to radio talk show programs.

- Do an analysis of front pages, articles or programs in preparation for the meeting. Ask about staff gender balance.

- Undertake a local monitoring effort that assesses the representation of women's issues in the mainstream media in your community.

From left to right: Donna Shalala, secretary of Health and Human Services, Veronica Biggens and Julia Taft — all members of the official U.S. delegation to the Fourth World Conference on Women — meet with U.S. participants at the NGO forum in Huariou.

Connecting with Other Campaigns

Facilitator's Note: Remind participants that members of UUSC's International Human Rights Network will receive information and action alerts concerning various campaigns, or they can contact these organizations directly. Addresses and telephone numbers of the organizations listed below are in the women's rights resource section.

- The Interfaith Office of Corporate Responsibility: Works to protect workers rights and the environment in today's globalized economy.

- The 50 Years Is Enough Campaign or the Women's Eyes on the Bank Program: Advocates an end to the failed structural adjustment programs of the World Bank and the International Monetary Fund.

- The Women's Environment and Development Organization: Helps to organize a local or state Contract with the American Women campaign.

- The Women's Budget Project: Works to include a women's perspective in the federal budget.

- The CEDAW Campaign: Helps groups to launch a local or state campaign to ratify the Women's Treaty/CEDAW.

3. If the group is larger than 10, ask participants to break into groups of five to six, depending on the size of the entire group, and develop an action plan that answers the four questions listed on the flip chart. Ask the groups to decide on one or two feasible activities such as those in the list above. (30 minutes)

Action Plan Questions

What issues do you want to work on?

What do you want to achieve?

What two actions could your group carry out in the next three to six months?

What contributions of time or talent are you willing to make?

4. About 15 minutes before the end of the session, bring everyone back into the large group. Ask the groups to briefly summarize their action plan on a flip chart.

5. Develop a joint plan combining the ideas of each group and plan a follow-up session to finalize these plans.

Facilitator's Note: "Developing an Action Plan" from the UUSC Busy Person's Guide to Social Action in the background and resource section may be useful for future planning if the group decides to form a women's rights taskforce.

Closing Circle

(10 minutes)

Objective

To provide closure for the group and to emphasize the bond between participants and among women worldwide.

Process

1. Ask participants to stand in a circle and state individually the commitments they are willing to make to follow through on the group's plan of action.

2. Ask participants to place their International Human Rights Network and Commitment to Action Sheets in the center of the circle and read "A Women's Creed" together. Urge participants to fill in the workshop evaluation form after the "Closing Circle."

A Women's Creed [3]

We are the female human beings poised on the edge of the new millennium. We are the majority of our species, yet we have dwelt in the shadows. We are the invisible, the illiterate, the laborers, the refugees, the poor.

We are the women who hunger — for rice, home, freedom, each other, ourselves.

We are the women who thirst — for clean water, laughter, literacy, and love.

We have existed at all times, in every society.

We are continuity, weaving future from past, logic with lyric.

We are the women who wear broken bones, voices, minds and hearts — but we are the women who dare whisper: No.

We are the women whose souls no fundamentalist cage can contain.

We are the women who refuse to permit the sowing of death in our gardens, air, rivers, seas.

We are each precious, unique, necessary. We are strengthened and blessed and relieved at not having to all be the same. We are daughters of longing. We are the mothers in labor to birth the politics of the 21st Century.

We are the women men warned us about.

We are the women who know that all issues are ours, who will reclaim our wisdom, reinvent our tomorrow, question and redefine everything, including power.

We have broken our silence, exhausted our patience...We are done with vague words and real waiting; famished for action, dignity, joy.

For we are the Old Ones, The New Breed, The Natives who came first but lasted, indigenous to an utterly different dimension. We are the girl-child in Zambia, the godmother in Burma, the woman in El Salvador and Afghanistan, Finland and Fiji.

3 Excerpted with permission from "A Women's Creed" written at the International Networking Women's Global Strategies Meeting, November 29-December 2, 1994, sponsored by the Women's Environmental and Development Organizations (WEDO) and attended by 148 women from 50 countries.

Bread. A clean sky. Active peace. A women's voice singing somewhere, melody drifting like smoke from the cookfires. The army disbanded, the harvest abundant. The wound healed, the child wanted, the prisoner freed, the body's integrity honored.

The labor equal, fair, and valued. Delight in the challenge for consensus to solve problems. No hand raised in any gesture but greeting. Secure interiors — of heart, home, land — so firm as to make secure borders irrelevant at last.

And everywhere laughter, care, celebration, dancing, contentment. A humble, earthly paradise, in the now.

Believe it. We are the women who will transform the world.

Journal Page

Workshop Evaluation

Please take a moment to share your thoughts on the contents of the workshop series. Write additional comments on the back.

1. What did you like most about the workshop series? Why?

   _____

   _____

   _____

2. What did you like least about it? Why?

   _____

   _____

   _____

3. What was the most important thing you learned?

   _____

   _____

   _____

4. How do you intend to put this knowledge to use?

   _____

   _____

   _____

5. Would you recommend that others participate in the workshop?
   ☐ yes   ☐ no

6. Were the sessions
   ☐ too short   ☐ too long   ☐ just right

7. Please rate group interaction:
   ☐ poor   ☐ fair   ☐ good   ☐ excellent

8. What could be have been done to improve interaction?

_____

_____

_____

9. Please rate the reading selections on the scale below:

DISAGREE   AGREE

Balanced

     1   2   3   4   5   6   7   8   9   10

Intellectually stimulating

     1   2   3   4   5   6   7   8   9   10

Comprehensible to non-experts

     1   2   3   4   5   6   7   8   9   10

Too much material

     1   2   3   4   5   6   7   8   9   10

Too little material

     1   2   3   4   5   6   7   8   9   10

10. Which exercise did you find most helpful? Why?

_____

_____

_____

11. Which exercise was the least helpful? Why?

_____

_____

_____

12. Were the background and resource sections helpful ☐
☐ too extensive   ☐ too brief

What ones did you appreciate most? Which ones did you like the least?

_____

13. Were the audio-visual programs helpful?

☐ yes   ☐ no

If yes, which one(s)?

_____

_____

14. What improvements do you suggest for the series?

_____

_____

_____

15. How many of the readings did you do?

☐ a few   ☐ most   ☐ all

16. Was the amount of reading

☐ too much   ☐ too little   ☐ just right

Please return to International Programs, UUSC, 130 Prospect St., Cambridge, MA 02139-1845

Notes

Session 6

Background and Resources

on Women and International Law and Organizing Strategies

Highlights of International Human Rights Law Relating to Women

1945 - United Nations Charter
U.S. status: ratified
Promotes "human rights, and fundamental freedoms for all, without distinction as to race, sex, language or religion."

1948 - Universal Declaration of Human Rights
U.S. status: automatically in agreement by virtue of U.N. membership
International "Bill of Rights" asserts equal rights of men and women, equal protection under law, support for families, and provision of basic necessities and services, such as health care and unemployment. Mothers and children designated to receive special attention.

1966 - International Covenant on Civil and Political Rights
U.S. status: ratified 1992
Assures equality before the law. Many of these rights describe areas of civil life where governments should not be involved or regulate, such as freedom of religion and of the press. Equal access to justice includes public trials, marriage rights, and legal protection of children as minors.

1966 - International Covenant on Economic, Social and Cultural Rights
U.S. status: not ratified
Services and policies through which a government is actively involved in citizens' economic, social and cultural lives. Commitment to women and children expanded: for example, marriages must be mutually consensual; pregnancy entitles mothers to work leave and adequate health care; and the abuse of working children should be avoided.

1981 - The Convention on the Elimination of All Forms of Discrimination Against Women
U.S. status: signed, not ratified
Among the international human rights treaties, the convention takes an important place in bringing the female half of humanity into the focus of human rights concerns. It establishes not only an international bill of rights for women, but also an agenda for action by countries to guarantee the enjoyment of those rights.

1989 - Convention on the Rights of the Child
U.S. status: not ratified
Girl and boy children assured equal status. Discrimination based on the status or actions of parents condemned. Children entitled to health care and education.

NOTE: See section "International Human Rights Law Adoption" on page 298.

1993 - Declaration on the Elimination of Violence Against Women
U.S. status: automatically in agreement by virtue of U.N. membership
While violence exists at all levels of society, women, minorities, refugees, youth, the elderly, the poor, and handicapped individuals are especially vulnerable. Governments are urged to support victims of violence and punish their persecutors.[4]

Committee on the Elimination of Discrimination Against Women (CEDAW)

CEDAW, a Committee of the United Nations, is the only United Nations women's human rights treaty body. It is responsible for monitoring the implementation of the convention. The committee met at the beginning of 1996 to review reports from countries that have ratified or acceded to the convention. These countries are legally bound to put into practice the convention's provisions and to submit national reports to the committee on measures taken to comply with these treaty obligations.

The committee can suggest specific measures as well as make general recommendations to the governments on eliminating discrimination against women. It may also invite U.N. specialized agencies to submit reports for consideration, and receive information from nongovernmental organizations.

In 1995, the committee made proposals on submitting to the Commission on the Status of Women the elements of a draft protocol to the convention, which would allow women and women's groups to petition the committee directly. A decision on the protocol is pending. If it is adopted, this will allow many more issues to be raised before the committee by nongovernmental organizations and individuals.

Iowa City Ratification of CEDAW

Following an aggressive public awareness campaign, the city council of Iowa City, Iowa, unanimously ratified the CEDAW treaty on August 5, 1995, becoming the first city to do so. Council members and activists say the ratification reflects the demand of the people of Iowa City and the people of the world for women's equality. Iowa City residents believed they sent a powerful mandate to the Senate to complete the obligation the U.S. made when it signed CEDAW in 1980. The U.S. is the only industrialized nation besides South Africa and Switzerland that has not ratified it. Sixty-eight members of the Senate signed a letter urging President Clinton to initiate the ratification of CEDAW during the spring of 1993. In the final days of the 103rd session of Congress (September 1994), the Senate Foreign Relations Committee approved the convention. However, an

4 Summarized from *The Human Rights of Women: A Reference Guide to Official United Nations Documents*, edited by Rita Maran. Compiled for the NGO Forum/U.N. Fourth World Conference on Women, 1995.

unnamed senator killed the treaty by blocking it from floor consideration. This sent the treaty back to the Senate Foreign Relations Committee of the 104th Congress where it now awaits action. In order to join the 151 other nations that have already ratified this international treaty, the Senate must approve CEDAW by a two-thirds majority, or 67 votes. Ratification would be strong evidence of the U.S. commitment to equality for all of its citizens. In addition, it would enhance the United States' effectiveness as a credible and effective supporter of women's rights at home and around the world.

Iowa City Ratification Statement

"Whereas CEDAW, sometimes called an international Bill of Rights for women, obligates those countries which have ratified it to take all appropriate measures to ensure the full development and advancement of women in all spheres — political, educational, employment, health care, economic, social, legal, marriage and family relations — as well as to modify the social and cultural patterns of conduct of men and women to eliminate prejudice, customs and all other practices based on the idea of inferiority or superiority of either sex.

Therefore, be it resolved, that the City of Iowa City go on record in support of United States ratification or accession to The Convention...and [urge that] immediate action begin on The Convention."[5]

Local government is an excellent place to begin advocating for national passage of CEDAW, and to begin instituting the convention's principles. Local government is often the most democratic, participatory, and responsive level to citizen demands. The united opinion of a city will help to focus the attention of elected officials in Washington, giving senators and representatives an incentive to address the mandates of their constituencies.

Guide for Action on CEDAW

Raising Awareness: People need to know what CEDAW says and how it addresses issues for women here and around the globe. By better understanding the goals of the women's movement and the commonality of women's struggles around the world, citizens are more inclined to support the ratification of CEDAW.

1. Enlist the help of the media.

2. Create events such as public discussion forums to provide information or public demonstrations to express support.

3. Coalition-building strengthens the commitment of members by formalizing their obligation to a local ratification effort. It helps generate new ideas and resources, and prevents duplication of effort.

5 Excerpted from Iowa City Council Resolution No. 95-222.

Reaching those outside of the existing circle of activists is important. Include locally elected officials that are sympathetic to the cause of women's rights, or vulnerable to women's votes!

4. Establish an organization that will monitor the implementation of the U.N. Fourth World Conference on Women's Platform for Action at the local level.

Drafting the Document: Create a proposal to be considered by the city council. Research is crucial for the document to withstand debate.

1. There may be state or local legislation that cites international covenants or sets a precedent for passing resolutions supporting the ratification of international treaties. For example, the city of New York under Mayor David Dinkins recognized the Universal Declaration of Human Rights as law.

2. Try to find existing legislation that supports the principles of CEDAW.

3. Use phrasing from other state or local resolutions as a model.

4. Include statistics on the status of women in your community and other related issues.

5. Solicit endorsements from community groups, churches, university programs, student groups, business associations, social organizations, etc. Attach these endorsements to the draft proposal that is submitted to the city council or state legislature.

Passing the Resolution: As all city governments vary, it is important to be aware of their management structure and legislative schedule.

1. Find out if there are any subcommittees or boards that have to be notified or that might be helpful. There may be a human rights commission that could endorse the draft and help promote the resolution.

2. Contact the city manager, or the equivalent, and discuss with him or her the appropriate route of action and establish a timetable. Most cities differentiate between ordinances, resolutions and proclamations. A proclamation is a sign of support having symbolic rather than legal value, such as a commemorative day. A resolution endorses a plan of action, binds the city to fulfill a contract, or calls upon the city to initiate a particular policy line. The Iowa City Council's action was a resolution. An ordinance carries with it the full force of law and mandates the local government to its implementation. There is no precedent for international law to be so mandated in a local community.

3. Bipartisan support at all levels is essential.

4. One method for raising support for CEDAW is to initiate a series of events leading up to the introduction of the resolution in the local government.

5. Another method is to dispatch a set of discussion questions to different organizations. Ask their constituencies to use the questions as a framework to consider how the community perceives the needs of women, how these concerns could be addressed. Ask for their responses and include them with the draft proposal to the council.

Regardless of the city's decision to endorse CEDAW or not, such a campaign is a catalyst for implementing the principles of CEDAW. The enthusiasm created can be harnessed to put related issues on the local agenda and activate programs such as: health care professionals donating time at inner-city clinics; school boards instituting a curriculum on women's contributions and working on steps to deal with gender stereotyping and discrimination in schools. An ongoing public forum series could be organized to increase the number of activists and maintain enthusiasm for the cause. CEDAW can be a standard by which to evaluate proposed laws, community practices, and the agendas of candidates or officials.[6] Finally, the commitment to CEDAW fosters a humane bond between local and global communities. For a complete package of information on the Iowa City ratification process, contact UUSC at (617) 868-6600.

Lobbying for the Ratification of CEDAW

The National Committee on the United Nations Convention on the Elimination of Discrimination Against Women is an informal network that provides valuable information about the status of CEDAW in the world as well as suggestions about what can be done to urge its ratification in the United States. To be placed on the mailing list, please contact: Billie Heller, Chair, National Committee on U.N./CEDAW, 520 North Camden Drive, Beverly Hills, CA 90210-3202, Tel: (310) 271-8087, Fax: (310) 271-2056.

6 Iowa Campaign to Ratify CEDAW, "Making International Law Work in Your Local Community."

U.S. Commitments to the Platform for Action

Health: U.S. AID has committed major resources to the health and well-being of women in the developing world. U.S. AID is working in more than 70 countries and with a number of public, private and nongovernmental organization partners in the areas of family planning, safe motherhood, sexually transmitted diseases and HIV/AIDS, breastfeeding, women's nutrition, adolescent reproductive health, post-abortion care and female genital mutilation. Comprehensive programs in these areas include: policy development; training, service delivery; education and communications; biomedical, operations, and social science research; and commodity procurement and logistics management. U.S. AID also supports the work of the International Planned Parenthood Federation, the World Health Organization, UNICEF and the U.N. Joint Commission on HIV/AIDs.[7]

Leadership Training: U.S. AID is planning two mutually-reinforcing initiatives concerning women's political participation and legal rights as well as an initiative on girls' and women's education. The political participation program will increase women's access to and participation in political processes and elections in both transitional and consolidating democracies around the world. It will provide assistance in political leadership training, support networking among politically active women and women's political organizations, educate women about voter rights, civic rights and responsibilities, and provide technical training and leadership services.[8]

Legal Rights Program: The women's legal rights program will disseminate knowledge about women's legal status, and strengthen the capacity of private voluntary organizations, NGOs and other actors to implement corrective programs. Goals will include strengthening women's legal literacy, integrating gender issues into law school curricula, providing gender-sensitive training to the judiciary, supporting legal clinics, engaging in dialogue with legislators to promote equitable laws and policies and facilitating partnerships and networks across sectors.[9]

Girls and Women's Education: U.S. AID will continue work on its initiative, announced at the World Summit for Social Development, to increase girls' primary school completion rates by demonstrating a 20 percent increase in 12 U.S. AID-assisted countries over the next decade. This will be done by assisting the governments involved in creating constituencies to promote girls' and women's education initiatives, identifying barriers to keeping girls in school and designing policy or program changes to overcome them, and designing community schools that specifically meet girls' requirements for work and safety. U.S. AID will work to involve

---

7 Contact: Elizabeth Maguire, Tel: (703) 875-4402 (U.S. AID).
8 Contact: Women's Political Participation — Melissa Brown, Tel: (202) 736-7979 (U.S. AID).
9 Contact: Women's Legal Rights — Cate Johnson, Tel: (703) 816-0266 (U.S. AID).

communities in activities to promote female education and train teachers to encourage girls' educational aspirations and attainment. U.S. AID will also work to increase women's literacy and young girls' school readiness in six U.S. AID assisted countries.[10]

The Platform for Action

Power and Decision-Making

(Section of Chapter IV. G — Strategic Objectives and Actions)

Strategic Objective

Strengthen factors that promote the full and active participation of women in power structures and decision making.

Actions to be taken by governments:

- Commit to establishing the goal of gender balance in governmental bodies and committees.

Actions to be taken by political parties:

- Consider examining party structures and procedures to remove discrimination against women's participation.

Actions to be taken by the United Nations:

- Develop a mechanism to appoint women to senior posts in U.N. organizations.
- Continue collection and disseminating data on decision making.

Actions to be taken by nongovernmental organizations:

- Build and strengthen solidarity among women through information and education.
- Seek accountability from elected public representatives on commitment to gender concerns.

Institutional Mechanisms for the Advancement of Women

(Section of Chapter IV. H — Strategic Objectives and Actions)

Strategic Objectives

Integrate gender-equality dimensions into policy, program planning and implementation.

Actions to be taken by governments:

- Create national mechanisms for women's advancement at the highest possible level.
- Carry out gender analysis before making policy decisions.

10 Contact: Girls' and Women's Education — Susie Clay, (703) 875-4179 (U.S. AID).

- Establish direct links with national, regional and international bodies dealing with women's advancement.
- Ensure the regular production of gender-statistical publications.

Actions to be taken by national and international statistical services:
- Collect, compile, analyze and present gender-disaggregated data.
- Improve data collection on measurement of poverty among women and men.

Actions to be taken by the United Nations:
- Promote better collection and analysis of data related to human rights of women.

Developing an Action Plan[11]

In order to define your group's goals and decide on a plan of action, answer the following questions:

Problem Definition

- What is your group's definition of the problem you want to address? Try to define it in one sentence.
- What is the underlying cause of the problem and what will your group do to remedy its root causes, not just its symptoms?

Alternative Solutions

- Brainstorm some possible actions your group might take to address this problem. Use newsprint paper or a blackboard. List as many ideas as possible — no matter how wild — for five minutes. Do not evaluate as you go along. These ideas can be evaluated and made "realistic" later. Encourage people to build on other people's suggestions.

Resources Available

- What personal investment is each person willing to make in order to work on this issue? How much time can each give (meeting time and/or time outside of meetings, etc.)?
- What knowledge, talents, skills, connections and money do you have or will you be able to assemble in order to implement these suggestions?

Reservations

- What barriers do you recognize within yourselves or within your congregation that may limit your ability to work effectively on this issue?

11 From "The Busy Person's Guide to Social Action," UUSC, 1984.

Selecting Alternatives

- Have each person select a few favorite actions from the brainstorming list which seem promising for effective group action.

- Outline the items selected in a few sentences — do not go into detail, do not evaluate. After all have suggested their favorites to the group, ask for additional ideas.

Choosing Projects

- Keeping in mind both resources and reservations, have the group select actions which are priorities.

- Remember to include some activities that are bound to succeed. For group morale it's essential to start on a positive note, so select a project that is doable, measurable, time-limited and energizing.

Overall Goal

- What is the overall goal of your group's actions?

Under Whom Should You Work?

- Under whose auspices can you most simply and effectively organize your actions? Your church or fellowship, the social action committee, UUSC, some other existing group or do you wish to create a totally independent organization?

Action Steps

Outline your plan detailing the actions you will take as a group. Ask yourself if these actions are:

- specific
- measurable
- achievable
- compatible with your overall goal.

Decide who will do what. Ask for volunteers.

Decide on Election Procedures

- Before going much further, you may decide that you want to elect or designate a group leader or group co-chairs for key functions.

- Decide whether you want to appoint a secretary, a treasurer or a public information coordinator.

- Clarify who will be accountable for what.

Writing Up and Carrying Out Your Plan

- List the steps in your action plan, the individual or group responsible, and estimated completion dates. Involve participants in decisions as to how to divide up the work.

- Be sure assigned responsibilities make the best use of resources and abilities. Don't give participants either too little or too much responsibility.

- Avoid conflicts with other projects or events in making up your schedules.

- If your program is a long-range one, develop some short-term activities that will produce tangible results. This will help to sustain interest and motivation over the long-term.

Assess progress and problems as you go along, modifying your strategy as circumstances warrant. Be ready to change direction or plans in response to an unexpected development.

- Keep project workers informed, inspired and involved.

- Introduce and orient all new members so they may truly become part of the group and understand its overall plans.

- Provide encouragement to members and acknowledge their efforts and participation.

- Consult members at key points in the project, either to obtain votes of confidence or to get advice and feedback.

- Issue progress reports to show your achievements and sustain motivation.

- If interpersonal problems arise, deal with them promptly — don't let conflicts escalate at the expense of group morale.

- Be professional, even though you are volunteers. Treat deadlines and commitments seriously.[12]

Evaluating Your Progress

- Build evaluation procedures into your plan from the start so you can both determine and respond effectively to your positive and negative results.

- As the project progresses, encourage participants to analyze and evaluate their efforts and to talk openly of disappointments, conflicts and anger.

- Analyze your expenses on a regular basis to make sure you are staying within your planned budget.

- After your project is completed, carefully analyze and evaluate your efforts and determine which techniques worked, which ones didn't and why.

- At regular intervals, and especially at the end of major phases of your program, ask whether the program should be continued, modified, or even abandoned.

- Try to anticipate consequences of your actions and make plans to deal with them as they occur. If, for example, your actions are likely to motivate people to become more involved, be ready to suggest constructive things they can do to help.

Once you've developed your action plan, you may want some ideas on how to strengthen your group as you carry out your activities.

12 Adapted from the American Association of University Women, Community Action Tool Catalog.

International Human Rights Law Adoption

- Nations become members of the United Nations by ratifying the U.N. Charter. There are now 185 member nations.

- The U.N. Charter, which became effective in 1945, opened the way for numerous international treaties (also called conventions and covenants) on human rights that have become law through the United Nations system.

- All members of the United Nations are automatically bound to declarations of the U.N. by virtue of membership. Therefore, the U.S., having ratified the charter, has automatically agreed to the Universal Declaration of Human Rights and the Declaration on the Elimination of Violence against Women.

- For a treaty to become effective, a specified number of member nations of the United Nations must ratify it.

- The process of ratification varies from country to country. In the U.S., the president signs an international treaty. Signing indicates intent to ratify at some future date. The U.S. Constitution requires a two-thirds consent by the Senate in order for an international treaty to be ratified.

- When ratifying a treaty, any country can legally place reservations on clauses it considers in conflict with national law or custom. This is called ratifying with reservations.

- When a treaty is ratified, governments are encouraged to incorporate its provisions into their national body of law.

The Contract with Women of the USA

The Contract with Women of the USA is a campaign that was initiated by the Women's Environment and Development Organization (WEDO). It is a call for public officials, advocates for women's rights, policy makers, organizations and individuals to signal their support for efforts to implement the Platform for Action.

The Contract wiith Women of the USA is a flexible and unifying way to initiate efforts to support and expand women's activism from the grassroots up to the local, state and national levels. The major objective of the contract is to provide a mechanism for monitoring and advocacy with policy makers and candidates.

WEDO works with women in many countries to formulate contracts based on the platform, which can be used to monitor governments' progress on empowering women.

For copies of the contract and sign-on sheets, contact: The Center for Women's Policy Studies, 2000 P St. NW, Suite 508, Washington DC 20036; Tel: (202) 872-1770, Fax: (202) 296-8962. For assistance in creating a contract at the state level contact: WEDO, 845 Third Avenue, 15th

Floor, New York, NY 10022, Tel: (212) 759-7982, Fax: (212) 759-8647, E-mail: wedo@igc.apc.org

The Contract with Women of the USA

As public officials, advocates for women's rights, policy makers, organizations and individuals, we sign this Contract with Women of the USA to implement the Platform for Action, adopted September 1995, at the United Nations Fourth World Conference on Women by 190 governments, including the United States of America.

We pledge our mutual commitment to the goal of equality and empowerment for American women, the continuing majority population of our nation and states.

We pledge to work together to overcome discrimination based on sex, race, class, age, immigration status, sexual orientation, religion and disability. We seek to end social, economic and political inequities, violence and the human rights abuses that still confront millions of American women and girls.

Looking to the 21st century, we enter into this Contract with Women of the USA for ourselves and for future generations to achieve our vision of a healthy planet and healthy nations, states and communities, with peace, equality and justice for all.

1. Empowerment of Women

We pledge to work for empowerment of women in all their diversity through their equal participation in decision making and equal access to shared power in government, in all spheres and at every level of society.

2. Sharing of Family Responsibilities

We pledge to work for equal sharing of family responsibilities by partners and individual members, to respect the diversity of families and promote practices and policies that enhance the multiple roles, security and well-being of women and girls, men and boys.

3. Ending the Burden of Poverty

We pledge to work to end the increasing burden of poverty on women and their children, a majority of the poor. Recognizing the value of women's unpaid and underpaid labor to our families, communities and economy, we support a significant increase in minimum wage rates and adequate funding for welfare and other social safety nets, child care, education and job training, and access to collateral-free credit for women-owned microenterprises.

4. High Quality, Affordable Health Care

We pledge to work to reaffirm the rights of women and girls, regardless of income or where they live, to high quality, accessible, affordable and respectful physical and mental health care based on sound women-focused research.

5. Sexual and Reproductive Rights

We pledge to work to reaffirm and uphold the sexual and reproductive rights of all women, including their individual right to control their own reproductive lives free of coercion, violence and harassment.

6. Workplace Rights

We pledge to work for guarantees of equal pay for work of comparable value and an end to discriminatory hiring and sexual harassment. We support family-friendly work practices, job training and opportunities programs, strengthening of affirmative action, employees' rights to organize unions and safe, healthy working environments.

7. Educational Equity

We pledge to work for educational equity for women and girls, including creation and strengthening of gender-fair curricula and teaching techniques, equal opportunities and access for girls and women throughout their lives to education, career development, training and scholarships, educational administration and policy making.

8. Ending Violence

We pledge to work for policies and programs to end violence against women and children in every form and to ensure that violence against women and children is understood as a violation of their human rights and civil rights.

9. Protecting a Healthy Environment

We pledge to work to end environmental degradation and eliminate toxic chemicals, nuclear wastes and other pollutants that threaten our health, our communities, country and planet. We uphold active roles by government at all levels and public and private sectors to continue and expand environmental protection programs.

10. Women as Peacemakers

We salute women's leading roles in peace movements and conflict resolution and pledge to work for their inclusion in policy making at all levels aimed at preventing wars, halting the international arms trade and eliminating nuclear testing and weapons. We also seek reductions in military spending and conversion of military facilities.

11. Honor Commitment and Ratify CEDAW

We pledge to support the commitments made by the U.S. government to implement the U.N. Platform for Action, which constitutes a contract with the world's women. We call on the U.S. Senate to ratify the Convention to Eliminate Discrimination Against Women (CEDAW) which the United States has signed.

12. A Long-Term Plan to Achieve Equality

We who are state and federal policy makers pledge to work in partnership with women's organizations to develop and enforce a long-term plan to achieve our goals of equality and empowerment for women. We support the re-establishment of a national Advisory Panel on Women and similar panels in each state to ensure that government at every level take the necessary steps to implement this contract.

Journal Page

Appendix A

Women's Rights Resources

SUBJECT SPECIFIC

Gender, Human Rights and Global Organizing

Publications

Domestic Violence, by Margi Laird McCue. Issues addressed include myths and statistics, effects on children, court actions, programs for victims and abusers, and a state-by-state directory of organizations. Deals primarily with the issue of male violence against women, though it also contains information on same-sex battering, elder abuse, abuse of disabled people, and abuse of men by women. $39.50 (CA residents, add $2.86 sales tax) Order from: ABC-CLIO, 130 Cremona Drive, P.O. Box 1911, Santa Barbara, CA 93116-1911, (800) 368-6868 x141.

Unspoken Rules: Sexual Orientation and Women's Human Rights, edited by Rachel Rosenbloom, with foreword by Charlotte Bunch, published by the International Gay and Lesbian Human Rights Commission. Includes an overview of reports from more than 30 countries. Contact: The International Gay and Lesbian Human Rights Commission, 1360 Mission Street, Suite 200, San Francisco, CA 94110, Tel: 415-255-8680, Fax: (415) 255-8662, E-mail: IGLHRC@igc.apc.org.

Standing Firm: Women's Rights and Reproductive Self Determination, describes four projects supported by the Unitarian Universalist Service Committee in partnership with women's organizations in India, Jamaica, Nicaragua and Eritrea. The projects, which were designed to advance the health and reproductive rights of women, represent the Unitarian Universalist Service Committee approach to women's projects that is based on the belief that reproductive choices are not made in a vacuum, but in a broad context that includes women's roles and their participation in the economic, social and political life of their communities. Released in 1996. Order from: The Unitarian Universalist Service Committee, 130 Prospect Street, Cambridge, MA 02139, (617)868-6600, Fax: (617) 868-7102, E-mail: postmaster@uusc.org.

Educational Materials

Doing the Gender Boogie: Power, Participation and Economic Justice, by Ten Days for World Development. An excellent publication designed to help groups join with people worldwide who are exploring gender and global justice. It includes five hands-on workshops and supportive materials needed to put together a workshop. Contact: The Inter-Church Committee for World Development Education, 85 St. Clair Avenue East, Toronto, Ontario, Canada M4T1M8, Tel: (416) 922-0591.

No Punching Judy: A Curriculum on the Prevention of Domestic Violence, created by Margi Lairot McCue for the Unitarian Universalist Service Committee. A multigenerational curriculum that promotes the prevention of domestic violence, originally developed for use in the Portland, Oregon, public schools, this curriculum has been adapted for use in religious education programs. Includes materials for ministers for sermons, and guidelines for an adult workshop that presents an analysis of the key components that foster domestic violence, including gender role stereotyping, poor communication, and lack of nonviolent conflict resolution skills. Core curriculum is for grades K through 12, and is designed to equip children and young adults with the means to overcome tendencies toward violence in interpersonal situations, as well as how to cope with violence in their homes. It also reviews community action against domestic violence. Video and curriculum are available for $65. Contact: The Unitarian Universalist Service Committee, 130 Prospect Street, Cambridge, MA 02138-1845, Tel: (617) 868-6600, Fax: (617) 868-7102, E-mail: postmaster@uusc.org.

Our Human Rights: A Manual for Women's Human Rights, by Julie Mertus, Mallika Dutt and Nancy Flowers, and the Organizing Committee for the People's Decade for Human Rights Education, New York. Comprehensive study guide is designed to educate readers about the international human rights of women. Available from: The Center for Women's Global Leadership, 27 Clifton Avenue, New Brunswick, NJ 08903, Tel: (908) 932-8782, Fax: (908) 932-1180.

The Human Rights Watch Global Report on Women's Human Rights, gathers evidence on the epidemic levels of violence against women and rampant sex discrimination around the world. Specific actions that governments and the international community should take to combat these violations are recommended. Contact: Human Rights Watch, 1522 K Street NW, Suite 910, Washington, DC 20005-1202, Tel: (202) 371-6592, Fax: (202) 371-0124 E-mail: hrwdc@hrw.org, Internet:gopher://gopher.humanrights.org:5000.

Organizations

Amnesty International's Women's Network, conducts a comprehensive program known as "Human Rights are Women's Rights." Their publication, *It's About Time!* covers topics such as women and war, fighting for justice, women at risk, and campaigning for women's human rights. Contact: Amnesty International U.S.A., National Office Publications, 322 Eighth Avenue, New York, NY 10001, Tel: (212) 807-8400, Fax: (212) 627-1451.

International Gay and Lesbian Human Rights Commission, provides documents relating to lesbian participation in the Fourth World Conference on Women. Contact: The International Gay and Lesbian Human Rights Commission, 1360 Mission Street, Suite 200, San Francisco, CA 94110, Tel: (415) 255-8680, Fax: (415) 255-8662, E-mail: IGLHRC@ igc.apc.org.

The International Women's Rights Action Watch (IWRAW), a global network of individuals and organizations that monitors implementation of the Convention on the Elimination of All Forms of Discrimination Against Women. IWRAW publicizes the work of the U.N. Committee on the Elimination of Discrimination Against Women (CEDAW). Their resources include a quarterly newsletter, special reports on the status of women, and international gatherings scheduled along with the Committee on the Elimination of All Forms of Discrimination Against Women meetings. Contact: IWRAW, Humphrey Institute of Public Affairs, University of Minnesota, 301 - 19th Avenue South, Minneapolis, MN 55455, Tel: (612) 625-5093, Fax: (612) 624-0068.

Health, Sexuality and Reproductive Rights

Videos

Bintou in Paris. (15 minutes) Tells the story of Bintou, a young Malian mother living in Paris faced with the critical decision of whether or not to excise her daughter. Her husband and mother-in-law put pressure on her to uphold the tradition while her older sister, a nurse, tries to convince her to resist. Produced by the Commission for the Abolishment of Female Genital Mutilations (CAMS). Contact Linda Weil-Curiel, Paris, Tel: (33 1) 45 49 04 00, Fax: (33 1) 45 49 16 71.

Organizations

Research Action & Information Network for Bodily Integrity of Women (RAINBO), an organization that disseminates innovative educational and training materials focused on the need to end female genital mutilation, and provides technical assistance, grants and leadership training and provides support to grass roots groups. Contact: RAINBO, 915 Broadway, Suite 1109, New York, NY 10010-7108, Tel: (212) 477-3318, Fax: (212) 447-4154, E-mail: NT61@Columbia.edu.

Women's International Network (WIN), produces a magazine with ongoing columns on women and health, women and development, women and the media/environment/violence/human rights, the United Nations and more. Regularly records information on genital/sexual mutilations; direct reports from Africa, the Middle East, Asia & Pacific, Europe and the Americas are featured in every issue. Contact: Fran P. Hosken, WIN News, 187 Grant Street, Lexington, MA 02173, Tel: (617) 862-9431, Fax: (617) 862-1734.

Value of Work and Economic Issues

Publications

50 Years Is Enough: The Case Against the World Bank and the International Monetary Fund, edited by Kevin Danaher. This book brings together more than 30 authors to examine the World Bank and the International Monetary Fund. It covers structural adjustment programs, failed development projects, the feminization of poverty, destruction of the environment, the internal workings of the World Bank and the International Monetary Fund, and the struggle to build alternatives to neoliberal policies. It addresses how women's struggles to achieve economic empowerment are inextricably linked to political gains. It also contains a guide to the many organizations involved in reform efforts. ($15.75) Contact: Global Exchange, 2017 Mission Street, Suite 303, San Francisco, CA 94110, Tel: (415) 255-7296, Fax: (415) 255-7498.

The Corporate Welfare Handbook, by Drew Dugan and Jan Ritchter. Describes the federal budget and the corporate tax code and explains why special tax breaks are unfair. Also provides basic tools to help convince Congress to reform corporate welfare. Contact: Tax Watch, 910 17th Street N.W., #413, Washington DC, 20006, Tel: (202) 776-0595, Fax: (202) 776-0599.

Gender, Poverty and Employment: Turning Capabilities into Entitlements, published by the International Labor Office in Geneva. Contains information about economic conditions worldwide with a special focus on the relationship between gender and poverty. Strategies undertaken in the last three decades to alleviate poverty are evaluated. Contact: Special Advisor on Women Workers' Questions, International Labor Office, 4, Route des Morillons, CH-1211 GENEVA 22, Tel: (79)9-69-30, Fax: (79)8-86-85.

Keeping Women and Children Last, by Ruth Sidel. Revisits the condition of America's poor women, with particular focus on the federal government's attempts to dismantle the welfare system. Shows how America, in its search for a post-Cold War enemy, has turned inward to target single mothers on welfare and how politicians have scapegoated and stigmatized female-headed families both as a method of social control and to divert attention from the severe problems that Americans face. Reveals the real victims of poverty — the millions of children who suffer from societal neglect, inferior education, inadequate health care, hunger, and homelessness. Cites statistics that are both terrifying and disturbing and delivers a chilling indictment of the current trends and political maneuvering that threaten to keep America's poor women and children last. Published by Penguin Books.

The Politics of Power and Empowerment, by Peggy Law, director of the National Radio Project, published by Share Publishing. Examines the politics of violence, the politics of poison, and international trade agreements. Distributed by: Share Publishing, 3130 Alpine Road, Suite 200-1009, Portola Valley, CA 94028, Tel: or Fax: (415) 851-0731.

Videos

Who's Counting? Marilyn Waring on Sex, Lies and Global Economics. (52 minutes) This provocative documentary from the National Film Board of Canada is directed by Oscar-winning director Terre Nash. It includes a rich collection of the ideas of Marilyn Waring, former member of the New Zealand Parliament, university professor, world-renowned political economist and author of *If Women Counted.* Ms. Waring demystifies the language of economics. ($59 purchase; $35 rental) Contact: Bullfrog Films, Tel: (800) 543-3764; Fax: (610) 370-1078, E-mail: Bullfrog@igc.apc.org.

Zoned for Slavery. (30 minutes) Documents conditions in the maquiladora system. Factories are leaving our communities to relocate abroad where workers, including children, are forced to accept wages as low as $.11 to $.30 per hour which are below survival level. Many of the women who work in these factories cannot afford to eat. The clothes they produce are being sold under well-known brand labels throughout the United States. This video presents this problem in an easy-to-understand format with moving footage of the actual factories, including interviews with workers, and analysis of the global economy that creates this situation. Contact: National Labor Committee, 14 Union Square, New York, NY 10020, Tel: (212) 242-0986.

Deadly Embrace: Nicaragua, The World Bank and The IMF. This 25 minute video, to be released in the summer of 1996, contains recent footage from the Sandinista TV station in Managua showing the police attack resulting in the death of two demonstrators in the December 1995 student uprising. The video demonstrates two disastrous consequences of structural adjustment — lack of credit for farmers and low wages and unemployment in urban areas. The film comes with an organizing guidebook that contains background information, personal stories and activities. ($35 for the video and guidebook) Available from: Deadly Embrace, Wentworth, NH 03282, Tel: (603) 764-9948.

Organizations

The 50 Years Is Enough Campaign, an organization that is challenging World Bank and the International Monetary Fund policies. Contact the Washington office for information on the National Campaign and referrals to local groups: 50 Years is Enough Campaign, 1025 Vermont Avenue, Washington, DC, Tel: (202) 463-2265, Fax: (202) 879-3186, E-mail: wb50years@igc.org.

Redefining Progress, a San Francisco-based research group interested in developing the concept of the Genuine Progress Indicator (GPI). The GPI adjusts for resource depletion, housework and other transactions, long-term environmental damage, unemployment, pollution and sustainable investments. Contact: Ted Halstead, 116 New Montgomery Street, Suite 209, San Francisco, CA 94105, Tel: (415) 543-6511.

Access to Education, the Media and Communications

Publications

A Media Guidebook for Women: Finding Your Public Voice, instructs groups on how to develop a media strategy, a media plan, press releases, tips on paste-up of published articles, interviews, print tools, electronic media, press conferences, press kits, speeches and presentations. Available from: The United States Information Agency, 301 4th Street, SW, Washington, DC 20547, Tel: (202) 619-4700.

The Burden of Girlhood: A Global Inquiry into the Status of Girls, by Neera Kuckreja Sohoni. Offers a fresh look at the issues facing girls worldwide. Contact: Third Party Publishing Co., P.O. Box 13306, Montclair Station, Oakland, CA 94661, Tel: (510) 339-2323, Fax: (510) 339-6729.

Case Studies on Girls. In light of the United Nations Fourth World Conference on Women, young women around the world have felt the need to express, in their own voices, their concerns and proposals for concrete solutions. The project grew into reality with contributions from UNFPA and UNICEF. Overall coordination was from Earth Council (Costa Rica) and the Women's Environment and Development Organization (WEDO, New York).

The studies range from violence against young women (South Africa, Nepal, Jordan, USA), education (Romania, Kenya), employment (Costa Rica, Venezuela, Jordan, the Philippines, Mexico), reproductive and sexual health (St. Vincent and the Grenadines, Spain, Togo), health of young women (Barbados) to participation in decision-making processes. Available from: the Women's Environment & Development Organization, 845 Third Avenue - 15th Floor, New York, NY 10022, Tel: (212) 759-7982, Fax: (212) 759-8647, E-mail: wedo@igc.apc.org.

The Difference: Growing up Female in America, by Judy Mann. A Washington Post columnist looks at the socialization of girls in the U.S. and shares her own insights and experiences with her daughter and her friends. ($22.95) Contact: Warner Books, 1271 Avenue of the Americas, New York, NY 10020, Tel: (212) 522-7200.

Failing At Fairness: How America's Schools Cheat Girls, by Myra and David Sadker. This landmark study documents gender bias in U.S. schools from kindergarten to higher education. ($12) Contact: Touchtone, Rockefeller Center, 1230 Avenue of the Americas, New York, NY 10020.

The Gender Primer: Helping Schoolgirls Hold Onto Their Dreams by Tim H. Flinders. A resource book for teachers and parents of pre-teen girls deals with gender stereotypes and other problems faced by girls in school. Available from: Two Rock Publications, P.O. Box 2773, Petaluma, CA 94953.

GirlNet, a newsletter that focuses on international issues of interest to girls, developed as a result of the Beijing women's conference. This newsletter is edited by girls and serves as a networking tool. Contact: GirlNet, 1850 Union Street #1033, San Francisco, CA 94123, E-mail: Girlnet@aol.com or Girlnet@linex.com.

Promoting Justice: A Media Guide, is designed to help volunteers and activists use the media to promote justice. Suggests effective ways to advocate for U.S. policies and legislation that support progressive international and domestic priorities. Offers how-to tips on writing press releases, getting on TV and sponsoring special events to elicit media coverage. It costs ($3) and is available from: Unitarian Universalist Service Committee, 130 Prospect Street, Cambridge, MA 02138-1845, Tel: (617) 868-6600, E-mail: postmaster@uusc.org.

Educational Materials

Action Guide for Girls' Education, by the San Francisco Bay Area Girls' Education Network. Contains exercises, discussion questions and valuable information and resources including: girls' access in education, girls' safety in school, course content and curriculum, equity in the school environment, action strategies. Contact: BAGEN via the Internet home page: http://www.well.net/bagen.

The Education Committee of the Northern California Division of the United Nations Association of the U.S.A. has published three curriculums for varied age groups that provide a wealth of information on global citizenship and the U.N., presented in age-appropriate styles.

The United Nations: My Human Family & My Home, The Earth, by Steve Ross. This is a three-week curriculum for grades K-3.

The United Nations: Living Together in the World Community, by Mary Granholm. This is a one-week curriculum for grades 4-8.

The United Nations: Yesterday, Today, and Tomorrow by Steve Ross. This is a one-week curriculum for high school.

Contact: Steve Ross or Mary Granholm, Education Committee, United Nations Association, Northern California Division, P.O. Box 291, Brookdale, CA 95007, Tel: (408) 338-6110.

Organizations

Gender Equity in Global Communication Networks: A Global Alert from WITS to Potential Strategic Partners, an interdisciplinary group of women scholars and academic professionals at the University of Illinois at Urbana-Champaign, formed to address gender equity issues in information technology. The women of WITS believe that women and girls should have integral roles in the conception, design, content, use, implementation, economics and legal policies of electronic communication networks at all levels. For more information contact: WITS, Center for Advanced Study, 912 W Illinois Street, Urbana, IL 61801, E-mail: cheris@UIUC.edu.

Global Media Monitoring Project: Women's Participation in the News, published by National Watch on Images of Women in the Media (MediaWatch). At the Women Empowering Communication Conference in Bangkok, Thailand in 1994, a project was launched to monitor the media. On January 18, 1995, hundreds of volunteers around the world monitored their news media — television, radio and daily newspapers. The result is a survey of 71 countries based on more than 49,000 data records. This document gives a global picture of women in the news in 1995 and a benchmark for future monitoring. Available from: MediaWatch - Suite 204, 517 Wellington Street West, Toronto, Ontario, Canada M5V 1G1, Tel: (416) 408-2065 Fax: (416) 408-2069, E-mail: mediawat@web.apc.org.

Media Literacy Project, is developing a curriculum to enhance media literacy for girls and young women. Contact: Suki Jones, Media Literacy Project Director, 960 West Hedding, Street 164, San Jose, CA 95126, Tel: (408) 261-7100, Fax: (408) 261-7110.

Environmental Sustainability

Publications

Building a Sustainable Community: An Organizer's Handbook by the Task Force for Sustainable Community Development, a primer on sustainability, and a resource for starting a campaign. Contact: Action Coalition for Global Change, 55 New Montgomery Street, Suite 219, San Francisco, CA 94105, Tel: (415) 896-2242.

Fight Global Warming: 29 Things You Can Do, by Sarah L. Clark, staff scientist for the Environmental Defense Fund. Explains the environmental, economic, and social consequences of the greenhouse effect and outlines what must be done on the local, national, and international level to slow the warming trend. Available from: Consumer Reports Books, 101 Truman Avenue, Yonkers, NY 10703, Tel: (914) 378-2000.

The Global War Against the Poor, by Richard Barnet, published by Servant Leadership Press. Barnet is the author of 14 books dealing with the institutions that make foreign policy, shape the physical and cultural environment, and create the global economic order. This work is distilled from two decades of thinking and writing about poverty, its causes and consequences. ($2.50) Available from: The Potter's House Book Service, 1658 Columbia Road, NW, Washington, DC 20009, Tel: (202) 232-5483.

How to Make the World a Better Place: 116 Ways You Can Make a Difference, by Jeffrey Hollender with Linda Catling. Shows how one person can make a difference in solving global, national and local problems, from protecting the environment, to helping the homeless, to making their community safer.

Rain Forest in Your Kitchen: The Hidden Connection Between Extinction and Your Supermarket, by Martin Teitel, foreword by Jeremy Rifkin. The biodiversity crisis — the extinction of thousands of species of plants and animals — is not just a faraway problem for scientists to solve. Instead, the crisis is as close as our backyards, our gardens and our refrigerator shelves. This practical guide is designed to appeal to the average citizen to wield their consumer power in favor of protecting the world's plant and animal species. Contact: Island Press, 1718 Connecticut Avenue, NW, Suite 300, Washington, DC 20009. Island Press is one of the leading presses that deals with environmental, population and development issues. For a catalog of their publications call: (800) 828-1302.

Shopping for a Better World: The Quick and Easy Guide to All Your Socially Responsible Shopping, serves the American consumer concerned with environmental and social issues. Presented in easy-to-use tables, this guide rates more than 2,000 brand names according to the leading indicators of social consciousness such as a company's policies on charitable giving, women and minority advancement, community outreach, the environment, family benefits, and other work place issues. Available from: The Council on Economic Priorities, 30 Irving Place, New York, NY 10003, Tel: (800) 729-4CEP.

Women's Handbook on Safe Energy, published by Plutonium Free Future Women's Network. This pamphlet covers uranium mining, plutonium, nuclear waste, and global warming and also explains energy efficiency, safe, renewable and sustainable energy, solar power and biomass. Available from: Plutonium Free Future Women's Network, P.O. Box 2589, Berkeley, CA 94702, Tel: (510) 540-7645, Fax: (510) 540-6159, E-mail: pff@igc.apc.org.

Organizations

Center for Community Action and Environmental Justice, publishes important studies including: Environmental Racism, Environmental Injustice, and Environmental Equity; Killing Legally with Toxic Chemicals: Women and the Environment in the USA; Women, Ecology and Health: Rebuilding Connections. Contact: Penny Newman, P.O. Box 33124, Riverside, CA 92519, Tel: (909) 360-8451.

The Sacred Grove Women's Forest Sanctuary, is a nonprofit land trust, dedicated to preserving forest habitat. Contact: Catherine Allport, The Women's Forest Sanctuary, 2828 1/2 Cherry Street, Berkeley, CA 94705, Tel: (510) 548-1693.

Developing Local and Global Plans for Action

Publications

The Busy Person's Guide to Social Action, a clear, concise, and effective how-to guide for people who want to work for change but have limited time. Outlines practical time-saving ways to organize community groups, maximize your involvement, plan and coordinate letter writing campaigns, and much more. Contact: The Unitarian Universalist Service Committee, 130 Prospect Street, Cambridge, MA 02138-1845, Tel: (617) 868-6600, Fax: (617) 868-7102, E-mail: postmaster@uusc.org

Insight and Action: How to Discover and Support a Life of Integrity and Commitment to Change, by Tova Green and Peter Woodrow with Fran Peavey. A how-to manual that makes the most of loving and supportive relationships with friends, colleagues and family members practical strategies sustaining commitments. Guide for activist organizations, religious communities and those striving to live their values. Available from: New Society Publishers, 4527 Springfield Avenue, Philadelphia, PA 19119, Tel: (215) 382-6543.

In the Tiger's Mouth: An Empowerment Guide for Social Action, by Katrina Shields, illustrations by Phil Somerville. Offers a wealth of ideas and approaches for curing stress and burnout, coping with the daily diet of bad news, developing accountability in groups, and listening to and supporting others as well as one's self. Full of exercises and success stories drawn from experience, the author provides ideas for building sustainable groups and activist lives. Available from: New Society Publishers, 4527 Springfield Avenue, Philadelphia, PA 19119, Tel: (215) 382-6543.

Educational Resources

Women Connecting Beyond Beijing: A Workshop in Response to the United Nations Fourth World Conference on Women, by Maria Riley. A workshop series is focused on how to formulate a local action plan. Available from: Center of Concern, 3700 13th. NE, Washington, DC 20017, Tel: (202) 635-2757, Fax: (202) 832-9494.

Organizations

Committee to Attain Ratification of the Convention on the Elimination of All Forms of Discrimination Against Women, provides information on activities and strategies in the efforts toward attainment of the ratification of CEDAW by the U.S. Contact: Kit Cosby, The National Spiritual Assembly of the Bahai Faith, 1320 19th Street, Suite 701, Washington, DC 22036, Tel: (202) 833-8990.

The National Committee on the United Nations Convention on the Elimination of Discrimination against Women, an informal network that provides valuable information about the status of the Convention on the Elimination of all forms of Discrimination Against Women (CEDAW) in the world as well as suggestions about what can be done to urge its ratification in the United States. To be placed on the mailing list, contact: Billie Heller, Chair, National Committee on U.N./CEDAW, 520 North Camden Drive, Beverly Hills, CA 90210-3202, Tel: (310) 271-8087, Fax: (310) 271-2056.

The Year 2000 Campaign to Redirect World Military Spending to Human Development, is a coalition of 67 citizen groups from around the world that have formed together to promote changes in the allocation of world resources. It calls for the appointment of United Nations regional envoys who would help countries negotiate mutual reductions in military forces with their neighbors. It aims to establish an international Code of Conduct to bar the export of arms to unelected governments, human rights violators and countries that engage in acts of armed aggression. The Campaign also opposes World Bank and International Monetary Fund loans to countries that fail to report complete and accurate military budgets. The goal of this effort is to provide more security for all human beings and more funds available for human development in all countries. Contact: Pamela Richardson, Demilitarization for Democracy/ The Year 2000 Campaign, 1601 Connecticut Avenue, N.W., Suite 600, Washington, DC 20009, Tel: (202) 319-7191, Fax: (202) 319-7194, E-mail: pdd@clark.net World Wide Web: http://www.fas.org/pub/gen/mswg/year2000/.

GENERAL RESOURCES

United Nations Publications

Beijing Declaration and Platform for Action, includes an overview and explanation of the Beijing Declaration and Platform for Action. ($7, plus $5 shipping and handling)

Convention on the Elimination of all Forms of Discrimination Against Women, is the central and most comprehensive document in the promotion of women's rights. The articles of the convention not only establish a Bill of Rights for women, but also provide an agenda for action by countries to guarantee the enjoyment of those rights. ($5)

The United Nations and the Advancement of Women, 1948-1995, chronicles the role played by the United Nations in promoting the status of women. Vital documents related to the promotion of gender equality are included in this comprehensive volume. ($29.95)

Methods of Measuring Women's Participation in the Informal Sector, explains the technique, based on linking employment with economic output, to calculate both remunerated and unremunerated work. Empirical illustrations are included. ($39)

Strategies for Confronting Domestic Violence: A Resource Manual, examines the causes of violence, and the need to improve the criminal justice system and respond to victims' needs. ($19.95)

Violence Against Women in the Family, provides an overall picture of the violence against women in the family and recommends short- and long-term strategies to confront this problem. ($27)

Women: Looking Beyond 2000, examines health and education, work and power, challenges, opportunities and action. ($14.95)

The World's Women 1995: Trends and Statistics, covers population growth, environment, health, education, work, power and violence. ($15.95)

Contact: United Nations Publications Sales Section, Room DC2-853, United Nations Plaza, New York, NY 10017, Tel: 1 (800) 253-9646, (212) 963-8302, Fax: (212) 963-3489, Internet: http://www.un.org.

General Publications

A Reference Guide to Official United Nations Documents, has been compiled in Arabic, Chinese, English, French, Russian, and Spanish and contains extracts of important U.N. documents which relate to women including the Convention on the Elimination of All Forms of Discrimination Against Women and the Declaration on the Elimination of Violence Against Women. Available through Amnesty International's Website: http://io.org/amnesty/overview.html.

Beijing in Your Backyard, is a condensed version of the Beijing Declaration and the Platform for Action with suggestions for action for individuals and for groups working in your community, including ideas on how to begin a constructive dialogue with your government. Contact: Quaker United Nations Office, 777 U.N. Plaza, New York, NY 10017, Tel: (212) 682-2745.

Beijing Women's Conference: United States Government Official Comments & Report from the White House, includes U.S. government commitments and reports made by the U.S. delegation and Hillary Clinton's remarks to the U.N. Plenary in Beijing. Contact: Meiklejohn Civil Liberties Institute, P.O. Box 673, Berkeley, CA 94701, Tel: (510) 848-0599.

Beyond the Numbers: A Reader on Population, Consumption, and the Environment, edited by Laurie Ann Mazur, including a foreword by Timothy E. Wirth. Examines topics such as: the interrelationships between population, economic growth, resource consumption, and development; the history of family planning efforts; gender equality and the empowerment of women; reproductive health and rights; and international migration and urbanization. Contact: South Island Press, Center for Resource Economics, 1718 Connecticut Avenue, N.W., Suite 300, Washington, DC 20009.

Bringing Beijing Home, published by the Women's Bureau, U.S. Department of Labor, and the President's Interagency Council on Women, the White House. A series of publications, the first four are titled, *On the Road to Beijing.* Contact: The Women's Bureau, 200 Constitutional Avenue, NW, Washington, DC 20036, Tel: (202) 219-6601.

Changing the Boundaries: Women-Centered Perspectives on Population and the Environment, by Janice Jiggins, foreword by Helen Rodriquez-Trias. Asserts that for women, a sustainable world is one in which societies address issues of excessive consumption, expenditures for destruction, and inequities based on class, race, gender, or ethnicity. Contact: South Island Press, Center for Resource Economics, 1718 Connecticut Avenue, N.W., Suite 300, Washington, DC 20009.

Covenant for the New Millennium, is the Platform for Action produced as a paperback book. ($10 each; $6 each for 51-100 copies; $4 each for more than 100 copies) Contact: Free Hand Books, P.O. Box 184, Tomales, CA 94971, Tel: 1 (800) 548-6682, E-mail: fhb.wco.com.

From Information to Education, was launched by the Panos Institute in October 1991. It adapts information from books, dossiers, press features and magazines into portfolios for educational use. Contact: Panos-Washington, The Panos Institute, 1717 Massachusetts Avenue, NW, Suite 301, Washington, DC 20036, Tel: (202) 483-0044, Fax: (202) 483-3059.

Girls: Challenging the World, a pamphlet for secondary-school students, provides information about the experiences of real people as a guide for young readers. (Free)

Global Gender Issues, by V. Spike Peterson and Anne Sisson Runyan. (Part of the *Dilemmas in World Politics Series*.) It connects inequalities between women and men with the world politics of power, security, economy and ecology. Through historical perspectives, visual imagery, empirical data, theoretical analysis, and other narrative techniques, the authors suggest connections between women's issues and wars of aggression, arms proliferation, global economic recession and environmental degradation. Contact: Westview Press, 5500 Central Avenue, Boulder, CO 80301-2877.

The New Field Guide to the U.S. Economy: A Compact and Irreverent Guide to Economic Life in America, by Nancy Folbre and the Center for Popular Economics, published by The New Press, 1995. Highlights issues associated with owners, workers, women, people of color, government spending, welfare, education, health, the environment, macroeconomics and the global economy. ($12.95) Contact: The Center for Popular Economics, P.O. Box 785, Amherst, MA 01004, Tel: (413) 545-0743.

When Corporations Rule the World, by David Korten. Exposes the harmful effects of globalization on economics, politics, society, and the environment. Presents ideas for creating a world responsive to human-needs desire, and the natural environment. Contact: Kumarian Press, 630 Oakwood Avenue, Suite 119, West Hartford, CT 06110.

Audiovisual Resources

Women's Rights Are Human Rights: Beijing, 1996. (15 minutes) Offers an overview of the Beijing Conference and the Unitarian Universalist Service Committee presence at the conference. Contact: The Unitarian Universalist Service Committee, 130 Prospect Street, Cambridge, MA 02139, Tel: (617) 868-6600, Fax: (617) 868-7102, E-mail: postmaster@uusc.org.

Beijing and Beyond. (35 minutes) A great introduction to the experience and purpose of the Beijing conference. Can be obtained for the cost of reproduction from: Dee L. Aker, Ph.D., Tel: (619) 428-2132 or Fax: (619) 428-8158, E-mail: DeeandBill@aol.com.

Leading to Beijing: Voices of Global Women, produced by KUOM-AM, distributed by Public Radio International. A six-minute tape and a 53-minute documentary that includes interviews and profiles of international women leaders. Contact: Radio KUOM-AM, 550 Rarig Center, 330 21st Avenue South, University of Minnesota, Minneapolis, MN 55455-0415.

Media Education Foundation, offers high quality videos on topics of interest to women, many targeting young women and students. Tapes are available at several rates depending on your usage — institutional, non-profit or individual. Preview tapes for free for 15 days. Among the titles are: Dreamworld Two — women in music videos; Slim Hopes — the obsession with thinness; The Killing Screens — violence in the media; Pack of Lies — tobacco industry's targeting women and children; Sexual Harassment — geared toward students on college campuses. Contact: Media Education Foundation, 26 Center Street, Northhampton, MA 01060, Tel: (800) 659-6882.

The National Radio Project, produces the nationwide radio program Making Contact, an alternative voice on national radio that covers progressive issues and broadens the public discourse. Making Contact is available, free of charge, to every public radio station in the United States and Canada. The program is uplinked via the National Public Radio satellite every Wednesday at noon. Stations without satellite dishes can have a broadcast-quality tape mailed to them each week, free of charge. Contact: The National Radio Project, 830 Los Trancos Road, Portola Valley, CA 94038, Tel: (415) 851-7256, Fax: (415) 851-0731, E-mail: contact@igc.apc.org

Power and Promise. (15 minutes) Explores a middle-school program that builds on the life-stories of courageous women to help sixth-grade girls support each other in coping with gender bias and to hold onto their self-confidence. ($15) Contact: Gender Fairness Program, Old Adobe USD, 845 Crinella Avenue, Petaluma, CA 94954.

Sister, Carry On. (90 minutes) Includes an audio cassette and book (1992). Produced and arranged by Carolyn McDade in collaboration with various musicians and singers. Many of the songs on the tape are sung and written by Carolyn McDade. The booklet Sister Carry On is a beautiful collection of songs, poems and essays that address the struggles of women worldwide. The pieces on the tape suggest that women should join together to share and analyze their common experiences. The desires of women to reach the goal of breaking the cycles of violence and oppression is the central focus of the work. From the description of how the song Come Sing a Song With Me "was recorded by women prisoners at MCI, Framingham, a Massachusetts Correctional Facility, to the essay entitled, Conflict Zones in El Salvador and the U.S.A.: Surviving, and Healing from, War and Sexual Abuse," the document provides a vehicle for women to express the music of their souls to one another. Audio cassette available for $12; book available for $10; cassette/book set available for $20. Distributed by Carolyn McDade Music, P.O. Box 510, Wellfleet, MA 02667.

Slides of Huairou and Beijing. (8 minutes) Provides a taste of the experience of the conference and China. Order at cost from: Off Center Video, 1300 A Shattuck Avenue, Berkeley, CA 94709, Tel: (510) 486-8010, Fax: (510) 644-2139, E-mail: MargotS999@AOL.com.

Through Women's Eyes. (31.5 minutes) Produced by Terri Berthiaume Hawthorne. This entertaining and instructive video allows viewers to visit Beijing with two women. Gives a unique perspective on both China and the Beijing Conference. ($18) Order from: TARA Educational Services, 65 Cretin Avenue, North, St. Paul, MN 55104-5701; Tel or Fax: (612) 645-0625.

Videos Recommended by UUSC

Available for a nominal rental fee from: UUSC, 130 Prospect Street, Cambridge, MA 02139, Tel: (617) 868-6600, Fax: (617) 868-7102, E-mail: postmaster@uusc.org.

Gender Justice: Women's Rights Are Human Rights. (40.5 minutes) Consists of four segments on the tape for use with UUSC's workshop series. Provides facilitators and participants with the opportunity to gain a deeper understanding of the information in the sessions. (For complete descriptions of these videos, see the following section entitled, "Other Recommended Videos.")

Segment 1: Excerpt from the Vienna Tribunal. (10:46) A condensed version of highlights from the Global Tribunal of Violations of Women's Rights. Segment 2: *A Matter of Interest.* (13:10) This segment uses fictional and factual examples of nations in debt to explain in simple terms how the debts of poor countries were incurred and what consequences of the debt crisis have been. It examines ethical questions about lenders in rich countries demanding full repayment from poor countries and aims to encourage citizens to put "people before profit" and support actions that demand solutions to Third World debt. Produced by Christian Aid and the Leed's Animation Project. Distributed by: Friendship Press, P.O. Box 37844, Cincinnati, OH, 45222, Tel: (513) 948-8733.

Segment 3: Structural Adjustment in Nicaragua — Excerpt from *Partners for Justice.* (6:09) It describes the realities of structural adjustment in Nicaragua in terms of cutbacks in health care and education and demonstrates the shift in support from large corporations to small privately owned businesses and how the potential impacts on workers rights. Produced by the Unitarian Universalist Service Committee. Segment 4: Excerpt from "Still Killing us Softly." (9:33) This segment highlights the award winning documentary that focuses on the portrayal of women in advertising. Available for rental for seven weeks for $10, or purchase for $20. Contact: UUSC, 130 Prospect Street, Cambridge, MA 92139, Tel: (617) 868-6600, Fax: (617) 868-7102, E-mail: postmaster@uusc.org.

Defending Our Lives/Defendiendo Nuestras Vidas. (30 minutes) Features women imprisoned for killing their batterers. Exposes the magnitude and severity of domestic violence in the United States and captures the cruel irony of imprisoning battering victims once they have finally escaped their abusers. Winner of the Academy Award for Best Short Documentary in 1994. Produced by Cambridge Documentary Films. Available in English or Spanish, video or film. Video available for $45 rental/$150 purchase; film available for $86 rental/$375 purchase; from Cambridge Documentary Films, P.O. Box 385, Cambridge, MA 02139, Tel: (617) 354-3677, Fax: (617) 492-7653.

Partners for Justice. (29 minutes) Produced by UUSC in 1992. Describes UUSC project partners in Central America. One segment describes the impact of structural adjustment in Nicaragua and another describes labor union repression in Guatemala.

In Her Own Image. (25 minutes) Focuses on the lives and struggles of women for their rights in Senegal, Bolivia, Egypt, Canada, India and the Philippines. By combining brief excerpts from several films, the video describes how women have joined together to overcome injustice in various circumstances. Produced by Media Network.

The Preferred Sex...The Desired Number: Women's Lives and Choices in India and Nigeria. (52 minutes) Gives personal insights into the issues of reproductive health and the status of women around the world. Includes the traditional Nigerian Ibu Eze ceremony which honors a woman who has given birth to nine children. Contrasting points of view about family planning are examined. Filmed in New Delhi, India, it tells the story of Lali Devi, a mother of five daughters who poisons herself and two of her children. Explores the circumstances surrounding Lali's death, including the psychological torment that led to the incident. Poignant circumstances of her life and death are described as well as the responses of family and community members to the tragedy. Examines the responsibilities that her husband, brother and father-in-law shared in these events. Produced by Nightingale Films. Available for $100 rental/$195 purchase from Nightingale Films, 5214 North Lakewood Avenue, Chicago, IL 60640, Tel: (312) 728-8233, Fax: (312) 728-0355.

The Vienna Tribunal. (48 minutes) Highlights of moving testimonies at the Global Tribunal on Violations of Women's Rights held in conjunction with the United Nations World Conference on Human Rights in Vienna, Austria, in 1993. Points out why women's rights must be seen as human rights and encourages the commitment of women to work to attain these rights. Produced by Women Make Movies. Available for $60 rental/$195 sale from Women Make Movies, Distribution Service, 462 Broadway, Suite 500 D, New York, NY 10013, Tel: (212) 925-0606, Fax: (212) 925-2052.

Still Killing Us Softly. (30 minutes) Jean Kilbourne, Ed.D, examines the relationship of media images to the problems of women in American society. Focuses on how advertising serves to shape ideals of female beauty and traditional male/female roles. Explores the way in which women are made into objects, which in turn perpetuates conditions that lead to violence against them. Produced by Cambridge Documentary Films. Available for $46 rental/$299 purchase from Cambridge Documentary Films, P.O. Box 385, Cambridge, MA 02139, Tel: (617) 354-3677, Fax: (617) 492-7653.

What's the Cost of Your Blouse? (18 minutes) Focuses on women garment workers in the California Bay Area, El Paso, Texas, and workers in the maquiladoras on the Mexican border. Told from the perspective of the human cost of the global economy. Some stories deal with issues of economic justice in the workplace in the U.S. and across the border, as U.S. corporations move parts of their production "offshore" to cut labor costs and avoid environmental, health and safety standards. Produced by Sydney Brown and Betty McAfee; A Project of the Northern California Interfaith Council, Oakland, CA, in collaboration with Open Window Images, Berkeley, CA 94703. ($30, plus $5 shipping and handling; CA residents add $2.47 sales tax)

Women's Rights Electronic Resources[1]

Institute for Global Communications (IGC), Association for Progressive Communications (APC) Networks: gopher.igc.apc.org or gopher://gopher.igc.apc.org:70/11/orgs.

Women's human rights conferences on IGC network: hr.women, hrnet.women, women.violence, women.media, women.info.src, un.cedaw.docs, un.csw.docs.

Womensnet, the women's network of the IGC and member of APC: http://www.igc.org/womensnet/

Center for Women's Global Leadership (CWGL): http://www.igc.apc.org/womensnet/beijing/ngo/cwgl.html gopher: gopher.igc.apc.org:70/11/orgs/cwgl

Women's Environment and Development Organization (WEDO): http://www.igc.apc.org/womensnet/beijing/ngo/wedo.html gopher: gopher.igc.apc.org:70/11/orgs/wedo

1 From the Woman Source Documentation Center and the International Women's Tribune Center.

Amnesty International: the www page gives an overview of the organization, and provides linkages with region-specific information: http://www.igc.apc.org/amnesty

PeaceNet Home Page: http://www.peacenet.org/peacenet/

The Global Democracy Network (GDN) (Bulletin Board): gopher.gdn.org

American Civil Liberties Union: http://www.aclu.org

United Nations Web Sites

Human Rights on CD-Rom: Compiled by the U.N. Library in Geneva. Contact: Chief Library Technical Unit. United Nations Office at Geneva. E-mail: maggie.wachter@itu.ch
United Nations Documents: http://undcp.or.at/unlinks.html

For UN information on the state of world population access the Population Information Network (POPIN) gopher://gopher.undp.org

Internet Accessible Resources on the Fourth World Conference on Women

The President's Interagency Council on Women
http://www.whitehouse.gov/WH/EOP/Women/IACW/html/IACWhome.html

International Institute of Sustainable Development (IISD), Linkages Fourth World Conference on Women
http://www.iisd.ca/linkages/women.html

Earth Negotiations Bulletin, produced by IISD:
http://www.igc.org/womensnet/beijing/beijing.html

U.N. Secretariat for the Fourth World Conference on Women: newsletter and other documents: http://www.undp.org/fwcw/daw1.html

U.N. Fourth World Conference on Women Platform for Action:
http://women.usia.gov/usia/beijpg.htm

APC conferences for relevant documents in English:
un.wcw.doc.eng, wcw.ngo.doc, un.cedaw.docs, un.csw.docs [2]

2 This list was compiled using the following sources: "Women's Issues Conferences on IGC/APC Network," Canada-US. Human Rights Information and Documentation Network: A Report on the November 3-5, 1994 CUSHRID Net Inaugural Meeting at the American Association for the Advancement of Science (AAAS), Women's International News Gathering Service (WINGS), Laura Hunt, Email: lhunt@cc.colorado.edu, World Wide Web Yellow Pages, 1995, NRP.

Organizations

Action for Development (ACFODE) is a Ugandan women's organization that has been working actively and publishing since the 1985 Third World Conference on Women in Nairobi. ACFODE produces a quarterly magazine called ARISE. The Spring 1996 issue featured, "Working in Solidarity for Gender Equity: From Nairobi to Beijing and the Way Forward." Contact: ACFODE House, Bukoto, P.O. Box 6729, Kampala, Uganda, Tel: (256-41) 532311; Fax: 530460.

Center for Women's Global Leadership, a project of Douglas College, Rutgers University. The center addresses issues of gender and politics with a focus on women's human rights. It coordinated the Global Campaign for Women's Human Rights at the World Conference on Human Rights in Vienna in June 1993. The center supplies excellent resources on activities being undertaken globally to counteract all forms of violence against women, supports the major annual international campaign 16 Days of Activism Against Gender Violence, and supplies information on how to organize activities in your area. The publications center provides the following resources on violence against women: *Testimonies of the Global Tribunal on Violations of Women's Human Rights* (1993); *Gender Violence: A Human Rights and Development Issue* by, Charlotte Bunch and Roxanna Carrillo; *and International Feminism: Networking Against Female Sexual Slavery*. Contact: Charlotte Bunch, Director, 27 Clifton Avenue, New Brunswick, NJ 08903, Tel: (908) 932-8782, Fax: (908) 932-1180.

Committee on Women, Population, and the Environment, a U.S.-based women's group that promotes the idea that environmental degradation stems not from over-population, but from: economic systems that exploit and misuse nature; rapid urbanization and poverty due to rural migration; disproportionate consumption patterns of the affluent; technologies that take from, but do not restore, nature; and militarization. Contact: Population and Development Program, Hampshire College, P.O. Box 5001, Amherst, MA 01002, Tel: (413) 582-5506, Fax: (413) 582-5620.

Forum for African Women Educationalists (FAWE), the organization that coordinated the major workshops in the African tent in Beijing. They have published a book that is an excellent follow-up to the conference entitled, *The Education of Girls and Women in Africa*. It can be obtained from: FAWE, 12th Floor, International House, Mama Ngina Street, P.O. Box 53168, Nairobi, Kenya, Tel: (254) 2 226590, Fax: (254) 2 210709.

Human Rights Advocates (HRA), a human rights membership organization open to those concerned with education, litigation, and supporting the United Nations. HRA published a Newsletter in December 1995 that focused on the Fourth World Conference on Women from a human rights perspective. To obtain a copy of the newsletter, write to: P.O. Box 5675 Berkeley, CA 94705.

The International Women's Tribune Centre (IWTC), works to end gender violence and promote sustainable development projects. Excellent information and training resources on women and development are available from this organization. The Tribune Center distributes *Women's Ink* through its publication division. *Women's Ink* is a listing of publications on women and development that includes information on: gender analysis and planning; women's rights; the environment; women's organizing; agriculture, science and technology; population and housing; small business; and development. Contact: International Women's Tribune Centre, 777 United Nations Plaza, New York, NY, 10017, Tel: (212) 687-8633, Fax: (212) 661-2704. E-mail: iwtc@igc.igc.apc.org.

The Learning Alliance, a nonprofit organization committed to developing empowering and participatory solutions to address the issues of our times. The Alliance offers workshops, conferences, training programs and cultural events. Contact: Dianne Williams, Program Coordinator, 324 Lafette Street, 10107, 7th Floor, New York, NY 10102, Tel: (212) 226-7171.

Unitarian Universalist Association (UUA), a liberal religious organization with Jewish- Christian roots made up of 1,000 independent congregations. The UUA's Department of Social Justice provides materials on a variety of social justice issues that relate directly or indirectly to women. In 1995, the general assembly of the UUA adopted for study a resolution entitled *Population and Development*, which deals with issues raised at the Conference on Population and Development held in Cairo in 1994. Contact: UUA, 25 Beacon Street, Boston, MA 01208-2800, Tel: (617) 742-2100.

Unitarian Universalist Association Office of Lesbian, Bisexual and Gay Concerns, conducts ongoing programming, including support for the curriculum designed for use in congregations entitled, *The Welcoming Congregation: Resources for Affirming Gay, Lesbian and Bisexual Persons.* Contact Keith Kron at: The Unitarian Universalist Association, 25 Beacon Street, Boston, MA 02108, Tel: (617) 742-2100 x465.

Unitarian Universalists Acting to Stop Violence Against Women, an organization that grew out of the Violence Against Women Resolution passed at the 1993 Unitarian Universalist Association's General Assembly. This group was organized to break the silence, provide a network for Unitarian Universalists and develop resources for education, support and action. Materials available include a 15-minute video that introduces the issue of violence against women, a study guide and a quarterly newsletter. Contact: Jody Shipley and Marilyn Gentile, Co-Chairs, 3221 Snyder Avenue, Modesto, CA 95356, Tel: (209) 545-2665.

The Unitarian Universalist Service Committee (UUSC), an independent membership organization focused on advancing justice in the United States, Latin America, the Caribbean, Africa and Asia. Building on the momentum of the U.N. conferences at Cairo and Beijing, UUSC is launching a new International Women's Rights Network to bring about justice, equality and human rights for women around the world. The network provides action alerts, access to educational materials on women's issues and connections to other activists. Contact: UUSC, 130 Prospect Street, Cambridge, MA 02139, Tel: (617) 868-6600, Fax: (617) 868-7102, E-mail: postmaster@uusc.org

The President's Interagency Council on Women, an office in the White House set up to provide information about U.S. follow-up efforts regarding the Fourth World Conference on Women. Contact: Martha Brown, The President's Interagency Council on Women, The White House, New Executive Office Building, Suite 3212, Washington, DC 20503, Tel: (202) 456-7350,
Internet: http://www.whitehouse.gov/WH\EOP/Women/IACW/html/IACWhome.html

The Stanley Foundation, a private nonprofit foundation that sponsors a variety of programs and activities designed to provoke thought and encourage dialogue on issues of global security, human rights, the United Nations, and sustainable development. The foundation has a special interest in women's issues and the Beijing Platform for Action. Contact: Joan D. Winship, Vice President, Outreach, The Stanley Foundation, 216 Sycamore Street, Suite 500, Muscatine, Iowa 52761-3831, Tel: (319) 264-1500, Fax: (319) 264-0864, E-mail: standfound-sf@mcimail.com.

Women's Environment & Development Organization (WEDO), initiated in 1990, is a global advocacy organization that networks with groups of women and men in every region of the world. WEDO works with labor, peace and environmental activists, parliamentarians, human rights networks, health and development organizations. Co-founded by Bella Abzug, WEDO has made an important contribution to critical issues such as: environment, health/population, development, and gender equality. Contact: WEDO, 355 Lexington Avenue, 3rd Floor, New York, NY 10017-6603, Tel: (212) 973-0325, Fax: (212) 973-0335,
E-mail: wedo@igc.apc.org, Gopher: gopher.igc.apc.org
Internet: http://www.igc.apc.org/womensnet/beijing/ngo/wedo.html.

Additional Women's Organizations

Alt-Wid
Elmira Nazombe
Office of World Community/ Church World Service
475 Riverside Drive, Room 670
New York, NY 10015

Church Women United
475 Riverside Drive
New York, NY 10115
Tel: (212) 870-2347
Fax: (212) 870-2338

DAWN
Peggy Antrobus
School for Continuing Studies, University of the West Indies
Pinelands, St. Michael, Barbados
Fax: (809) 426-3006

International Center for Research on Women
1717 Massachusetts Avenue, N.W.
Washington, DC 20036
Tel: (202) 797-0007
Fax: (202) 797-0020

International Women's Health Coalition
24 East Twenty-First Street
New York, NY 10010
Tel: (212) 979-8500
Fax: (212) 979-9009

International Women's Media Foundation
1001 Connecticut Avenue, N.W. Suite 1201
Washington, DC 20036
Tel: (202) 496-1992
Fax: (202) 496-1977

Women's International League for Peace and Freedom
National Office
1213 Race Street
Philadelphia, PA 19107-1691
Tel: (215) 563-7110
Fax: (215) 563-5527

Women's Treaty (CEDAW) Working Groups
c/o Bahais of the United States
1320 Nineteenth Street, N.W.
Suite 701
Washington, DC 20036
Tel: (202) 833-8990
Fax: (202) 833-8988

Young Women's Christian Association (YWCA)
276 Broadway
New York, NY 10003
Tel: 1 (800) 992-2871
Fax: (212) 677-9716

Acronym Guide

AFDC	Aid to Families with Dependent Children program
ACFODE	Action for Development
AIDS	Acquired Immune Deficiency Syndrome
ATC	Agricultural Workers' Union
AWHRC	Asian Women's Human Rights Council
CBO	Congressional Budget Office
CDFI	Community Development Financial Institutions
CEDAW	Convention on the Elimination of All Forms of Discrimination Against Women
DAWN	Development Alternatives with Women for a New Era
DCHWP	Delhi Community Health Workers
DHHS	Department of Health and Human Services
DOL	Department of Labor
DOS	Department of State
ECOSOC	Economic and Social Council of the United Nations
ED	Department of Education
EPZ	Export Processing Zone
FDA	(United States) Food and Drug Administration
FGM	Female Genital Mutilation
FUMEDI	Methodist Foundation for Integrated Development
FY	Fiscal Year
GATT	General Agreement on Tariffs and Trade
GDP	Gross Domestic Product
GNP	Gross National Product
HDI	Human Development Index
HDR	Human Development Report
HIV	Human Immune Virus
IAC	African Committee Against Harmful Traditional Practices
IFG	International Forum on Globalization
ICCR	Interfaith Center on Corporate Responsibility
ICPD	International Conference on Population and Development
ICWBE	Interagency Committee on Women's Business Council

ICPD	International Conference on Population and Development
IFG	International Forum on Globalization
ILO	International Labor Organization
IMF	International Monetary Fund
INSTRAW	United Nations Commission on the Status of Women
IUD	Intrauterine Device
IMF	International Monetary Fund
IWHC	International Women's Health Coalition
NAFTA	North American Free Trade Agreement
NOW	National Organization of Women
NCTPE	National Committee on Traditional Practices in Ethiopia
NUEW	National Union of Eritrean Women
NGO	Non-Governmental Organization
OPEC	Organization of Petroleum Exporting Countries
OSHA	Occupational Safety and Health Administration
PBS	Public Broadcasting System
PPAE	Planned Parenthood Association of Eritrea
PVO	Private Voluntary Organization
RuWSEC	Rural Women's Social Education Center
TNC	Transnational Corporation
SAP	Structural Adjustment Program
SIEDS	Society for Informal Education and Development Studies
SLORC	State Law and Order Restoration Committee (in Burma)
STD	Sexually Transmitted Disease
UN	The United Nations
UNCED	United Nations Conference on Environment and Development
UNITE	Union of Needle Trades, Industrial and Textile Employees
UN/CSW	United Nations Commission on the Status of Women
UN/DAW	United Nations Division for the Advancement of Women
UNESCO	United Nations Educational, Scientific and Cultural Organization
UNICEF	United Nations Children's Fund

UNIFEM	United Nations Development Fund for Women
UNFPA	United Nations Population Fund
U.S. AID	United States Agency for International Development
U.S./GLEP	United States/Guatemala Labor Education Project
UUA	Unitarian Universalist Association
UUSC	Unitarian Universalist Service Committee
VP	Volunteer Presenter
VVF	Vesico-Vaginal Fistulae
WAGN	Women Are Good News
WAND	Women's Action for A New Direction
WB	World Bank
WEDO	Women's Environment and Development Organization
WCHR	United Nations World Conference on Human Rights
WHO	World Health Organization

About the Authors

ELIZABETH FISHER is a professional writer and editor who has been active in the women's movement for more than 25 years, and who attended the Fourth World Conference on Women NGO Forum in Huairou in 1995. A Unitarian Universalist for many years, she has a particular interest in women, religion and social justice, providing leadership in both areas at the local, regional and international levels. She is author of the curriculum *Rise Up and Call Her Name: A Woman-honoring Journey into Global, Earth-based Spiritualities*, published by the Unitarian Universalist Women's Federation.

LINDA GRAY MACKAY, who has been involved in social justice work for the last 30 years, has a deep commitment to women's rights. She has been a teacher, social worker and public administrator and has served on the staff of the Unitarian Universalist Service Committee since 1984. She also served as a Peace Corps volunteer in El Salvador in the late 1960s. Author of *A Journey to Understanding: A Central American Study Guide* and *The Busy Person's Guide to Social Action*, two highly acclaimed UUSC publications, she also produced and directed two UUSC videos: *Partners for Justice* and *El Salvador In Crisis*, which served as the centerpiece of UUSC's nationwide campaign, "End Our Forgotten War."

Notes

Notes

Notes